HOUGHTON MIFFLIN HARCOURT

WRITE SOURCE

TEACHER'S EDITION

Grade 1

Authors

Dave Kemper, Patrick Sebranek, and Verne Meyer

Illustrator

Chris Krenzke

GREAT
SOURCE.

HOUGHTON MIFFLIN HARCOURT

23413

Reviewers

WRITE SOURCE Online
www.hmheducation.com/writesource

Program Overview

How does *Write Source* work? **TE-6**

What are the main components of *Write Source?* **TE-8**

How does the Teacher's Edition support instruction? **TE-9**

How is *Write Source* organized? **TE-10**

How does *Write Source* support today's digital-age learners? **TE-12**

Professional Development for Writing

THE FORMS, THE PROCESS, AND THE TRAITS

How does *Write Source* teach the forms of writing? **TE-18**

How does the program integrate the writing process and the six traits? **TE-19**

WRITING WORKSHOP AND GRAMMAR

How can I implement a writing workshop? **TE-20**

How is grammar presented? **TE-22**

WRITING ACROSS THE CURRICULUM, ACADEMIC VOCABULARY,
AND TEST PREPARATION

How is writing across the curriculum addressed? **TE-24**

How does *Write Source* teach academic vocabulary? **TE-25**

How is test preparation covered? **TE-26**

DIFFERENTIATION

How is differentiation handled in the Student Edition? **TE-28**

How is differentiation handled in the Teacher's Edition? **TE-29**

RESEARCH

What research supports the *Write Source* program? **TE-30**

Teacher Resources

Yearlong Timetable **TE-32**

Reading-Writing Connection **TE-36**

Scope and Sequence **TE-44**

Meeting the Common Core State Standards **TE-56**

Getting-Started Activities **TE-62**

Contents

The Process of Writing

Why Write? 11

THE WRITING PROCESS

Using the Writing Process 14
One Writer's Process 16
Working with a Partner 26
Understanding the Writing Traits 28
Learning About a Rubric 36
Publishing Your Writing.. 38
Using a Portfolio 40

The Forms of Writing

SENTENCES AND PARAGRAPHS

Writing a Sentence 44
Kinds of Sentences 54
Writing a Paragraph 56

DESCRIPTIVE WRITING

Descriptive Start-Up 62
Descriptive Paragraph 64
Across the Curriculum.. 80

NARRATIVE WRITING

Narrative Start-Up 84
Narrative Paragraph 86
Across the Curriculum 102
Writing for Assessment 104

EXPOSITORY WRITING

Expository Start-Up 108
Expository Paragraph 110
Across the Curriculum 126
Writing for Assessment 128

PERSUASIVE WRITING

Persuasive Start-Up 132
Persuasive Paragraph 134
Across the Curriculum 139

RESPONDING TO LITERATURE

Reviewing a Fiction Book 142
Reviewing a Nonfiction Book.................................... 150
Writing for Assessment 158

CREATIVE WRITING

Writing Stories.. 162
Writing Poems 170

REPORT WRITING

Finding Information 180
Writing a Report.. 188

The Tools of Learning

Speaking to Others 202
Learning to Listen 204
Learning to Interview 206
Writing in Journals 208
Using Learning Logs 210
Being a Smart Viewer 212
Taking Tests 214

Words

Words 218

A Writer's Resource

A Writer's Resource 240

Proofreader's Guide

Using Punctuation 270
Using Capital Letters 275
Making Plurals 278
Checking Spelling 279
Using the Right Word 284
Understanding Opposites 287
Understanding Sentences 288
Using the Parts of Speech 291

Theme Words

People 300
Places 302
Things 304
Animals 306
Foods 308
Activities 310

Copy Masters

Editing and Proofreading Marks 316
Benchmark Papers 317
Graphic Organizers 333
Worksheets 340
Family Connection Letters 395
Unit-Planning Worksheets 413
Getting-Started Activities 415
Credits 419

Index

Index 420

How does *Write Source* work?

Write Source is a complete language arts curriculum focused on writing and grammar in print and digital formats.

With writing instruction at the core, grammar, usage, and mechanics are taught in an authentic writing context.

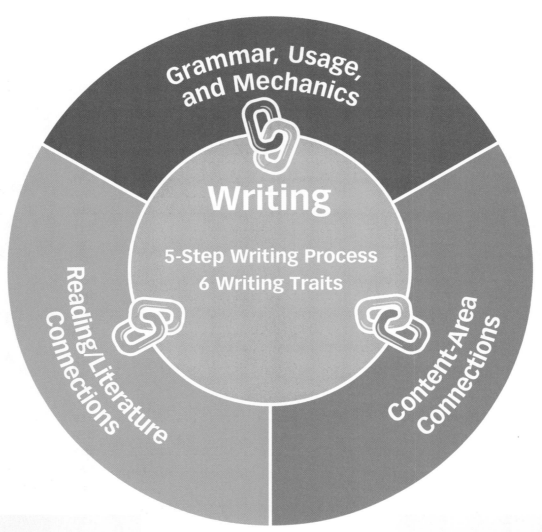

The Six Traits of Effective Writing

- Ideas
- Organization
- Voice
- Word Choice
- Sentence Fluency
- Conventions

Steps of the Writing Process

- Prewriting
- Writing
- Revising
- Editing
- Publishing

Introduce the writing form:

- **Read authentic real-world fiction or nonfiction** that models the writing form.
- Preview the form by learning about its content and/or structure.
- Discuss ideas for a paragraph.

Each core forms of writing unit follows the same instructional path—a consistent writing curriculum across all grade levels.

Explore the writing form:

- Analyze a model paragraph.
- Use the writing process to write a paragraph.
- Revise and then edit the writing for **conventions**.

Write in the content areas:

- Write a piece in the same writing form **across two of the major content areas**—science, social studies, math, and the arts.

Write for the assessment:

- Using the unit's writing form, write a paragraph for assessment.

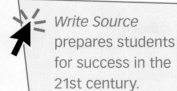

Write Source prepares students for success in the 21st century.

What are the main components of *Write Source?*

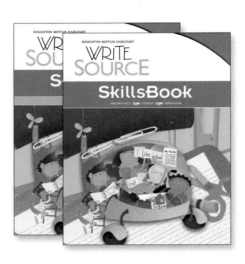

The Assessment book provides a pretest, progress tests, and a post-test.

The **Daily Language Workouts** build student conventions skills through quick, daily editing and proofreading activities.

The *Write Source* **Student Edition** reflects the latest research on writing instruction. The **Teacher's Edition** has all the support you need to help students become confident, proficient writers.

The **SkillsBook** helps students practice and improve grammar, usage, and mechanics skills.

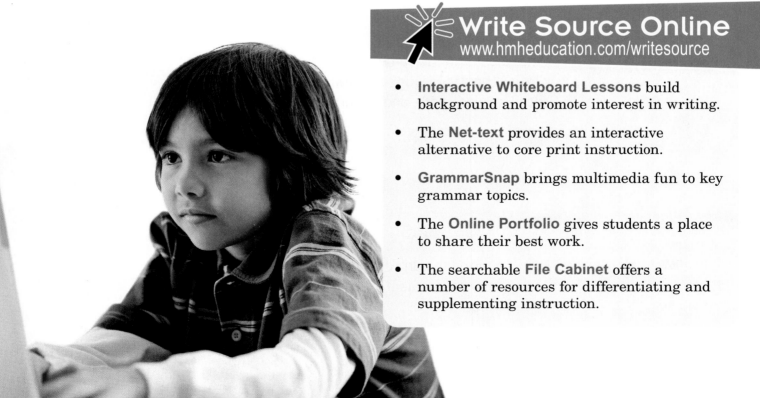

Write Source Online
www.hmheducation.com/writesource

- **Interactive Whiteboard Lessons** build background and promote interest in writing.

- The **Net-text** provides an interactive alternative to core print instruction.

- **GrammarSnap** brings multimedia fun to key grammar topics.

- The **Online Portfolio** gives students a place to share their best work.

- The searchable **File Cabinet** offers a number of resources for differentiating and supplementing instruction.

How does the Teacher's Edition support instruction?

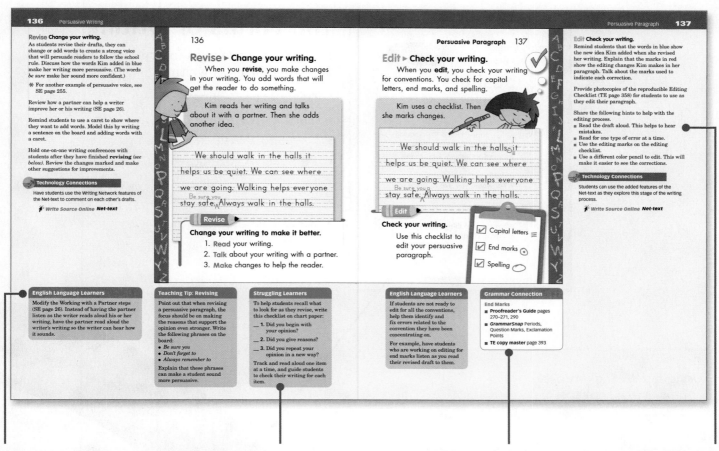

Revise Change your writing.

As students revise their drafts, they can change or add words to create a strong voice that will persuade readers to follow the school rule. Discuss how the words Kim added in blue make her writing more persuasive. (The words *be sure* make her sound more confident.)

✳ For another example of persuasive voice, see SE page 255.

Review how a partner can help a writer improve her or his writing (SE page 26).

Remind students to use a caret to show where they want to add words. Model this by writing a sentence on the board and adding words with a caret.

Hold one-on-one writing conferences with students after they have finished **revising** *(see below)*. Review the changes marked and make other suggestions for improvements.

Technology Connections

Have students use the Writing Network features of the Net-text to comment on each other's drafts.

🏃 *Write Source Online* **Net-text**

136

Revise ▶ Change your writing.

When you **revise**, you make changes in your writing. You add words that will get the reader to do something.

Kim reads her writing and talks about it with a partner. Then she adds another idea.

> We should walk in the halls it
> helps us be quiet. We can see where
> we are going. Walking helps everyone
> Be sure you
> stay safe. Always walk in the halls.

Revise

Change your writing to make it better.
1. Read your writing.
2. Talk about your writing with a partner.
3. Make changes to help the reader.

Edit ▶ Check your writing.

When you **edit**, you check your writing for conventions. You check for capital letters, end marks, and spelling.

Kim uses a checklist. Then she marks changes.

> We should walk in the halls it
> helps us be quiet. We can see where
> we are going. Walking helps everyone
> Be sure you a
> stay safe. Always walk in the halls.

Edit

Check your writing.

Use this checklist to edit your persuasive paragraph.

☑ Capital letters ≡
☑ End marks ⊙
☑ Spelling ◯

Edit Check your writing.

Remind students that the words in blue show the new idea Kim added when she revised her writing. Explain that the marks in red show the editing changes Kim makes in her paragraph. Talk about the marks used to indicate each correction.

Provide photocopies of the reproducible Editing Checklist (TE page 358) for students to use as they edit their paragraph.

Share the following hints to help with the editing process.
■ Read the draft aloud. This helps to hear mistakes.
■ Read for one type of error at a time.
■ Use the editing marks on the editing checklist.
■ Use a different color pencil to edit. This will make it easier to see the corrections.

Technology Connections

Students can use the added features of the Net-text as they explore this stage of the writing process.

🏃 *Write Source Online* **Net-text**

English Language Learners

Modify the Working with a Partner steps (SE page 26). Instead of having the partner listen as the writer reads aloud his or her writing, have the partner read aloud the writer's writing so the writer can hear how it sounds.

Teaching Tip: Revising

Point out that when revising a persuasive paragraph, the focus should be on making the reasons that support the opinion even stronger. Write the following phrases on the board:
• *Be sure you*
• *Don't forget to*
• *Always remember to*
Explain that these phrases can make a student sound more persuasive.

Struggling Learners

To help students recall what to look for as they revise, write this checklist on chart paper:
___ 1. Did you begin with your opinion?
___ 2. Did you give reasons?
___ 3. Did you repeat your opinion in a new way?
Track and read aloud one item at a time, and guide students to check their writing for each item.

English Language Learners

If students are not ready to edit for all the conventions, help them identify and fix errors related to the convention they have been concentrating on.
For example, have students who are working on editing for end marks listen as you read their revised draft to them.

Grammar Connection

End Marks
■ *Proofreader's Guide* pages 270–271, 290
■ *GrammarSnap* Periods, Question Marks, Exclamation Points
■ **TE copy master** page 393

The Teacher's Edition provides consistent support for **English language learners**.

Differentiated Instruction for struggling learners and advanced learners is provided throughout the core instructional units.

Grammar Connections support grammar, usage, and mechanics instruction.

Teaching suggestions and activity answers provide the support you need to implement writing instruction.

Additional Resources

- Common Core State Standards Correlation
- Yearlong Timetable
- Professional Development for Writing

- Reading–Writing Connection
- "Getting Started" Copy Masters
- Benchmark Papers
- Graphic Organizers
- Family Letters

How is *Write Source* organized?

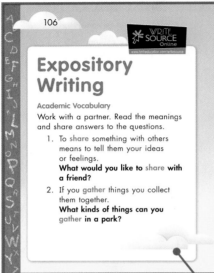

106

Expository Writing

Academic Vocabulary

Work with a partner. Read the meanings and share answers to the questions.

1. To share something with others means to tell them your ideas or feelings.
   What would you like to share with a friend?

2. If you gather things you collect them together.
   What kinds of things can you gather in a park?

The Forms of Writing

Write Source provides instruction in the following forms of writing:

- Descriptive Writing
- Narrative Writing
- Expository Writing
- Persuasive Writing
- Responding to Literature
- Creative Writing
- Report Writing

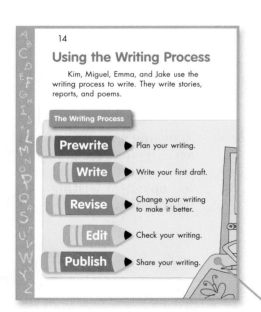

14

Using the Writing Process

Kim, Miguel, Emma, and Jake use the writing process to write. They write stories, reports, and poems.

The Writing Process

Prewrite ▶ Plan your writing.

Write ▶ Write your first draft.

Revise ▶ Change your writing to make it better.

Edit ▶ Check your writing.

Publish ▶ Share your writing.

The Writing Process

This unit introduces students to the steps in the writing process and integrates instruction on the six traits of writing.

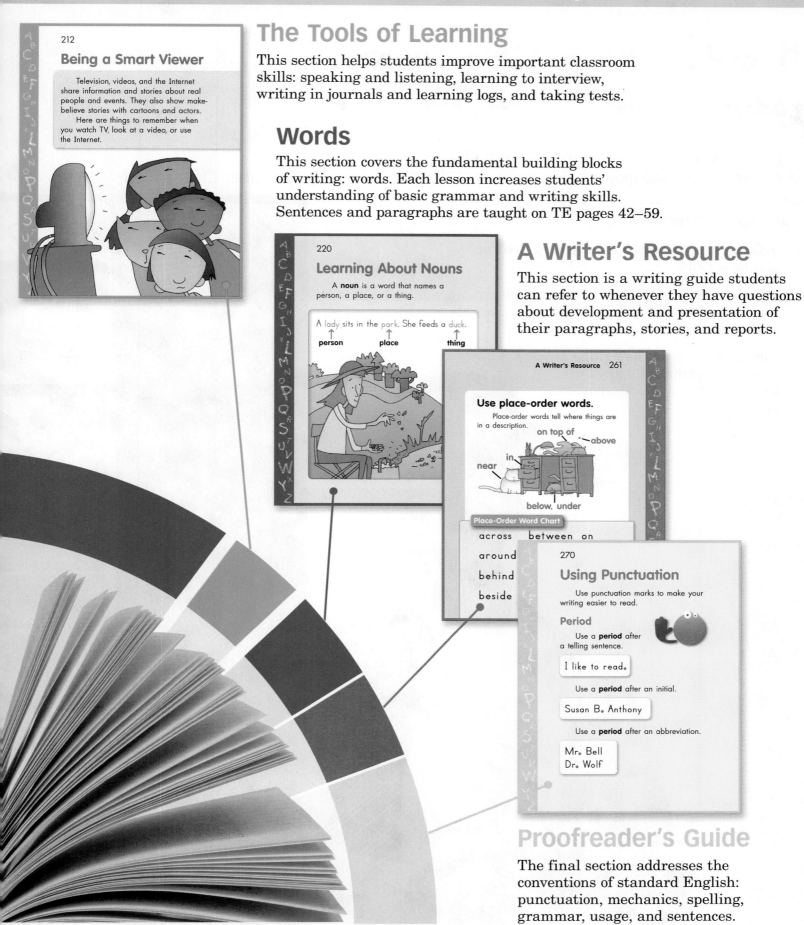

212

Being a Smart Viewer

Television, videos, and the Internet share information and stories about real people and events. They also show make-believe stories with cartoons and actors.

Here are things to remember when you watch TV, look at a video, or use the Internet.

The Tools of Learning

This section helps students improve important classroom skills: speaking and listening, learning to interview, writing in journals and learning logs, and taking tests.

Words

This section covers the fundamental building blocks of writing: words. Each lesson increases students' understanding of basic grammar and writing skills. Sentences and paragraphs are taught on TE pages 42–59.

220

Learning About Nouns

A **noun** is a word that names a person, a place, or a thing.

A lady sits in the park. She feeds a duck.

person   place   thing

A Writer's Resource

This section is a writing guide students can refer to whenever they have questions about development and presentation of their paragraphs, stories, and reports.

A Writer's Resource   261

Use place-order words.

Place-order words tell where things are in a description.

on top of   above

in

near

below, under

Place-Order Word Chart

across   between   on

around

behind

beside

270

Using Punctuation

Use punctuation marks to make your writing easier to read.

Period

Use a **period** after a telling sentence.

I like to read.

Use a **period** after an initial.

Susan B. Anthony

Use a **period** after an abbreviation.

Mr. Bell
Dr. Wolf

Proofreader's Guide

The final section addresses the conventions of standard English: punctuation, mechanics, spelling, grammar, usage, and sentences.

How does *Write Source* support today's digital-age learners?

*W*rite Source Online taps into the power of interactivity and motivation to deliver a coordinated, comprehensive technology program that empowers teachers to . . .

- build an early **foundation in writing and key grammar skills**

- deliver **interactive instruction** using Net-text, an easy-to-use online application featuring complete writing support

- engage students in the writing process through **customizable avatars, dashboards,** and **electronic portfolios**

Teacher Dashboard

Mr. Rodriguez

Class:
Third Period English

Change   Sign out

WRITE SOU

Narrative Wri

Punctuation

FFLIN HARCOURT

Write Source Online
www.hmheducation.com/writesource

**Preparing students and teachers
for success in the 21st century.**

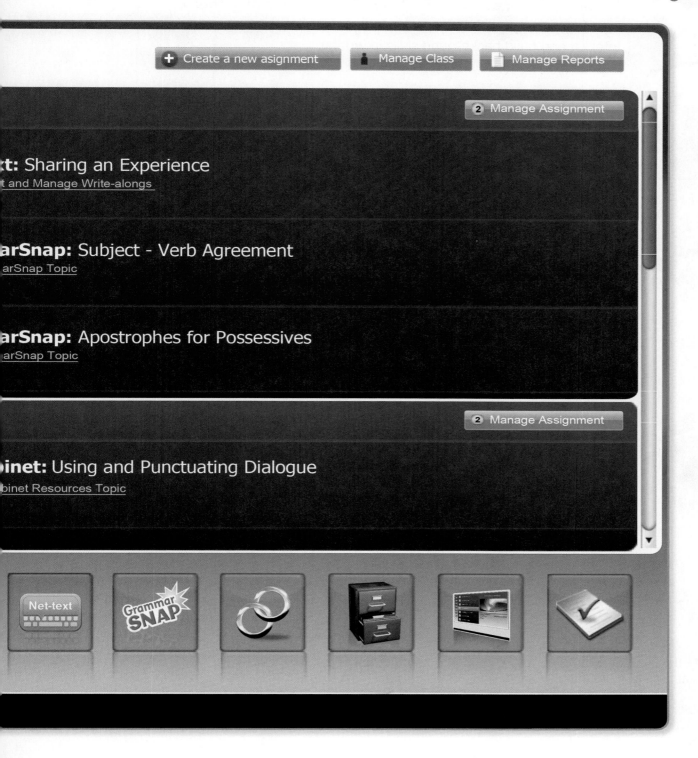

+ Create a new asignment   **Manage Class**   **Manage Reports**

2 Manage Assignment

t: Sharing an Experience
t and Manage Write-alongs

arSnap: Subject - Verb Agreement
arSnap Topic

arSnap: Apostrophes for Possessives
arSnap Topic

2 Manage Assignment

inet: Using and Punctuating Dialogue
binet Resources Topic

Net-text   Grammar SNAP

What are the components of *Write Source Online?*

Set the stage for success with Interactive Whiteboard Lessons, high-functioning multimedia presentations that help you promote interest and build background skills in writing.

Transform students into aspiring young writers with Net-text, an online application that features full audio, click-and-reveal instruction, useful checklists, and more.

Put the fun into grammar with GrammarSnap, a multimedia application that builds foundation in key topics through videos, games, and quizzes.

Students can use **SkillSnap points earned in GrammarSnap to unlock a variety of accessories** for their personal avatar.

Tap into the power of publishing with the *Write Source Online* Portfolio, a customizable resource that gives students an authentic forum for sharing their writing.

With teacher support, students can connect with each other in **My Network** to share their published pieces.

Simplify the management of daily work with the Assignment Manager, a tool that delivers automatic student notifications about due dates and next steps.

Energize instruction with an innovative, integrated online writing program.

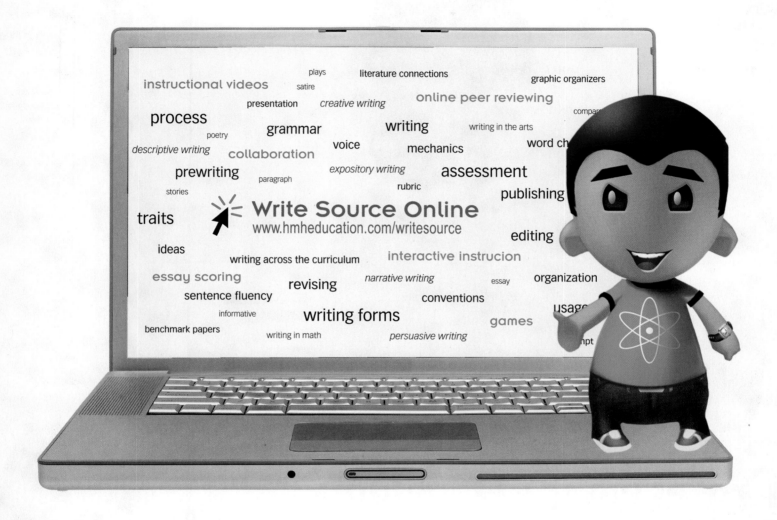

Additional Resources

- **Bookshelf** *Write Source* print component eBooks
- **File Cabinet** Additional resources, such as blackline masters and additional assessments, that help you minimize planning time and differentiate instruction

Professional Development for Writing

This section of the *Write Source* Teacher's Edition provides information to help you make the most of *Write Source* in your classroom. The program's instructional design includes comprehensive support for the topics that matter most to teachers: grammar, writing workshops, academic vocabulary, test preparation, the use of technology, and so much more. Whether you are a new teacher or a veteran, the information in the following pages will show how *Write Source* can help you meet your classroom goals.

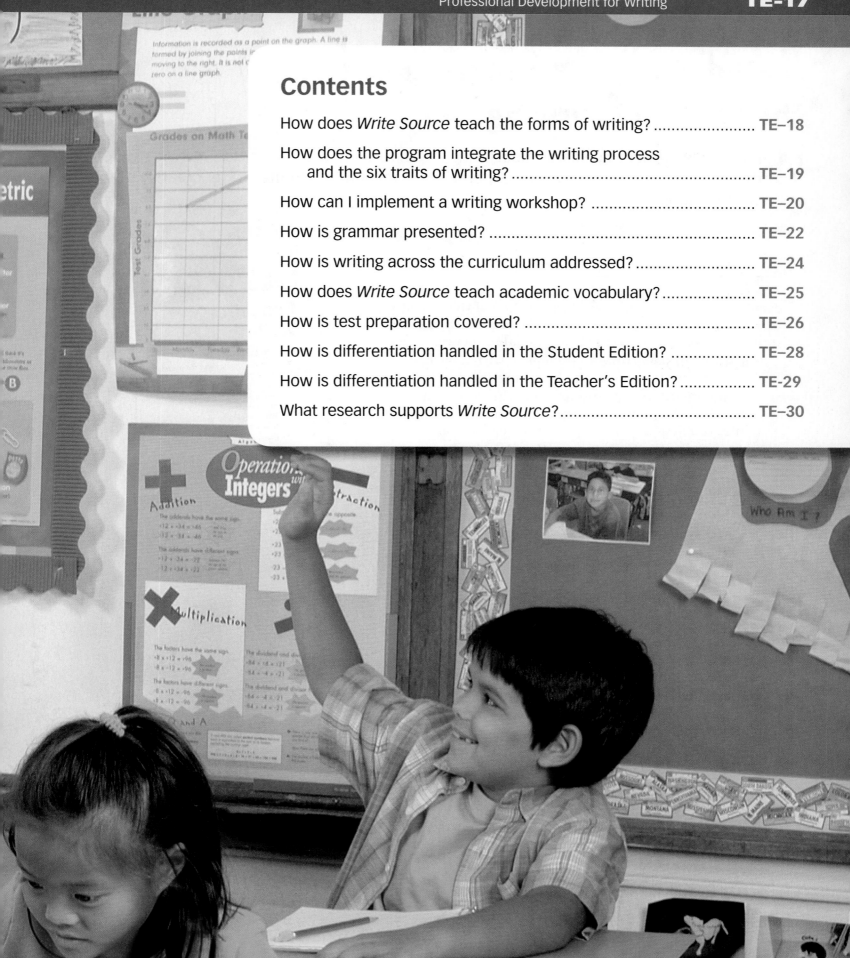

Contents

How does *Write Source* teach the forms of writing? TE–18

How does the program integrate the writing process
    and the six traits of writing? TE–19

How can I implement a writing workshop? TE–20

How is grammar presented? TE–22

How is writing across the curriculum addressed? TE–24

How does *Write Source* teach academic vocabulary? TE–25

How is test preparation covered? TE–26

How is differentiation handled in the Student Edition? TE–28

How is differentiation handled in the Teacher's Edition? TE-29

What research supports *Write Source*? TE–30

How does *Write Source* teach the forms of writing?

Write Source provides numerous models and assignments for each major form of writing: **descriptive, narrative, expository, persuasive, responding to literature, creative,** and **report writing**.

Writing Assignments

The core writing units provide students with comprehensive, research-based exploration of the narrative, expository, and persuasive forms of writing. Each of these units employs the following instructional sequence:

- a **start-up assignment**—complete with a writing sample that introduces the form of writing
- a **paragraph assignment**—complete with writing model, in-depth step-by-step guidelines, and integration of traits and grammar instruction
- one or more **Writing Across the Curriculum assignments**—complete with writing models and writing tips
- an **assessment writing assignment**—complete with a model response to a prompt plus writing tips

Writing Skills and Strategies

As students develop their writing in each unit, they gain valuable experience in working with the following skills and strategies:

- reading and responding to texts (writing models)
- working with **the writing process integrated into the writing traits**
- using graphic organizers
- developing beginnings, middles, and endings
- publishing (presenting) writing
- reflecting on writing
- **responding to an assessment prompt**

How does the program integrate the writing process and the six traits?

Throughout each core forms of writing unit, the six traits of effective writing are integrated into the steps of the writing process. As students develop their writing, they acquire an understanding of and appreciation for each trait of writing. In addition, a rubric, checklists, guidelines, and activities are used to ensure that each piece of writing is completely traits based.

The Process and the Traits in the Core Units

Understand Your Writing Goal

The beginning of each core paragraph assignment helps students understand the goal of their writing. A chart listing the traits of writing helps students meet that goal.

Revising and Editing for the Traits

When students are ready to revise and edit, they will find guidelines and strategies to help them improve their writing for each of the featured traits.

Goals for the Core Units

The trait-based goals (usually featuring three traits) at the beginning of core units focus student writing and serve as an evaluation tool.

Special Note: For more information about the writing traits, we recommend *Creating Writers Through 6-Trait Writing Assessment and Instruction*, 4th ed., by Vicki Spandel (Addison Wesley Longman, 2005) and *Write Traits®* by Vicki Spandel and Jeff Hicks (Houghton Mifflin Harcourt, 2011).

How can I implement a writing workshop?

Write Source supports a workshop approach through both print and technology resources. The program includes minilessons for instruction, high-quality models to encourage writing, support for whole-class sharing, and much more.

Integrated Minilessons

As a starting point, **Interactive Whiteboard Lessons** provide short, focused teaching opportunities designed to lay a foundation in key concepts. Students build on this foundation as they move through the core forms of writing units, where each step in the writing process presents additional opportunities for minilessons targeting individual needs. Both the print book and the **Net-text** teach students to:

- preview the trait-based goal of a writing project
- select a topic
- gather details using a graphic organizer
- organize details
- create a strong paragraph
- revise the paragraph
- edit and proofread for conventions
- publish a finished piece

Mon	Tues	Wed	Thurs	Fri
		Writing Minilessons (10 minutes as needed)		
		Status Checks (2 minutes) Find out what students will work on for the day.		
		Individual Work (30 minutes) Writing, Revising, Editing, Conferencing, or Publishing		
		Whole-Class Sharing Session (5 minutes)		

Graphic Organizers

Write Source contains a wealth of graphic organizers that can serve as the subjects of minilessons. The graphic organizers modeled in print and technology include the following:

Web	Gathering grid	Time line	Sequence chart
Cluster	5 W's chart	List	Order chart
Sensory chart	Topic list	Bar graph chart	
Storyboard	Picture diagram	Story map	

High-Quality Models

Each core unit in the print book and the **Net-text** begins with a high-interest model, complete with annotations pointing out key features. Once students have read and analyzed each model, they will be ready—and excited—to begin their own writing. Other models and examples throughout each unit offer specific techniques that students can use in their own writing.

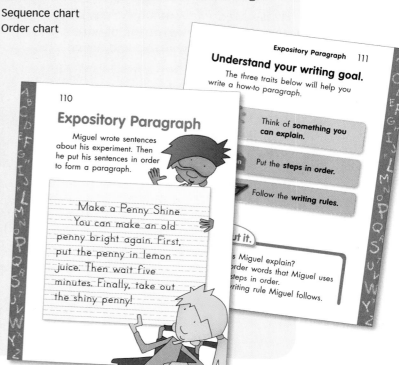

110

Expository Paragraph

Miguel wrote sentences about his experiment. Then he put his sentences in order to form a paragraph.

Make a Penny Shine
You can make an old penny bright again. First, put the penny in lemon juice. Then wait five minutes. Finally, take out the shiny penny!

Expository Paragraph   111

Understand your writing goal.
The three traits below will help you write a how-to paragraph.

Think of **something you can explain.**

Put the **steps in order.**

Follow the **writing rules.**

Individual Writing

Write Source print and technology resources make it easy for writing-workshop students to work on their own. They also provide specific help whenever students have questions about their writing. Here are some of the areas that are addressed:

- catching the reader's interest
- developing strong paragraphs
- elaborating (adding facts, examples, anecdotes, etc.)
- organizing ideas by time and location
- quoting
- using transitions

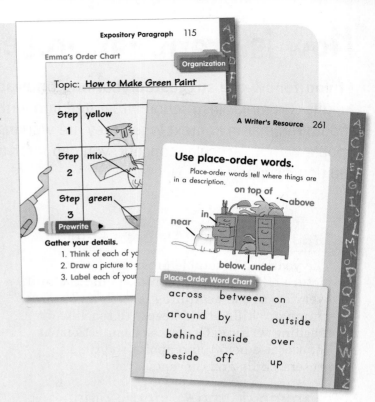

Peer and Teacher Response

Write Source teaches peer responding and provides a peer response sheet. Consistent integration of the traits into the writing process allows students and teachers to speak a common language as they conduct responding sessions. Traits-based conventions checklists and rubrics help pinpoint just what is working—and what could work better—in each piece of writing.

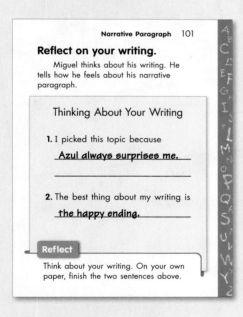

Whole-Class Sharing

Write Source helps students prepare their work for whole-class sharing— whether in a traditional presentation or in the public section of the **Online Portfolio**. In addition, the program provides a wealth of suggestions for publishing in a variety of forms and for a variety of audiences.

How is grammar presented?

If you follow the suggested yearlong timetable, you will cover all the key grammar skills. Grammar instruction integrated into writing instruction allows students to learn about grammar in context when they are working on their own writing. If students have trouble with a particular concept, you can refer to a wealth of print and online resources for additional support.

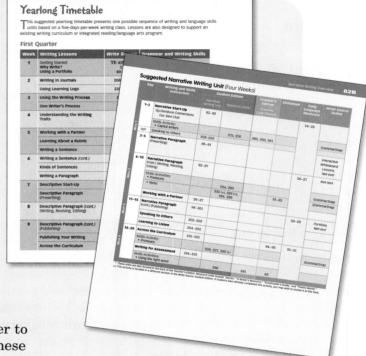

Grammar in the Teacher's Edition

The yearlong timetable provides the big picture of grammar integration, and the unit overview at the beginning of each unit shows grammar skills and concepts to teach while teaching writing. Grammar Connections at point of use help you pinpoint the time to present skills and concepts.

Grammar in the Student Edition

Forms of Writing

Each core unit includes grammar instruction integrated within the revising and editing steps.

Basic Grammar and Writing

For more grammar in the context of writing, refer to "Words" and "Sentences and Paragraphs." Use these minilessons to teach specific grammar and style topics that students can apply to their writing. These pages include examples of each skill, as well as practice activities.

Proofreader's Guide

This unit serves as a complete conventions guide, providing grammar, usage, and mechanics rules, instruction, examples, and practice.

Grammar in Other Program Components

The *SkillsBook* provides more than 130 grammar, usage, punctuation, mechanics, spelling, and sentence-construction activities. For key topics at each grade, GrammarSnap provides interactive instruction, practice, and basic skills reinforcement through videos, minilessons, games, and quizzes. The *Assessment* book contains a pretest, benchmark tests, and a post-test for basic writing and editing skills. *Daily Language Workouts* includes a year's worth of sentences (daily) and paragraphs (weekly) for editing practice.

Planning Grammar Instruction

Should I implement all of the suggested basic grammar activities?

In the course of the year, if you assigned every grammar exercise listed in the unit scope and sequence charts (located in the unit overviews of your Teacher's Edition), your students would complete **all** of the "Basic Grammar and Writing," "Proofreader's Guide," *SkillsBook*, and **GrammarSnap** activities.

Because the most effective teaching of grammar happens in context, grammar instruction appears at appropriate times during the revising and editing steps of the core writing forms units. As the teacher, you must choose the type and amount of instruction that will best meet the needs of your students.

How are all the grammar resources related?

The *Write Source SkillsBook* grammar activities parallel and expand on the rules and exercises found in the "Proofreader's Guide." In "Basic Grammar and Writing," brief exercises function well as minilessons and may be assigned on an as-needed basis. **GrammarSnap** offers additional support for key grammar topics in an engaging, interactive format.

How do I use the unit scope and sequence charts?

The sample below from the persuasive writing unit is followed by an explanation of how to read and use the charts.

Suggested Persuasive Writing Unit (Four Weeks)

Day	Writing and Skills Instruction	Student Edition		Teacher's Edition	SkillsBook	Daily Language Workouts	Write Source Online
		Persuasive Writing Unit	Resource Units*	Grammar Copy Masters			
1–2	**Persuasive Start-Up** ◔ Literature Connections "Three Reasons Why Pets Are Great"	131–133				38–41	
	Skills Activities: • Opposites		287	392	66		
opt.	*Speaking to Others*	202–203					
3–5	**Being a Smart Viewer**	212–213					

1. The Resource Units column indicates the Student Edition pages that cover rules, examples, and exercises for corresponding skills activities.
2. The *SkillsBook, Daily Language Workouts*, and **Write Source Online** columns indicate pages and information from those particular resources.

How do I use *Daily Language Workouts*?

Daily Language Workouts is a teacher resource that provides a high-interest sentence for each day of the year and weekly paragraphs for additional editing and proofreading practice. This regular practice helps students develop the objectivity they need to effectively edit their own writing.

How is writing across the curriculum addressed?

*W*rite Source provides a wide variety of writing-across-the-curriculum activities and assignments. It promotes *writing to show learning, writing to learn new concepts,* and *writing to reflect on learning.*

Writing to Show Learning

Writing to show learning is the most common type of writing that content-area teachers assign. The following forms of writing covered in the program are commonly used for this purpose.

- descriptive paragraph
- narrative paragraph
- expository paragraph
- persuasive paragraph
- response paragraph book review
- response to nonfiction
- response to a poem
- research report

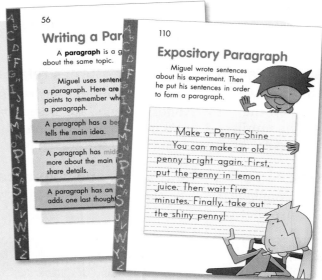

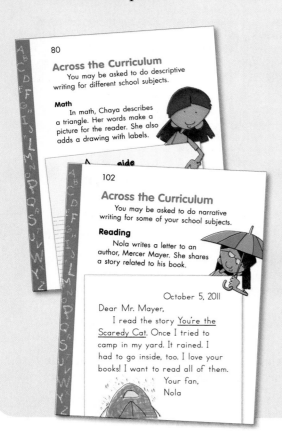

Sample Writing-Across-the-Curriculum Assignments

Descriptive Writing
    Math: A Shape
    Science: A Classroom Pet

Narrative Writing
    Reading: Letter to an Author
    Music: Personal Story

Expository Writing
    Math: Explain a Math Problem
    Social Studies: A Report

Persuasive Writing
    Health: Healthy Food Choice

How does *Write Source* teach Academic Vocabulary?

Write Source gives students the opportunity to learn and use academic vocabulary so essential for success in school.

Academic Vocabulary in *Write Source*

Academic vocabulary refers to the words students must know in order to understand the concepts they encounter in school. Academic vocabulary such as *share, gather,* and *describe* are not specific to any one subject but rather denote key ideas and skills relevant to many subject areas. In a sense, academic vocabulary is the language of school. To be successful in school, students must understand and be able to use academic vocabulary as they write about and discuss what they learn in class.

The *Write Source* Academic Vocabulary feature gives students the opportunity to learn and practice using new academic vocabulary in a collaborative activity. This feature, which appears at the beginning of each unit of the Student Edition, provides a brief explanation of each academic vocabulary word, followed by a prompt that motivates students to practice using the term.

- Academic vocabulary is taken from words appearing in the unit.
- Students work with a partner to read the explanations of the academic vocabulary.
- Each explanation is accompanied by an activity or question that prompts students to demonstrate their understanding of the word.

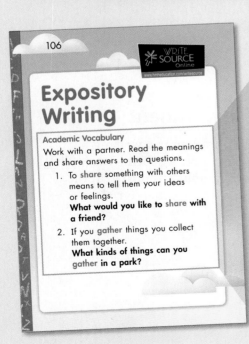

Academic Vocabulary

Work with a partner. Read the meanings and share answers to the questions.

1. To **share** something with others means to tell them your ideas or feelings.
   What would you like to share with a friend?

2. If you **gather** things you collect them together.
   What kinds of things can you gather in a park?

How is test preparation covered?

Each core forms of writing unit in the Student Edition prepares students for responding to testing prompts. **If students complete their work in each of the core units, they will have learned the skills necessary for success on any type of writing assessment.** Here are some of the main features in the Student Edition that address testing.

Core Writing Units

The *Write Source* program teaches descriptive, narrative, expository, and persuasive writing, and responding to literature—the main forms of writing included on writing assessments.

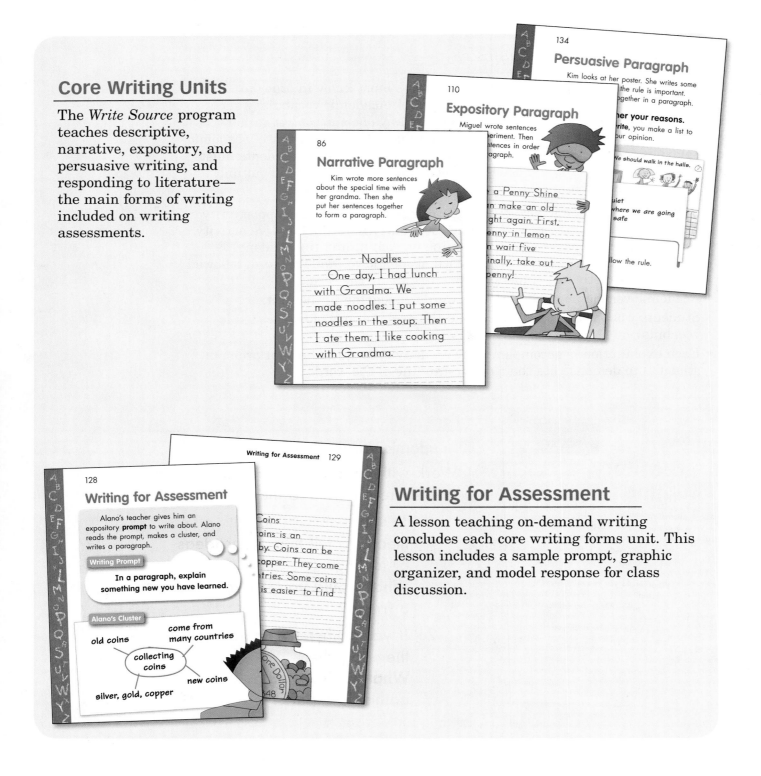

Writing for Assessment

A lesson teaching on-demand writing concludes each core writing forms unit. This lesson includes a sample prompt, graphic organizer, and model response for class discussion.

Responding to Literature

Special attention is given to assessing literary response. Included in this unit is a response to a poem.

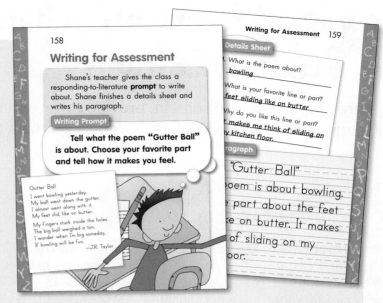

Taking Tests

The chapter on taking tests includes examples of the four main types of tests.

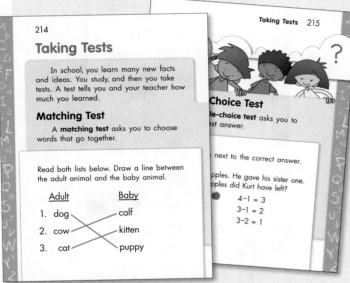

Writing Across the Curriculum

The writing-across-the-curriculum assignments at the end of the core forms of writing units help students prepare for on-demand writing in content-based tests.

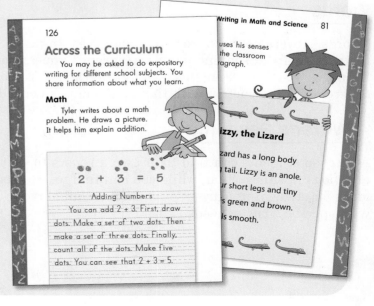

How is differentiation handled in the Student Edition?

Write Source **texts,** by design, **provide differentiation** in writing instruction—from struggling learners and English-language learners to advanced, independent students.

Core Form of Writing Units

Implementation Options: You can implement the forms of writing units, one assignment after another, as delineated in the yearlong timetable (pages TE-32–TE-35), helping individuals or small groups of students as needed. Or you can differentiate instruction in any number of ways. Here are three of the many possibilities:

- Have **struggling learners** focus on the start-up activity and generate as complete a writing assignment as possible (perhaps a list or a sentence or two) while other students complete the paragraph assignment.
- Have **advanced learners** work individually or in small groups on the paragraph assignment while you guide struggling learners step-by-step through the development of the paragraph.
- Conduct a **writing workshop** (pages TE-20–TE-21), asking advanced learners to develop an assignment (perhaps an additional across-the-curriculum assignment) in the unit at their own pace.

Words

"Words," covers nouns, verbs, and adjectives. In-depth instruction about sentences and paragraphs appears on SE pages 42–49 in "Sentences and Paragraphs." You can differentiate instruction with these chapters as needed.

A Writer's Resource

Advanced students can find their own answers to writing questions in this section, while you can find minilesson ideas for struggling learners and English language learners with specific writing needs.

84
Narrative Start-Up

In a **personal narrative,** you write a story about something you did.

Kim writes about a special time.
Kim remembers a day with her grandma. She writes a first sentence about it.

Here are two points to remember when you write a personal narrative.

86
Narrative Paragraph

Kim wrote more sentences about the special time with her grandma. Then she put her sentences together to form a paragraph.

Noodles
One day, I had lunch with Grandma. We made noodles. I put some

218
Words

Academic Vocabulary
Work with a partner. Read the meanings and share answers to the questions.

1. A person is a man, woman, or child. **What kind of** person **is your teacher?**
2. Something that is happening is going on or taking place. **What is** happening **in your**

240
A Writer's Resource

Academic Vocabulary
Work with a partner. Read the meanings and share answers to the questions.

1. When you finish something, you come to the end of it. **What do you do with your homework when you** finish **it?**
2. A chart is a drawing that shows information. **Is information easier to read in a** chart? **Explain.**
3. To connect two things means to join them together. **What might** connect **one room to another?**

How is differentiation handled in the Teacher's Edition?

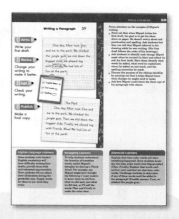

The Teacher's Edition provides point-of-use differentiation for struggling learners, English language learners, and advanced learners.

Struggling Learners

The Struggling Learners notes allow you to customize lessons to meet the needs of students who may have difficulty completing the work. These notes provide alternative approaches, extra practice, or additional insights.

Struggling Learners

To help students understand the difference between the naming and telling parts, write the following sentence frames on sentence strips:

The children _____.
The animals _____.

Explain that each pair of words is the naming part of a sentence.

Have students brainstorm some action words, and write each word on a word card. Help students read the words. Explain that these words could be used as the telling part in sentences. Have students take turns slotting the word cards in the blanks to complete each sentence. Help students read the sentences aloud to make sure that they express complete thoughts.

English Language Learners

If students choose as a topic a food that is unfamiliar to you, you will be unable to offer vocabulary support. Therefore, encourage students to think of other topics. Before students fill out their list, review Emma's list. Identify each item by name and category (hamster, mouse/pet; train, doll/toy). Encourage students to think of toys, pets, or other categories to include on their list.

English Language Learners

The English Language Learners notes help you to guide students with limited language skills through the lessons. These notes provide extra practice, alternative approaches, connections to first languages, glossaries of new terms, demonstration ideas, and more.

Advanced Learners

The Advanced Learners notes help you enhance the lessons for students who need to be challenged. Some of the notes extend the lessons.

Advanced Learners

Challenge students to think of a first sentence that not only introduces the topic but makes their readers want to find out more.
- Flat beginning: *My aunt bakes great calzones.*
- Interesting beginning: *Who makes the biggest, cheesiest, tastiest calzones? My aunt Angie makes them every summer when I visit her!*

What research supports the *Write Source* program?

Write Source reflects the best thinking and research on writing instruction.

Applying the Process Approach to Writing

Research: The process approach, discussed by educators Donald M. Murray and Donald H. Graves, among others, breaks writing down into a series of steps—prewriting through publishing. Research has shown that students write more effectively and thoughtfully if they approach their work as a process rather than as an end product.

Graves, Donald. H. *Writing: Teachers and Children at Work.* Heinemann, 2003.

Murray, Donald. M.; Newkirk, Thomas; Miller, Lisa C. *The Essential Don Murray: Lessons from America's Greatest Writing Teacher.* Boynton/Cook Heinemann, 2009.

Write Source: All writing units and assignments are arranged according to the steps in the writing process. This arrangement helps students manage their work, especially in the case of longer essay or research report assignments.

Sequencing Assignments

Research: Writing instructor and researcher James Moffett developed a sequence of writing assignments—known as the "universe of discourse"—that has over the years served countless English/language arts classrooms. Moffett sequences the modes of writing according to their connection or immediacy to the writer. Moffett suggests that students first develop descriptive and narrative pieces because the students have an immediate, personal connection to this type of writing. Next, they should develop informational pieces that require some investigation before moving on to more challenging, reflective writing, such as persuasive essays and position papers.

Moffett, James. *Teaching the Universe of Discourse.* Boynton/Cook, 1987.

Related Title: Fleischer, Cathy; Andrew-Vaughn, Sarah. *Writing Outside Your Comfort Zone: Helping Students Navigate Unfamiliar Genres.* Heinemann, 2009.

Write Source: The writing units and assignments in the *Write Source* texts are arranged according to the "universe of discourse," starting with descriptive and narrative writing, moving on to expository writing, and so on. These assignments are designed to be used in a sequence that supports an existing writing curriculum or integrated reading/language arts program.

Implementing a Writing Workshop

Research: Countless respected writing instructors and researchers have advocated the importance of establishing a community of writers in the classroom. Teachers can establish such a community by implementing a writing workshop. In a writing workshop, students are immersed in all aspects of writing, including sharing their work with their peers.

Atwell, Nancie. *In the Middle: New Understandings About Writing, Reading, and Learning.* Heinemann, 1998.

Write Source: The instruction in *Write Source* is clearly presented so that most students can work independently on their writing in a workshop. In addition, the core forms of writing units contain innumerable opportunities for workshop minilessons.

Producing Writing with Detail

Research: Rebekah Caplan learned through her teaching experience that students don't automatically know how to add details to their personal, informational, and persuasive writing. She discovered with her students that adding detail to writing is a skill that must be practiced regularly. To address this problem, Caplan came up with the "show-me" sentence strategy, in which students begin with a basic idea—"My locker is messy"—and create a brief paragraph that shows rather than tells the idea.

Caplan, Rebekah. *Writers in Training: A Guide to Developing a Composition Program.* Dale Seymour Publications, 1984.

Related Title: Bernabi, Gretchen S.; Hover, Jayne; Candler, Cynthia. *Crunchtime: Lessons to Help Students Blow the Roof Off Writing Tests—and Become Better Writers in the Process.* Heinemann, 2009.

Write Source: *Daily Language Workouts* contains a series of show-me sentences that teachers can implement as a regular classroom warm-up.

Meeting Students' Diverse Needs

Research: Many students in today's classrooms struggle with writing. For struggling students, following the writing process is not enough. According to the research done by James L. Collins, struggling students need specific strategies and aids to help them become better writers. Collins found that these students benefit from skills instruction integrated into the process of writing, color coding and signposts in the presentation of instructional material, the use of graphic organizers, instructions presented in discreet chunks of copy, and so on.

Collins, James L. *Strategies for Struggling Writers.* Guilford Press, 1998.

Related Title: Cruz, M. Colleen; Calkins, Lucy. *A Quick Guide to Reaching Struggling Writers, K–5.* FirstHand/Heinemann, 2008.

Write Source: The core writing forms units contain all the key features from Collins's work. As a result, the units are well suited to struggling learners and English language learners.

Yearlong Timetable

This suggested yearlong timetable presents one possible sequence of writing and language skills units based on a five-days-per-week writing class. Lessons are also designed to support an existing writing curriculum or integrated reading/language arts program.

First Quarter

Week	Writing Lessons	Write Source	Grammar and Writing Skills
1	Getting Started **Why Write?** **Using a Portfolio**	TE 415–417 11 40–41	
2	**Writing in Journals**	208–209	Writing dates, capitalize days, ABC order
	Using Learning Logs	210–211	
3	**Using the Writing Process**	14–15	Capitalize first word, ABC order
	One Writer's Process	16–25	
4	**Understanding the Writing Traits**	28–35	Sentences—Complete thought, sentence word order, singular and plural nouns
5	**Working with a Partner**	26–27	
	Learning About a Rubric	36–37	
	Writing a Sentence	44–47	Sentences—Complete thought, word order, naming part, telling part
6	**Writing a Sentence** (cont.)	48–53	
	Kinds of Sentences	54–55	Telling sentence, asking sentence, exclamatory sentence
	Writing a Paragraph	56–59	
7	**Descriptive Start-Up**	62–63	Adjectives
	Descriptive Paragraph (Prewriting)	64–69	
8	**Descriptive Paragraph** (cont.) (Writing, Revising, Editing)	70–75	Adjectives, action and linking verbs, present and past tenses, place-order words
9	**Descriptive Paragraph** (cont.) (Publishing)	76–79	Place-order words, pronouns, using the right word
	Publishing Your Writing	38–39	
	Across the Curriculum	80–81	

Second Quarter

Week	Writing Lessons	*Write Source*	Grammar and Writing Skills
1	**Narrative Start-Up**	84–85	Capitalize first word
	Narrative Paragraph (Prewriting)	86–91	
2	**Narrative Paragraph** (cont.) (Writing, Revising, Editing)	92–97	Pronouns, linking verbs
	Working with a Partner	26–27	
3	**Narrative Paragraph** (cont.) (Publishing)	98–101	
	Speaking to Others	202–203	
	Learning to Listen	204–205	
4	**Across the Curriculum**	102–103	Pronouns, using the right word
	Writing for Assessment	104–105	
	Portfolio Review		
5	**Expository Start-Up**	108–109	Nouns, plurals (singular and plural nouns), sentences—end punctuation
	Expository Paragraph (Prewriting)	110–115	
6	**Expository Paragraph** (cont.) (Writing, Revising, Editing)	116–121	
7	**Expository Paragraph** (cont.) (Publishing)	122–125	
	Across the Curriculum	126–127	Proper nouns, capital letters (names and titles), using the right word
	Writing for Assessment	128–129	
8	**Reviewing a Fiction Book**	142–146	Proper nouns, capital letters (special names)
	Working with a Partner	26–27	
9	**Fiction Book** (cont.)	147–149	Spelling
	Writing for Assessment	158–159	Irregular plurals
	Taking Tests	214–217	
	Portfolio Review		

Third Quarter

Week	Writing Lessons	Write Source	Grammar and Writing Skills
1	Persuasive Start-Up	132–133	Opposites
2	Being a Smart Viewer	212–213	
	Persuasive Paragraph (Prewriting)	134	End punctuation
3	Persuasive Paragraph (cont.) (Writing, Revising, Editing)	135–137	
	Working with a Partner	26–27	
4	Persuasive Paragraph (cont.) (Publishing)	138	
	Across the Curriculum	139	Commas in a series
5	Writing Stories (Prewriting)	162–166	Apostrophes
6	Stories (cont.) (Writing, Revising, Editing)	167–168	Kinds of sentences, spelling
	Working with a Partner	26–27	
7	Stories (cont.) (Publishing) Speaking to Others	169 202–203	
8	Reviewing a Nonfiction Book (Prewriting)	150–153	Pronouns
9	Nonfiction Book (cont.) (Writing, Revising, Editing, Publishing)	154–157	End punctuation

Fourth Quarter

Week	Writing Lessons	*Write Source*	Grammar and Writing Skills
1	**Finding Information**	180–183	
2	**Finding Information** *(cont.)*	184–187	
	Learning to Interview	206–207	
3	Writing a Friendly Letter	102, 272–273	Capitalize days and months, punctuation review
4	**Writing a Report** (Prewriting)	188–191	
5	**Report** *(cont.)* (Writing)	192–195	Verbs (action and linking), sentence review, capital-letter review
	Working with Partners	26–27	
6	**Report** *(cont.)* (Revising, Editing, Publishing)	196–199	Plurals, subject-verb agreement
7	**Writing Poems**	170–173	Adjectives, parts of speech review, spelling
8	**Poem** *(cont.)* (ABC poem, rhyming poem)	174–177	
9	Writing Project (Choice) Journal and Portfolio Review		

Reading-Writing Connection

The literary works listed on pages TE-36–TE-43 provide high-interest **mentor texts** that you can use to inspire your students as you teach the different forms of writing. Use these texts to accentuate **writer's craft**:

- Read **strong beginnings** or **strong endings** to inspire students as they create their own beginnings and endings.
- Read paragraphs that **elaborate ideas** or demonstrate **strong organization**.
- Read from two different examples to **contrast voice** and **word choice**.
- Read from different authors to examine their **sentence fluency**.

Narrative Books for Grades 1–2

First Year Letters
Julie Danneberg, 2003

My Great-Aunt Arizona
Gloria Houston, 1997

Fireflies
Julie Brinckloe, 1986

I Know a Lady
Charlotte Zolotow, 1992

The Relatives Came
Cynthia Rylant, 2005

Owl Moon
Jane Yolen, 1987

Something Beautiful
Sharon Dennis Wyeth, 2002

The Wednesday Surprise
Eve Bunting, 1989

Apple Picking Time
Michele B. Slawson, 1998

A Chair for My Mother
Vera B. Williams, 1982

All the Places to Love
Patricia MacLachlan, 1994

Icy Watermelon/ Sandía Fría
Mary Sue Galindo, 2008

Bravo, Amelia Bedelia!
Herman Parish, 1997

Mama Played Baseball
David A. Adler, 2003

Uptown
Bryan Collier, 2007

Marianthe's Story: Painted Words and Spoken Memories
Aliki, 1998

Uncle Andy's: A Faabbbulous Visit with Andy Warhol
James Warhola, 2003

Alexander and the Terrible, Horrible, No Good, Very Bad Day
Judith Viorst, 1972

The Listening Walk
Paul Showers, 1991

There's an Alligator Under My Bed
Mercer Mayer, 1987

If I Could Drive a Fire Truck!
Michael Teitelbaum, Uldis Klavins,
Jeff Walker, 2001

I Took My Frog to the Library
Eric A. Kimmel, 1992

My Daddy is a Soldier
Kirk Hilbrecht, 2000

The Gardener
Sarah Stewart, 1997

Mr. Yee Fixes Cars
Alice K. Flanagan, 1998

Pen Pals
Joan Holub, 1997

Junie B. Jones and the Stupid Smelly Bus
Barbara Park, 1992

My First Kwanzaa
Karen Katz, 2003

The Hello, Goodbye Window
Norton Juster, 2005

Music, Music for Everyone
Vera B. Williams, 1988

Wash Day
Barbara H. Cole, 2004

The Cool Crazy Crickets
David Elliott, 2001

The Day I Had to Play With My Sister
Crosby Bonsall, 1999

Fishing Day
Andrea Davis Pinkney, 2003

Red Rubber Boot Day
Mary Lyn Ray, 2000

My Day in the Garden
Miela Ford, 1999

Harry Gets an Uncle
Barbara Ann Porte, 2002

Show & Tell Day
Anne Rockwell, 2000

I Live in Brooklyn
Mari Takabayashi, 2004

**Charlie and Lola:
Snow is My Favorite and My Best**
Lauren Child, 2006

Expository Books for Grades 1–2

Planting a Rainbow
Lois Ehlert, 1992

My Five Senses
Aliki, 1989

Sleep is for Everyone
Paul Showers, 1997

Air Is All Around You
Franklyn M. Branley, 2006

Animals in Winter
Henrietta Bancroft and
Richard G. Van Gelder, 1997

Sounds All Around
Wendy Pfeffer, 1995

What Makes a Shadow?
Clyde Robert Bulla, 1994

*The Furry News: How to Make
a Newspaper*
Loreen Leedy, 1993

*How to Make a Rainbow: Great Things to
Make and Do for 7 Year Olds*
Deborah Manley, 1994

Watch Me Make a Bird Feeder
Jack Otten, 2002

Watch Me Build a Sandcastle
Jack Otten, 2002

Watch Me Plant a Garden
Jack Otten, 2002

Watch Me Make a Mask
Jack Otten, 2002

Watch Me Make a Birthday Card
Jack Otten, 2002

Let's Make Tacos
Mary Hill, 2002

Let's Make Pizza
Mary Hill, 2002

Let's Make Cookies
Mary Hill, 2002

*I Can Play Games: Fun-to-Play
Games for Younger Children*
Petra Boase, 2000

Let's Jump Rope
Sarah Hughes, 2000

Let's Play Hopscotch
Sarah Hughes, 2000

Let's Play Jacks
Sarah Hughes, 2000

Let's Play Tag
Sarah Hughes, 2000

Let's Play Hide-And-Seek
Sarah Hughes, 2000

*How High Can a Dinosaur Count?:
And Other Math Mysteries*
Valorie Fisher, 2006

I Face the Wind
Vicki Cobb, 2004

Arrowhawk
Lola M. Schaefer, 2004

Garden of the Spirit Bear
Dorothy Hinshaw Patent, 2004

Pupniks: The Story of Two Space Dogs
S. Ruth Lubka, 2004

They Call Me Woolly: What Animal Names Can Tell Us
Keith DuQuette, 2002

Brrr: A Book About Polar Animals
Melvin & Gilda Berger, 2001

Flotsam
David Wiesner, 2006

Water Hole
Zahavit Shalev, 2005

Octopuses
Lola M. Schaefer, 2006

Bug Faces
Darlyne A. Murawski, 2000

An Island Grows
Lola M. Schaefer, 2006

What Do You Do With a Tail Like This?
Steve Jenkins and Robin Page, 2003

My Family Plays Music
Judy Cox, 2003

On the Go
Ann Morris, 1994

Houses and Homes
Ann Morris, 1995

Me on the Map
Joan Sweeney, 1996

Persuasive Books for Grades 1–2

I Wanna Iguana
Karen Kaufman Orloff, 2004

Dear Mrs. La Rue: Letters From Obedience School
Mark Teague, 2004

Dear Mr. Blueberry
Simon James, 1996

Don't Take Your Snake for a Stroll
Karin Ireland, 2003

The Perfect Pet
Margie Palatini, 2003

Maybe You Should Fly a Jet! Maybe You Should Be a Vet!
Theo LeSieg, 2001

Take Care Of Your Teeth
Don L. Curry, 2005

Take Care Of Your Eyes
Don L. Curry, 2004

The Great Kapok Tree: A Tale of the Amazon Rain Forest
Lynne Cherry, 2001

Priscilla and the Pink Planet
Nathaniel Hobbie, 2004

Go Away, Dog
Joan L. Nodset, 1999

Cows Can't Fly
David Milgrim, 2000

Allie's Basketball Dream
Barbara E. Barber, 1998

Grandpa's Corner Store
DyAnne DiSalvo-Ryan, 2000

Bernelly & Harriet: The Country Mouse and the City Mouse
Elizabeth Dahlie, 2002

Hundred Million Reasons for Owning an Elephant: (Or at Least a Dozen I Can Think of Right Now)
Lois G. Grambling, 1990

The Environment (The Reason Why Series)
Irving Adler, Peggy Adler, 1976

Why Should I Eat Well? (Why Should I? Books)
Claire Llewellyn, 2005

Fruits Are Fun
Amanda Rondeau, 2002

Why Should I Eat This Carrot?
Angela Royston, 2004

Drink More Water
Cindy Devine Dalton, 2000

Bengal Tiger (Save Our Animals)
Richard Spilsbury, 2007

Asian Elephant (Save Our Animals)
Richard Spilsbury, 2007

Operation Turtle (Save Our Species)
Jill Bailey, 1992

Rainforests (Save Our World)
Jane Parker, 1999

Books About Responding to Literature for Grades 1–2

Alexander and the Terrible, Horrible, No Good, Very Bad Day
Judith Viorst, 1972

The Hello, Goodbye Window
Norton Juster, 2005

The Stories Julian Tells
Ann Cameron, 1989

Get Ready for Second Grade, Amber Brown
Paula Danziger, 2003

The Case of the Spooky Sleepover (Jigsaw Jones Mystery)
James Preller, 2001

The New Girl . . . and Me
Jacqui Robbins, 2006

How I Became a Pirate
Melinda Long, 2003

Henry and Mudge: The First Book
Cynthia Rylant, 1996

Mr. George Baker
Amy Hest, 2004

Ready, Freddy!: Don't Sit on My Lunch
Abby Klein, 2005

A Fine, Fine School
Sharon Creech, 2001

Why Do Leaves Change Color?
Betsy Maestro, 1994

And So They Build
Bert Kitchen, 1995

Bottle Houses: The Creative World of Grandma Prisbrey
Melissa Eskridge Slaymaker, 2004

Snakes! Strange and Wonderful
Laurence Pringle, 2004

Bill Pickett: Rodeo-Ridin' Cowboy
Andrea Pinkney, 1999

Sunken Treasure
Gail Gibbons, 1990

Welcome to the Green House
Jane Yolen

Welcome to the Ice House
Jane Yolen

Alexander and the Wind-Up Mouse
Leo Lionni

The 20th Century Children's Poetry Treasury
Jack Prelutsky, 1999

Kids Pick The Funniest Poems
Bruce Lansky

I Like This Poem
Kaye Webb, 1999

Shadows and Reflections
Tana Hoban, 1990

Books About Creative Writing for Grades 1–2

The Kingfisher Treasury of Animal Stories
Jane Olliver, 1992

The Very Hungry Caterpillar
Eric Carle, 1994

Guess How Much I Love You
Sam McBratney, 1996

Click, Clack, Moo: Cows That Type
Doreen Cronin, Betsy Lewin, 2003

Frog and Toad Together
Arnold Lobel, 1999

Henny Penny
Vivian French, 2006

The Bremen-Town Musicians
Ilse Plume, 1998

Stone Soup
Marcia Brown, 1999

There Was an Old Lady Who Swallowed a Fly
Simms Taback, 1997

Gingerbread Baby
Jan Brett, 1999

Forecasting Fun: Weather Nursery Rhymes
Paula Knight, Melissa Carpenter, 2004

The Kingfisher Book of Nursery Tales
Terry Pierce, 2004

The Best Hawaiian Style Mother Goose Ever! Hawai'i's Version of 14 Very Popular Verses
Kevin Sullivan, 1995

The Neighborhood Mother Goose
Nina Crews, 2003

Mother Goose Rhyme Time People
Kimberly Faurot, 2006

"I Did It Because...": How a Poem Happens
Loris Lesynski, 2006

Grasshopper Pie and Other Poems: All Aboard Poetry Reader
David Steinberg, 2004

Chanting Rhymes (First Verses Series)
John Foster, 1998

Read A Rhyme, Write A Rhyme
Jack Prelutsky, 2005

Busy Buzzing Bumblebees and Other Tongue Twisters (An I Can Read Book)
Alvin Schwartz, 1992

Creepy Crawly Critters and Other Halloween Tongue Twisters
Nola Buck, 1996

The Kingfisher Book of Children's Poetry
Michael Rosen, 1993

Doodle Dandies: Poems That Take Shape
J. Patrick Lewis, 2002

Hippopotamus Stew and Other Silly Animal Poems
Joan Horton, 2006

The Kingfisher Book of Family Poems
Belinda Hollyer, 2003

Reference Books for Grades 1–2

The American Heritage First Dictionary
Edited by Editors of The American Heritage Dictionaries, 2006

The World Almanac for Kids 2007
Editors of World Almanac, 2006

Kingfisher First Encyclopedia of Animals
Editors of Kingfisher, 2005

Kingfisher First Thesaurus
George Beal, Martin Chatterton, 2004

The Kingfisher First Encyclopedia
Editors of Kingfish, 2005

First Nature Encyclopedia
DK Publishing, 2006

Look-it-up: Animals On The Move
Gallimard Jeunesse, 2002

Look-it-up: Baby Animals In The Wild
Gallimard Jeunesse, 2002

Look-it-up: Animal Homes
Gallimard Jeunesse, 2002

Birds (Kingfisher Young Knowledge)
Nicola Davies, 2003

Smithsonian Kids' Field Guides: Birds of North America West
DK Publishing, 2001

Parrots and Parakeets As Pets (A True Book)
Elaine Landau, 1998

Complete Library Skills (Grade K–2)
School Specialty Publishing, 2004

"L" Is for Library
Sonya Terry, 2006

A Day in the Life of a Librarian (First Facts)
Judy Monroe, 2004

Scope and Sequence

Skills taught and/or reviewed in the *Write Source* program, grades K–8, are featured in the following scope and sequence chart.

FORMS OF WRITING Grades	K	1	2	3	4	5	6	7	8
Narrative Writing									
sentences	■	■							
paragraph	■	■	□	■	■	■	■	■	■
narrative prompts		■	□	■	■	■	■	■	■
narrative essay			□	■	■	■	■	■	■
phase autobiography								■	■
Expository Writing									
sentences	■	■							
paragraph		■	□	■	■	■	■	■	■
expository prompts		■	□	■	■	■	■	■	■
expository essay			□	■	■	■	■	■	■
classification essay							■		■
cause-and-effect essay								■	
comparison-contrast essay								■	■
Persuasive Writing									
sentences		■							
paragraph		■	□	■	■	■	■	■	■
persuasive prompts			□	■	■	■	■	■	■
persuasive letter			□	■	■	■	■	■	■
persuasive essay				■	■	■	■	■	■
editorial								■	■
problem-solution essay								■	■
personal commentary									■
position essay									■
Response to Literature									
sentences		■							
paragraph		■	□	■	■	■	■	■	■
response prompts		■	□	■	■	■	■	■	■
book review		■	□	■	■	■	■	■	■
journal response					■	■	■	■	■
response to literature							■	■	■
letter to an author									■
theme analysis									■

Grades

	K	1	2	3	4	5	6	7	8
Descriptive Writing									
sentences	■	■							
paragraph		■	□	■	■	■	■	■	■
descriptive essay			□	■	■	■	■	■	■
descriptive prompts				■	■	■			
Creative Writing									
poetry		■	□	■	■	■	■	■	■
story	■	■	□	■	■	■	■	■	■
play			□	■	■	■			
Research Writing									
research report	■	■	□	■	■	■	■	■	■
multimedia presentation			□	■	■	■	■	■	■
summary paragraph				■	■	■	■	■	■
Research Skills									
interview an expert		■	□	■	■	■	■	■	■
online research/using the Internet		■	□	■	■	■	■	■	■
understanding the parts of a book		■	□	■	■	■	■	■	■
using a dictionary, a thesaurus, or an encyclopedia		■	□	■	■	■	■	■	■
using diagrams, charts, graphs, and maps		■	□	■	■	■	■	■	■
using reference sources		■	□	■	■	■	■	■	■
using the library		■	□	■	■	■	■	■	■
note taking/summarizing		■	□	■	■	■	■	■	■
using a card catalog			□	■	■	■	■	■	■
using periodicals or magazines			□	■	■	■	■	■	■
using time lines			□	■	■	■	■	■	■
asking questions				■	■	■	■	■	■
bibliography (works cited)				■	■	■	■	■	■
The Tools of Learning									
improving viewing skills		■	□	■	■	■			
interviewing skills	■	■	□	■	■	■	■	■	
giving speeches		■	□	■	■	■	■	■	■
journal writing	■	■	□	■	■	■	■	■	■
learning logs		■	□	■	■	■	■	■	■
listening in class	■	■	□	■	■	■	■	■	■
taking classroom tests		■	□	■	■	■	■	■	■
note taking				■	■	■	■	■	■
completing writing assignments							■	■	■

THE WRITING PROCESS Grades

	K	1	2	3	4	5	6	7	8
Prewriting									
Selecting a Topic									
draw pictures		■	■						
make lists	■	■	■	■	■	■	■	■	■
sentence starters		■	■	■	■	■	■	■	■
chart			■	■	■	■	■	■	■
cluster			■	■	■	■	■	■	■
brainstorm				■	■	■	■	■	■
character chart					■	■		■	■
freewrite				■	■	■	■	■	■
Gathering Details									
drawing	■	■							
story map		■	■	■					
cluster	■	■	■	■	■	■	■	■	■
answer questions		■	■	■	■	■	■	■	■
details chart/sheet		■	■	■	■	■	■	■	■
gathering grid		■	■	■	■	■	■	■	■
list details/reasons		■	■	■	■	■	■	■	■
sensory chart	■	■	■	■	■	■	■	■	■
selecting main reasons			■	■	■	■	■	■	■
five W's	■		■	■	■	■	■	■	■
time line	■			■	■	■	■	■	■
table diagram					■	■	■	■	■
opinion statement							■	■	■
counter an objection								■	■
Organizing Details									
time order	■	■	■	■	■	■	■	■	■
Venn diagram			■	■	■	■	■	■	■
plot chart				■	■	■	■	■	■
time line				■	■	■	■	■	■
note cards				■	■	■	■	■	■
outline ideas				■	■	■	■	■	■
order of importance					■	■	■	■	■
order of location				■	■	■	■	■	■
Writing									
topic sentence	■	■	■	■	■	■	■	■	■
opinion statement		■	■	■	■	■	■	■	■
facts, examples	■	■	■	■	■	■	■	■	■
supporting details/reasons		■	■	■	■	■	■	■	■
interesting facts/details			■	■	■	■	■	■	■

	K	1	2	3	4	5	6	7	8
Grades									
make comparisons				■	■	■	■	■	■
dialogue				■	■	■	■	■	■
transitions				■	■	■	■	■	■
call to action				■	■	■	■	■	■
closing sentences				■	■	■	■	■	■
final comment/interesting thought				■	■	■	■	■	■
focus or thesis statement				■	■	■	■	■	■
action words				■	■	■	■	■	■
direct quotations				■	■	■	■	■	■
sensory details				■	■	■	■	■	■
high point of story				■	■	■	■	■	■
explain theme				■	■	■	■	■	■
reflect on a change, a feeling, an experience, a person				■	■	■	■	■	
restate opinion/thesis					■	■	■	■	■
summarize					■	■	■	■	■
personal details						■	■	■	■
propose a solution							■	■	■
summarize a problem								■	■
share a new insight								■	■
counter an objection						■	■	■	■
emphasize a key idea								■	■
point-by-point discussion									■

Revising

Ideas

	K	1	2	3	4	5	6	7	8
sensory details	■	■		■	■	■	■	■	■
topic sentence				■	■	■	■	■	■
supporting details	■			■	■	■	■	■	■
dialogue				■	■	■	■	■	■
unnecessary details				■	■	■	■	■	■
focus statement					■	■	■	■	■

Organization

	K	1	2	3	4	5	6	7	8
order of ideas/details	■	■		■	■	■	■	■	■
transition words		■		■	■	■	■	■	■
order of importance				■	■	■	■	■	■
overall organization				■	■	■	■	■	■
order of location	■			■	■	■	■	■	■
logical order	■			■	■	■	■	■	■
clear beginning				■	■	■	■	■	■
time order	■			■	■	■	■	■	■

	K	1	2	3	4	5	6	7	8
Voice									
natural		■	■	■	■	■	■	■	■
convincing				■	■	■	■	■	■
interested				■	■	■	■	■	■
dialogue					■	■	■	■	■
fits audience/purpose					■	■	■	■	■
formal/informal					■	■	■	■	■
knowledgeable					■	■	■	■	■
Word Choice									
sensory words/details	■	■	■	■	■	■	■	■	■
specific nouns	■		■	■	■	■	■	■	■
action verbs				■	■	■	■	■	■
connotation					■	■	■	■	■
modifiers					■	■	■	■	■
onomatopoeia						■	■	■	■
descriptive words						■	■	■	■
vivid verbs						■	■	■	■
Sentence Fluency									
complete sentences	■	■	■	■	■	■	■	■	■
variety of lengths			■	■	■	■	■	■	■
kinds of sentences			■	■	■	■	■	■	■
combining sentences				■	■	■	■	■	■
compound sentences				■	■	■	■	■	■
complex sentences					■	■	■	■	■
expanded sentences					■	■	■	■	■
variety of beginnings						■	■	■	■
types of sentences					■	■	■	■	■
Editing									
capitalization	■	■	■	■	■	■	■	■	■
grammar/punctuation/spelling	■	■	■	■	■	■	■	■	■
proper nouns	■		■	■	■	■	■	■	■
proper adjectives				■	■	■	■	■	■
Publishing									
publish in a variety of ways	■	■	■	■	■	■	■	■	■
review own work to monitor growth		■	■	■	■	■	■	■	■
self- and peer-assessing writing			■	■	■	■	■	■	■
use portfolios to save writing		■	■	■	■	■	■	■	■
use published pieces as models for writing		■	■	■	■	■	■	■	■

WRITING ACROSS THE CURRICULUM

Grades	K	1	2	3	4	5	6	7	8
Narrative Writing									
reading		■							
music	■	■	■						
social studies	■		■			■	■	■	■
practical				■			■	■	■
science	■			■	■		■	■	■
Expository Writing									
social studies	■	■		■		■	■	■	■
math	■	■			■	■	■	■	■
reading *		■	■	■	■	■	■	■	■
science	■		■			■	■	■	■
practical			■	■	■	■	■	■	■
Persuasive Writing									
health		■							
science			■	■	■	■	■	■	■
social studies			■			■	■	■	■
practical				■	■	■	■	■	■
math						■	■	■	■
Descriptive Writing									
math	■	■	■				■	■	■
science		■	■		■	■	■	■	■
practical			■				■	■	■
social studies	■				■	■	■	■	■

* The models included in the "Response to Literature" section demonstrate expository writing within the reading curriculum.

GRAMMAR

Understanding Sentences	K	1	2	3	4	5	6	7	8
word order	■	■	■	■					
declarative		■	■	■	■	■	■	■	■
exclamatory		■	■	■	■	■	■	■	■
interrogative		■	■	■	■	■	■	■	■
complete sentences and fragments	■	■	■	■	■	■	■	■	■
simple subjects			■	■	■	■	■	■	■
simple predicates		■	■	■	■	■	■	■	■
correcting run-on sentences		■	■	■	■	■	■	■	■
compound			■	■	■	■	■	■	■
imperative			■	■	■	■	■	■	■
complete predicates				■	■	■	■	■	■

Understanding Sentences (Continued)	K	1	2	3	4	5	6	7	8
complete subjects				■	■	■	■	■	■
compound predicates				■	■	■	■	■	■
compound subjects				■	■	■	■	■	■
prepositional phrases				■	■	■	■	■	■
appositive phrases					■	■	■	■	■
clauses, dependent and independent					■	■	■	■	■
complex					■	■	■	■	■
modifiers					■	■	■	■	■
noun phrases					■	■	■	■	■
verb phrases					■	■	■	■	■

Using the Parts of Speech

Nouns

	K	1	2	3	4	5	6	7	8
singular and plural	■	■	■	■	■	■	■	■	■
common/proper	■	■	■	■	■	■	■	■	■
possessive			■	■	■	■	■	■	■
singular/plural possessive			■	■	■	■	■	■	■
specific				■	■	■	■	■	■
abstract/concrete					■	■	■	■	■
appositives					■	■	■	■	■
collective/compound					■	■	■	■	■
object					■	■	■	■	■
predicate					■	■	■	■	■
subject					■	■	■	■	■
gender					■	■	■	■	■

Verbs

	K	1	2	3	4	5	6	7	8
contractions with *not*		■	■	■	■	■	■	■	■
action	■	■	■	■	■	■	■	■	■
linking		■	■	■	■	■	■	■	■
past tense		■	■	■	■	■	■	■	■
present tense	■	■	■	■	■	■	■	■	■
subject-verb agreement		■	■	■	■	■	■	■	■
future tense			■	■	■	■	■	■	■
helping			■	■	■	■	■	■	■
singular/plural			■	■	■	■	■	■	■
irregular				■	■	■	■	■	■
simple tense				■	■	■	■	■	■
active/passive voice					■	■	■	■	■
direct objects					■	■	■	■	■
indirect objects					■	■	■	■	■
perfect tense					■	■	■	■	■

	K	1	2	3	4	5	6	7	8
transitive/intransitive					■	■	■	■	■
participles						■	■	■	■
continuous tense							■	■	■
gerunds							■	■	■
infinitives							■	■	■
Pronouns									
personal	■	■	■	■	■	■	■	■	■
antecedents		■	■	■	■	■	■	■	■
singular and plural		■	■	■	■	■	■	■	■
possessive		■	■	■	■	■	■	■	■
subject and object			■	■	■	■	■	■	■
demonstrative/interrogative					■	■	■	■	■
gender					■	■	■	■	■
indefinite					■	■	■	■	■
intensive and reflexive					■	■	■	■	■
relative					■	■	■	■	■
Adjectives									
adjectives	■	■	■	■	■	■	■	■	■
comparative/superlative		■	■	■	■	■	■	■	■
articles			■	■	■	■	■	■	■
compound				■	■	■	■	■	■
positive					■	■	■	■	■
proper				■	■	■	■	■	■
demonstrative					■	■	■	■	■
equal					■	■	■	■	■
indefinite					■	■	■	■	■
predicate					■	■	■	■	■
Interjections			■	■	■	■	■	■	■
Adverbs									
of manner			■	■	■	■	■	■	■
of place	■		■	■	■	■	■	■	■
of time			■	■	■	■	■	■	■
that modify verbs			■	■	■	■	■	■	■
of degree					■	■	■	■	■
that modify adjectives and adverbs					■	■	■	■	■
comparative/superlative					■	■	■	■	■
comparing with adverbs					■	■	■	■	■
irregular forms					■	■	■	■	■
positive					■	■	■	■	■

	K	1	2	3	4	5	6	7	8
Grades									
Conjunctions									
coordinating			■	■	■	■	■	■	■
correlative					■	■	■	■	■
subordinating					■	■	■	■	■
Prepositions									
prepositions	■		■	■	■	■	■	■	■
prepositional phrases				■	■	■	■	■	■
Mechanics									
Capitalization									
pronoun "I"		■	■	■	■	■	■	■	■
days, months, holidays		■	■	■	■	■	■	■	■
first words	■	■	■	■	■	■	■	■	■
names of people	■	■	■	■	■	■	■	■	■
proper nouns		■	■	■	■	■	■	■	■
titles used with names		■	■	■	■	■	■	■	■
titles		■	■	■	■	■	■	■	■
beginning of a quotation		■	■	■	■	■	■	■	■
geographic names			■	■	■	■	■	■	■
abbreviations			■	■	■	■	■	■	■
proper adjectives				■	■	■	■	■	■
words used as names				■	■	■	■	■	■
names of historical events					■	■	■	■	■
names of religions, nationalities					■	■	■	■	■
organizations					■	■	■	■	■
particular sections of the country					■	■	■	■	■
trade names/official names					■	■	■	■	■
letters to indicate form or direction							■	■	■
specific course names							■	■	■
Plurals									
irregular nouns		■	■	■	■	■	■	■	■
most nouns		■	■	■	■	■	■	■	■
nouns ending with *sh*, *ch*, *x*, *s*, and *z*			■	■	■	■	■	■	■
nouns ending in *y*			■	■	■	■	■	■	■
adding 's					■	■	■	■	■
compound nouns					■	■	■	■	■
nouns ending with *f* or *fe*					■	■	■	■	■
nouns ending with *ful*					■	■	■	■	■
nouns ending with *o*					■	■	■	■	■

	K	1	2	3	4	5	6	7	8
Abbreviations									
days and months			■	■	■	■	■	■	■
state postal abbreviations				■	■	■	■	■	■
titles of people		■	■	■	■	■	■	■	■
addresses			■	■	■	■	■	■	■
acronyms				■	■	■	■	■	■
initialisms				■	■	■	■	■	■
Numbers									
numbers 1 to 9				■	■	■	■	■	■
numbers only				■	■	■	■	■	■
sentence beginnings				■	■	■	■	■	■
very large numbers				■	■	■	■	■	■
numbers in compound modifiers							■	■	■
time and money							■	■	■

Punctuation

	K	1	2	3	4	5	6	7	8
Periods									
after an initial/an abbreviation		■	■	■	■	■	■	■	■
at the end of a sentence	■	■	■	■	■	■	■	■	■
as a decimal point				■	■	■	■	■	■
after an indirect question							■	■	■
Question Marks									
after questions	■	■	■	■	■	■	■	■	■
after tag questions					■	■	■	■	■
to show doubt					■	■	■	■	■
Exclamation Points									
for words, phrases, and sentences	■	■	■	■	■	■	■	■	■
for interjections		■	■	■	■	■	■	■	■
Commas									
in a series			■	■	■	■	■	■	■
in dates			■	■	■	■	■	■	■
in friendly letters			■	■	■	■	■	■	■
after introductory words			■	■	■	■	■	■	■
with interjections			■	■	■	■	■	■	■
in a compound sentence			■	■	■	■	■	■	■
in addresses			■	■	■	■	■	■	■
to set off dialogue			■	■	■	■	■	■	■
in direct address			■	■	■	■	■	■	■
in numbers				■	■	■	■	■	■
to separate equal adjectives				■	■	■	■	■	■
to set off appositives				■	■	■	■	■	■

Grades

Commas (Continued)	K	1	2	3	4	5	6	7	8
to set off interrupters					■	■	■	■	■
to set off phrases					■	■	■	■	■
to set off titles of people							■	■	■
Apostrophes									
in contractions	■	■	■	■	■	■	■	■	■
to form plural possessive nouns			■	■	■	■	■	■	■
to form singular possessive nouns			■	■	■	■	■	■	■
to form some plurals					■	■	■	■	■
to replace omitted numbers/letters					■	■	■	■	■
with indefinite pronouns					■	■	■	■	■
to show shared possession					■	■	■	■	■
in possessives w/compound nouns							■	■	■
to express time or amount							■	■	■
Underlining and Italics									
for titles	■	■	■	■	■	■	■	■	■
for special words					■	■	■	■	■
for scientific and foreign words							■	■	■
Quotation Marks									
for direct quotations			■	■	■	■	■	■	■
for titles			■	■	■	■	■	■	■
for special words					■	■	■	■	■
for quotations within a quotation							■	■	■
Colons									
between hour and minutes				■	■	■	■	■	■
in business letters				■	■	■	■	■	■
to introduce a list of items				■	■	■	■	■	■
for emphasis							■	■	■
to introduce sentences							■	■	■
Hyphens									
in word division				■	■	■	■	■	■
in compound words					■	■	■	■	■
in fractions					■	■	■	■	■
to create new words					■	■	■	■	■
to join letters and words					■	■	■	■	■
to avoid confusion or awkward spelling							■	■	■
to make adjectives							■	■	■

Grades

	K	1	2	3	4	5	6	7	8
Parentheses									
to add information				■	■	■	■	■	■
Dashes									
for emphasis					■	■	■	■	■
to show a sentence break					■	■	■	■	■
to show interrupted speech					■	■	■	■	■
Ellipses									
to show a pause					■	■	■	■	■
to show omitted words					■	■	■	■	■
Semicolons									
in a compound sentence					■	■	■	■	■
to separate groups (that have commas) in a series	■	■	■	■	■				
with conjunctive adverbs							■	■	■
Usage									
Spelling									
high-frequency words	■	■							
consonant endings				■	■	■	■	■	■
i before *e*				■	■	■	■	■	■
silent *e*				■	■	■	■	■	■
words ending in *y*				■	■	■	■	■	■
Using the Right Word	■	■	■	■	■	■	■	■	■
Penmanship									
word space, letter space	■	■							
writing legibly	■	■	■	■	■	■	■	■	■
margins/spaces				■	■	■	■	■	■

Meeting the Common Core State Standards

The following correlation clearly shows how the *Write Source* program helps students meet grade-specific **Common Core State Standards** for English Language Arts and Literacy in History/Social Studies, Science, and Technical Subjects. The Common Core standards translate their companion **College and Career Readiness standards** into grade-appropriate expectations that students should meet by the end of the school year.

Pages referenced below appear in the Teacher's Edition as well as the Student Edition.

Writing Standards

Text Types and Purposes

College and Career Readiness Standard 1. Write arguments to support claims in an analysis of substantive topics or texts, using valid reasoning and relevant and sufficient evidence.

Grade 1 Standard 1. Write opinion pieces in which they introduce the topic or name the book they are writing about, state an opinion, supply a reason for the opinion, and provide some sense of closure.	**Student Edition pages:** 132–136, 255 **Net-text:** Persuasive Writing

College and Career Readiness Standard 2. Write informative/explanatory texts to examine and convey complex ideas and information clearly and accurately through the effective selection, organization, and analysis of content.

Grade 1 Standard 2. Write informative/explanatory texts in which they name a topic, supply some facts about the topic, and provide some sense of closure.	**Student Edition pages:** 64–73, 110–119, 142–147, 150–155, 190–197, 254–255 **Net-text:** Descriptive Writing, Expository Writing, Responding to Literature, Report Writing

College and Career Readiness Standard 3. Write narratives to develop real or imagined experiences or events using effective technique, well-chosen details, and well-structured event sequences.

Grade 1 Standard 3. Write narratives in which they recount two or more appropriately sequenced events, include some details regarding what happened, use temporal words to signal event order, and provide some sense of closure.	**Student Edition pages:** 86–95, 162–168, 254 **Net-text:** Narrative Writing, Creative Writing

Production and Distribution of Writing

College and Career Readiness Standard 4. Produce clear and coherent writing in which the development, organization, and style are appropriate to task, purpose, and audience.

Standard 4. (Begins in grade 3)

College and Career Readiness Standard 5. Develop and strengthen writing as needed by planning, revising, editing, rewriting, or trying a new approach.

Grade 1 Standard 5. With guidance and support from adults, focus on a topic, respond to questions and suggestions from peers, and add details to strengthen writing as needed.

Student Edition pages: 16–17, 20–21, 26–27, 36–37, 58, 64–73, 86–95, 110–119, 132–136, 142–147, 150–155, 162–168, 170–174, 190–197

Interactive Whiteboard Lessons: Sentences and Paragraphs, Descriptive Writing, Narrative Writing, Expository Writing, Persuasive Writing, Responding to Literature, Creative Writing, Report Writing

Net-text: Sentences and Paragraphs, Descriptive Writing, Narrative Writing, Expository Writing, Persuasive Writing, Responding to Literature, Creative Writing, Report Writing

College and Career Readiness Standard 6. Use technology, including the Internet, to produce and publish writing and to interact and collaborate with others.

Grade 1 Standard 6. With guidance and support from adults, use a variety of digital tools to produce and publish writing, including in collaboration with peers.

Student Edition pages: 38–39, 266–267

Interactive Whiteboard Lessons: Sentences and Paragraphs, Descriptive Writing, Narrative Writing, Expository Writing, Persuasive Writing, Responding to Literature, Creative Writing, Report Writing

Research to Build and Present Knowledge

College and Career Readiness Standard 7. Conduct short as well as more sustained research projects based on focused questions, demonstrating understanding of the subject under investigation.

Grade 1 Standard 7. Participate in shared research and writing projects (e.g., explore a number of "how-to" books on a given topic and use them to write a sequence of instructions).

Student Edition pages: 188–197
Net-text: Report Writing

Research to Build and Present Knowledge (continued)

College and Career Readiness Standard 8. Gather relevant information from multiple print and digital sources, assess the credibility and accuracy of each source, and integrate the information while avoiding plagiarism.

Grade 1 Standard 8. With guidance and support from adults, recall information from experiences or gather information from provided sources to answer a question.	**Student Edition pages:** 190–191 **Net-text:** Report Writing

College and Career Readiness Standard 9. Draw evidence from literary or informational texts to support analysis, reflection, and research.

Standard 9. (Begins in grade 4)

Range of Writing

College and Career Readiness Standard 10. Write routinely over extended time frames (time for research, reflection, and revision) and shorter time frames (a single sitting or a day or two) for a range of tasks, purposes, and audiences.

Standard 10. (Begins in grade 3)

Language Standards

Conventions of Standard English

College and Career Readiness Standard 1. Demonstrate command of the conventions of standard English grammar and usage when writing or speaking.

Grade 1 Standard 1. Demonstrate command of the conventions of standard English grammar and usage when writing or speaking.

a. Print all upper- and lowercase letters.	**Student Edition pages:** 77, 99, 123, 138, 149, 169, 199 **Net-text:** Descriptive Writing, Narrative Writing, Expository Writing, Persuasive Writing, Responding to Literature, Creative Writing, Report Writing

Conventions of Standard English (continued)

b. Use common, proper, and possessive nouns.	**Student Edition pages:** 71, 93, 117, 119, 135, 145–146, 153–154, 167–168, 174, 190–195, 220–222, 291 **Net-text:** Descriptive Writing, Narrative Writing, Expository Writing, Persuasive Writing, Responding to Literature, Creative Writing, Report Writing **GrammarSnap:** Nouns, Common and Proper Nouns, Apostrophes for Possessives
c. Use singular and plural nouns with matching verbs in basic sentences (e.g., *He hops; We hop*).	**Student Edition pages:** 71, 93, 117, 135, 174, 193, 195, 223, 234–235, 289, 292 **Net-text:** Descriptive Writing, Narrative Writing, Expository Writing, Persuasive Writing, Creative Writing, Report Writing **GrammarSnap:** Subject-Verb Agreement
d. Use personal, possessive, and indefinite pronouns (e.g., *I, me, my; they, them, their, anyone, everything*).	**Student Edition pages:** 71, 93, 84–85, 135, 145–146, 153–154, 167, 224–227, 293 **Net-text:** Descriptive Writing, Narrative Writing, Persuasive Writing, Responding to Literature, Creative Writing **GrammarSnap:** Pronouns: I and Me, Pronouns: We and Us, Pronouns: They and Them
e. Use verbs to convey a sense of past, present, and future (e.g., *Yesterday I walked home; Today I walk home; Tomorrow I will walk home*).	**Student Edition pages:** 93, 95, 230–233, 295–296 **Net-text:** Narrative Writing **GrammarSnap:** Action Verb Tenses, Linking Verb Tenses
f. Use frequently occurring adjectives.	**Student Edition pages:** 68–73, 117, 170–174, 167, 192–195, 238–239, 258–259, 297 **Net-text:** Descriptive Writing, Expository Writing, Creative Writing, Report Writing **GrammarSnap:** Adjectives, Adjectives to Compare
g. Use frequently occurring conjunctions (e.g., *and, but, or, so, because*).	**File Cabinet:** Conjunctions Overview
h. Use determiners (e.g., articles, demonstratives).	**File Cabinet:** Using A, An, and The; Using This, That, These, and Those
i. Use frequently occurring prepositions (e.g., *during, beyond, toward*).	**Student Edition pages:** 71, 117, 119, 167, 193, 195, 261 **Student Edition pages:** 71, 117, 119, 167, 193, 195, 261 **Net-text:** Descriptive Writing, Expository Writing, Creative Writing, Report Writing

Conventions of Standard English (continued)

j. Produce and expand complete simple and compound declarative, interrogative, imperative, and exclamatory sentences in response to prompts.	**Student Edition pages:** 44–55, 70–73, 92–95, 116–119, 135–136, 146–147, 154–155, 167–168, 174, 192–197, 290 **Net-text:** Sentences and Paragraphs, Descriptive Writing, Narrative Writing, Expository Writing, Persuasive Writing, Responding to Literature, Creative Writing, Report Writing **GrammarSnap:** Understanding Sentences, Kinds of Sentences

College and Career Readiness Standard 2. Demonstrate command of the conventions of standard English capitalization, punctuation, and spelling when writing.

Grade 1 Standard 2. Demonstrate command of the conventions of standard English capitalization, punctuation, and spelling when writing.

a. Capitalize dates and names of people.	**Student Edition pages:** 59, 145–146, 153–154, 276–277 **Net-text:** Sentences and Paragraphs, Responding to Literature **GrammarSnap:** Capital Letters: Names and Titles; Capital Letters: Days of the Week, Months, Holidays
b. Use end punctuation for sentences.	**Student Edition pages:** 22–23, 35, 53, 55, 59, 74–75, 96–97, 120–121, 137, 148, 156, 175, 198–199, 270–271, 288 **Net-text:** Sentences and Paragraphs, Descriptive Writing, Narrative Writing, Expository Writing, Persuasive Writing, Responding to Literature, Creative Writing, Report Writing **GrammarSnap:** Periods, Question Marks, Exclamation Points, End Marks
c. Use commas in dates and to separate single words in a series.	**Student Edition pages:** 272–273 **GrammarSnap:** Commas in a Series, Commas in Dates and Letters
d. Use conventional spelling for words with common spelling patterns and for frequently occurring irregular words.	**Student Edition pages:** 223, 278 **GrammarSnap:** Irregular Plurals
e. Spell untaught words phonetically, drawing on phonemic awareness and spelling conventions.	**File Cabinet:** Spelling Unknown Words

Knowledge of Language

College and Career Readiness Standard 3. Apply knowledge of language to understand how language functions in different contexts, to make effective choices for meaning or style, and to comprehend more fully when reading or listening.

Standard 3. (Begins in grade 2)

Getting-Started Activities

The *Write Source* student edition is full of helpful resources that students can access throughout the year while they are developing their writing skills.

Getting-started activities are provided as copy masters on TE pages 415–417. (See the answer keys on TE page 418.) These activities will

- help students discover the kinds of information available in different sections of the book,
- teach students how to access that information
- familiarize students with the layout of the book

The more familiar students are with the text, the more proficient they will be in using it as a resource.

Scavenger Hunts

Students enjoy using scavenger hunts to become familiar with a book. The scavenger hunts we provide can be done in small groups or as a class. They are designed for oral answers, but you may want to photocopy the pages for students to write on. You may also vary the procedure by first having students take turns finding the items and then, on the next scavenger hunt, challenging students to "race" for the answers.

After your students have completed each scavenger hunt, you can challenge them to create their own versions. For example, small groups can work together to create "Find the Twos" or "Search for Fours" scavenger hunts and then exchange their "hunts" with other groups.

Special Challenge: Develop questions that teams of students try to answer, using the book. Pattern this activity after a popular game show.

Other Activities

- **All-School Reference** Have students write down all the subject areas they study and list under each heading the parts of the *Write Source* text that might help them in that subject.
- **Pen Pal Letter** Have students imagine that they are each going to send a copy of *Write Source* to a pen pal in another state or country. Ask students to write letters telling their pen pals about the book.
- **Favorite Feature** Give your students the following assignment: Find one page, one short section, one set of guidelines, one illustration, one writing sample, or one chart you think is interesting, entertaining, stimulating, valuable, and so on. Students should prepare to share their discoveries with members of their discussion group or with the entire class.
- **5 W's and H** Have students develop *Who? What? When? Where? Why?* and *How?* questions from *Write Source*—for example, *What is step one in the writing process?* Students should then exchange questions with a partner and search for answers in the book. Afterward, partners may discuss each other's answers. (This activity can also be used as a search contest.)

HOUGHTON MIFFLIN HARCOURT

WRITE SOURCE

Authors
Dave Kemper, Patricia Reigel, and Patrick Sebranek

Illustrator
Chris Krenzke

GREAT
SOURCE.

HOUGHTON MIFFLIN HARCOURT

Welcome to the Teacher's Edition!

Every child needs to learn about the world—and the world needs to learn about every child. Writing is the key to achieving both goals. With the *Write Source* program, your students will learn about the world as they learn to write, and they'll discover their unique voices in the process.

The student edition will guide your students on their journey. Along the way, they'll hear the voices of other writers speaking to them from the many accessible models.

The teacher's edition will guide you on this journey as well. In the following pages, you'll find not only lesson objectives and instructions, but also these special features at point of use:
- Teaching Tips
- Grammar Connections
- Literature Connections
- Writer's Craft Connections
- Technology Connections
- Notes for English Language Learners
- Accommodations for Struggling Learners
- Enrichments for Advanced Learners

Welcome to the journey! Welcome to *Write Source*.

Thanks to the Teachers!

This program would not have been possible without the input of many teachers and administrators from across the nation. As we originally developed this K–12 series, we surveyed hundreds of teaching professionals, and as we revised this series, we have implemented the feedback of even more. Our grateful thanks go out to each of you. We couldn't have done it without you!

2

Reviewers

Genevieve Bodnar NBCT
Youngstown City Schools
Youngstown, Ohio

Daniel Bower
Blackbird Elementary
Harbor Springs, Michigan

Kay E. Dooley
East Maine School District 63
Des Plaines, Illinois

Mary M. Fischer
Arlington Public Schools
Arlington, Massachusetts

Cynthia Fontenot
Green T. Linden Elementary
Lafayette, Louisiana

Marsha Ganz
School Board of Broward
   County
Ft. Lauderdale, Florida

Tracey Leatherwood
St. Charles Boromeo School
New York, New York

Lynn A. Lein
Goffstown SAU19
Goffstown, New Hampshire

Lynn Sholes
Broward County Schools
Ft. Lauderdale, Florida

Renee Wiley
P.S. 309
Brooklyn, New York

WRITE SOURCE Online
www.hmheducation.com/writesource

Quick Guide

3

11 Why Write?

OVERVIEW OF THE PROCESS

The Writing Process

14 The Writing Process
16 One Writer's Process
26 Working with a Partner
28 Traits of Good Writing
36 Rubrics
38 Publishing
40 Portfolios

Sentences and Paragraphs

44 Writing a Sentence
54 Kinds of Sentences
56 Writing a Paragraph

THE FORMS OF WRITING

Descriptive Writing

62 Descriptive Start-Up
64 Descriptive Paragraph
80 Across the Curriculum

Narrative Writing

84 Narrative Start-Up
86 Narrative Paragraph
102 Across the Curriculum

Expository Writing

108 Expository Start-Up
110 Expository Paragraph
126 Across the Curriculum

Persuasive Writing

132 Persuasive Start-Up
134 Persuasive Paragraph
139 Across the Curriculum

Responding to Literature

142 Fiction Book
150 Nonfiction Book

Creative Writing

162 Stories
170 Poems

Report Writing

180 Finding Information
188 Report

THE TOOLS OF LEARNING

202 Speaking to Others
204 Listening
206 Interviewing
208 Journals
210 Learning Logs
212 Viewing
214 Taking Tests

WORDS

220 Nouns
224 Pronouns
228 Verbs
238 Adjectives

A WRITER'S RESOURCE

242 Ideas
248 Organization
254 Voice
256 Word Choice
260 Sentence Fluency
262 Presentation

PROOFREADER'S GUIDE

270 Punctuation
275 Capital Letters and Plurals
279 Spelling
284 Using the Right Word
288 Sentences
291 Parts of Speech

THEME WORDS

300 People
302 Places
304 Things
306 Animals
308 Foods
310 Activities

The *Write Source* Voice

For more than 30 years, our student books have spoken directly to students. We see ourselves as writers speaking to other writers.

As a result, the *Write Source* voice is always encouraging, like an older classmate who genuinely wants a younger one to succeed. We believe that every student can learn to write and that every writer can improve. Throughout this book, your students will hear a voice that says, "You can do it!"

In the same way, the material in the wraparound text speaks directly to you. After all, we are teachers speaking to other teachers, and so we use the same encouraging voice.

Whether you're a seasoned writing teacher or a fresh new face, we are certain that these materials in your hands can make a big difference for your students. We hope you agree!

The Process of Writing

The first section of the book provides an introduction to the writing process.

- Prewrite ▶
- Write ▶
- Revise ▶
- Edit ▶
- Publish ▶

The chapter "One Writer's Process" lets students see how another first-grade writer works through the process of prewriting, writing, revising, editing, and publishing.

The Six Traits

The six traits of writing give you and your students a common language for talking about what makes writing great.

- Strong **ideas**
- Clear **organization**
- Natural **voice**
- Solid **word choice**
- Smooth **sentences**
- Correct **conventions**

Wraparound Feature

Teaching Tip

Throughout the wraparound, you'll find special strategies for making the lesson come alive for your students.

4

Contents

The Process of Writing

11 Why Write?

The Writing Process   12

14 Using the Writing Process

16 One Writer's Process
   STUDENT MODEL "My Butterfly"

26 Working with a Partner

28 Understanding the Writing Traits
   STUDENT MODEL "The Zoo"

36 Learning About a Rubric

38 Publishing Your Writing

40 Using a Portfolio

Contents   5

Sentences and Paragraphs   42

44 Writing a Sentence

54 Kinds of Sentences

56 Writing a Paragraph
STUDENT MODEL "The Park"

The Forms of Writing

Descriptive Writing   60

62 Descriptive Start-Up

64 Descriptive Paragraph
STUDENT MODEL "Our Tire Swing"
STUDENT MODEL "Delicious!"

80 Across the Curriculum
- Math: Sentences
  STUDENT MODEL "A Triangle"
- Science: A Paragraph
  STUDENT MODEL "Lizzy, the Lizard"

Narrative Writing   82

84 Narrative Start-Up

Creating the Forms of Writing

The writing units in *Write Source* focus on creating the fundamental forms of writing:
- Descriptive
- Narrative
- Expository
- Persuasive
- Response to Literature
- Creative
- Report

Each writing assignment includes instruction, examples, and activities that lead students through the writing process.

Writing Across the Curriculum

Special assignments after each of the major forms help your students write in their content areas: social studies, math, science, art, and music. Whether you teach these subjects or partner with team teachers, these content-area assignments can help your students succeed throughout their day.

Wraparound Features

Materials

At the beginning of each unit, consult this box to find out what materials you need to have on hand to teach the lesson.

Copy Masters

These features tell you what classroom presentation aids exist to help you deliver the lesson.

Benchmark Papers

Check this feature to find out what benchmark papers you can use to show your students a range of performance.

Teaching the Core Units

Each unit begins with an accessible model with response questions, helping students make the reading-writing connection.

Afterward, the text leads students step-by-step through the process of creating a similar piece of writing. Concrete activities help students do the following:

- select a topic;
- gather details;
- organize details;
- write a strong draft;
- revise their writing;
- edit for conventions;
- publish work with polished presentation; and
- assess writing using trait-based rubrics.

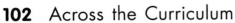

6

86 Narrative Paragraph
STUDENT MODEL "Noodles"
STUDENT MODEL "Leaping Lizard"

102 Across the Curriculum
- Reading: A Friendly Letter
STUDENT MODEL "Dear Mr. Mayer"
- Music: A Paragraph
STUDENT MODEL "Powwow"

104 Writing for Assessment
STUDENT MODEL "Pumpkin Farm"

Expository Writing 106

108 Expository Start-Up

110 Expository Paragraph
STUDENT MODEL "Make a Penny Shine"
STUDENT MODEL "Make Green Paint"

126 Across the Curriculum
- Math: A Process Paragraph
STUDENT MODEL "Adding Numbers"
- Social Studies: An Informative Paragraph
STUDENT MODEL "Collar Makers"

128 Writing for Assessment
STUDENT MODEL "Coins"

Wraparound Feature

Grammar Connection

Each unit overview suggests grammar activities to cover in the unit. Grammar Connection boxes then help you pinpoint the places to integrate instruction.

Contents 7

Persuasive Writing 130

132 Persuasive Start-Up
STUDENT MODEL Persuasive Poster

134 Persuasive Paragraph
STUDENT MODEL "Please Walk"

139 Across the Curriculum
• Health: A Note
STUDENT MODEL "Dear Mom"

Responding to Literature 140

142 Reviewing a Fiction Book
The Mysterious Tadpole
STUDENT MODEL "Growing Up"

Yoko
STUDENT MODEL "Sushi Cat"

150 Reviewing a Nonfiction Book
I *Want to Be an Astronaut*
STUDENT MODEL "Riding in Space"

What Is a Scientist?
STUDENT MODEL "Scientists"

158 Writing for Assessment
STUDENT MODEL "Gutter Ball"

Connecting to Literature

Write Source is designed to work with your existing reading program by providing writing-based opportunities for students to explore reading.

■ Reviewing a fiction book
■ Reviewing a nonfiction book
■ Responding to literature in assessments

The text also teaches students to write two literary forms: stories and poems. By learning the basic vocabulary of prose and poetry through writing, your students will be better ready to read these forms.

Wraparound Features

 Literature Connections

These features help you use age-appropriate literary works to teach students special writing techniques. You'll find fresh ways to use literature to teach writing.

 Writer's Craft

These features help you inspire students to write the way professional writers do. They feature techniques used by the great writers as well as interesting anecdotes and quotations.

Differentiating Instruction

The teacher's edition provides numerous **accommodations** to help students work at their own levels. Suggestions for English language learners, struggling learners, and advanced learners help you adjust the lesson to keep everyone moving forward.

Also, because the *Write Source* series follows a consistent format throughout its K–12 line, students who need further differentiation can work at a grade below (or above) their classmates. These **modifications** provide separate assignments to deepen differentiation.

8

Creative Writing   160

162   Writing Stories
STUDENT MODEL   "Suzi's Missing Hiss"
STUDENT MODEL   "Herman's New Home"

170   Writing Poems
STUDENT MODEL   "Cats"
STUDENT MODEL   "Silly Spaghetti"

Report Writing   178

180   Finding Information
188   Writing a Report
STUDENT MODEL   "Leafy Sea Dragon"

The Tools of Learning

202   Speaking to Others
204   Learning to Listen
206   Learning to Interview
208   Writing in Journals
210   Using Learning Logs
212   Becoming a Smart Viewer
214   Taking Tests

Wraparound Feature

English Language Learners

These boxes provide differentiation tips to help English language learners.

Struggling Learners

Consult this feature to adjust the lesson for those who are struggling.

Advanced Learners

These boxes feature tips for challenging students who excel.

Words

220 Learning About Nouns

224 Using Pronouns

228 Learning About Verbs

238 Using Adjectives

A Writer's Resource

242 How can I find a good topic?

248 How can I organize my ideas?

254 What is a writing voice?

256 How can I learn new words?

260 How can I connect sentences?

262 What can I add to my writing?

Words

The blue pages help your students practice working with the basic building blocks of language: nouns, pronouns, verbs, and adjectives. With clear rules, simple explanations, engaging examples, and fun activities, this section helps students understand and apply the fundamentals of grammar.

Creating Resourceful Writers

This section equips students with specific, traits-based strategies that they will use over and over during the writing process. Each new concept is introduced by a question that many of your students have asked at one time or another—followed by an answer to the question and a specific strategy for implementing the answer.

Wraparound Features

 Technology Connections

In these features, you'll see connections to *Write Source Online* www.hmheducation.com/writesource. *Write Source Online* includes Interactive Whiteboard Lessons, Net-text, Bookshelf, GrammarSnap, Portfolio, and the File Cabinet.

Teaching Conventions

The "Proofreader's Guide" provides a handy reference to the basic rules of English, along with activities to practice the rules.

As you work through the writing units earlier in the book, you will find cross-references to the "Proofreader's Guide" and "Words." You'll also find cross references to every grammar activity in the *SkillsBook* and the *Interactive Writing Skills* CD-ROM. Integrated grammar instruction allows students to use the rules in context and understand not just the "what" of grammar, but also the "why."

You can use all the grammar that is suggested—or can target the grammar to your students' specific needs. The choice is yours.

10

Proofreader's Guide

270 Using Punctuation

275 Using Capital Letters

278 Making Plurals

279 Checking Spelling

284 Using the Right Word

287 Understanding Opposites

288 Understanding Sentences

291 Using the Parts of Speech

Theme Words

300 People

302 Places

304 Things

306 Animals

308 Foods

310 Activities

11

Why Write?

You write to share your thoughts and feelings with other people. Sometimes you write just for yourself.

Writing will help you . . .

- **share with others.** You can write notes, cards, letters, and e-mail messages to family and friends.

- **remember more.** You can write down interesting facts and make reports.

- **learn more about yourself.** You can write about your thoughts and feelings.

- **have fun.** You can write poems, stories, and jokes.

Why Write?

Gather writing samples, such as notes, cards, letters, e-mail messages, safety tips, poems, posters, and comic strips, to share with students.

Tell students that people write to share ideas. Read aloud the writing samples and ask students to identify the ideas each writer shares. List the ideas on the board.

Read aloud the answer to *Why Write?* Compare it to the ideas listed on the board.

Then read aloud the *Writing will help you . . .* box. To help students relate these reasons for writing to their own experiences, invite them to talk about times when they drew or wrote
- to tell a friend or family member about something they did,
- to remember an interesting fact,
- to tell how they were feeling, or
- to make someone laugh.

Create a writing environment (*see below*) that encourages students to write for a variety of purposes.

Teaching Tip: Create a Writing Environment

To make students aware of the many reasons for writing, provide daily writing experiences. Begin each day by writing a morning message. After reading aloud the message, point out your reason for writing it. For example, the purpose of completing:
- a paragraph about a personal experience is to share with others.
- a how-to report for an art project is to remember the steps.

- a sentence frame, such as *Today I feel _____ because _____,* is to learn more about yourself.
- a riddle is to have fun.

Add special features to your writing center.
- Set up a post office. To get students started, write letters that ask them for responses.

- Display a notice board for posting announcements and classroom jobs. Encourage students to get in the habit of looking for and leaving messages on the board.

For students who need support with writing, offer drawing and dictation as options.

The Writing Process Overview

Common Core Standards Focus

Writing 5: With guidance and support from adults, focus on a topic, respond to questions and suggestions from peers, and add details to strengthen writing as needed.

Language 1: Demonstrate command of the conventions of standard English grammar and usage when writing or speaking.

Language 2: Demonstrate command of the conventions of standard English capitalization, punctuation, and spelling when writing.

Writing Process

- **Prewriting** List ideas, choose a topic, and draw a picture about the topic.
- **Writing** Look at the drawing for ideas and write sentences about the topic.
- **Revising** Read the writing to a partner, listen to the partner's questions, and change the writing by adding words.
- **Editing** Check capitalization, punctuation, and spelling.
- **Publishing** Think of a title, make a neat final copy, finish the drawing, and share the writing with others.

Focus on the Traits

- **Ideas** Thinking of a good topic and listing words about it
- **Organization** Putting words and sentences in order
- **Voice** Sounding as if talking to a friend
- **Word Choice** Choosing words that make a clear picture in the reader's mind
- **Sentence Fluency** Writing long and short sentences
- **Conventions** Checking for errors in capitalization, punctuation, and spelling

Technology Connections

 Write Source Online
www.hmheducation.com/writesource

- *Net-text*
- *Bookshelf*
- *GrammarSnap*
- *Portfolio*
- *Writing Network features*
- *File Cabinet*

 Interactive Whiteboard Lessons

Suggested Writing Process Unit (Five Weeks)

	Day	Writing and Skills Instruction	Student Edition		Teacher's Edition	SkillsBook	Daily Language Workouts	Write Source Online
			Writing Process Unit	Resource Units*	Grammar Copy Masters			
WEEK 1	1–5	Getting Started activities, **Why Write?** **Using a Portfolio**	11 40–41		415–418		4–5	
WEEK 2	6–10	**Writing in Journals** **Using Learning Logs**	208–209 210–211			88	6–7	
		Skills Activities: • Writing dates		272–273, 277	379, 382, 383	27–28		
		• Spelling		279–281	384, 385, 386	49–50, 51–52, 53–54		
WEEK 3	11–15	**Using the Writing Process**	14–15				8–9	
		One Writer's Process Prewriting, Writing, Revising, Editing, Publishing	16–25					
		Skills Activities: • Capital letters		222, 275		35–36		*GrammarSnap*
		• ABC order		281–283	387, 388	55–56, 57–58, 59–60		
WEEK 4	16–20	**Understanding the Writing Traits**	28–35				10–11	
		Skills Activities: • Word order	(31)			7–8		*GrammarSnap*
		• Plurals		223, 278, 292		71–72		*GrammarSnap*
		Learning to Listen	204–205					
WEEK 5	21–25	**Working with a Partner**	26–27				12–13	
		Skills Activities: • Spelling		279–283		7–8		
		Learning About a Rubric	36–37					

* These units are also located in the back of the *Teacher's Edition*. Resource Units include "Words," "A Writer's Resource," "Proofreader's Guide," and "Theme Words."
(+) This activity is located in a different section of the *Write Source Student Edition*. If students have already completed this activity, you may wish to review it at this time.

Teacher's Notes for The Writing Process

The overview for the writing process includes some specific teaching suggestions for the unit.

Using the Writing Process (pages 14–15)

Children rarely have a problem telling stories, made-up or true. The challenge is putting those stories on paper in a way that makes sense to other people. Young children learn to write through imitation and instruction, experimenting with pens, pencils, crayons, markers, and even keyboards. Gradually, they learn to write words, then sentences and paragraphs. This chapter introduces students to the five steps of writing.

One Writer's Process (pages 16–25)

Kim's story about a butterfly illustrates how children can go from seeing to writing about what they have seen.

Working with a Partner (pages 26–27)

This chapter stresses the importance of listening and talking during the revising process. Partners can learn to ask good questions.

Understanding the Writing Traits (pages 28–35)

Good writing has six traits: ideas, organization, voice, word choice, sentence fluency, and conventions. A student's work with the traits shows how each trait adds to her or his story.

Learning about a Rubric (pages 36–37)

Children may have an adult mark how tall they are on a doorjamb and add another mark later as a comparison. A rubric is a yardstick for writers.

Publishing Your Writing (pages 38–39)

Whenever students put their writing in a form that others can read and enjoy, that is publishing.

Using a Portfolio (pages 40–41)

One way for young writers to chart their progress is to keep a portfolio. Over the year, they can see how their writing has changed and improved as well as where their writing needs to be improved.

Academic Vocabulary

Read aloud the academic terms, as well as the descriptions and questions. Model for students how to read one question and answer it. Have partners monitor their understanding and seek clarification of the terms by working through the meanings and questions together.

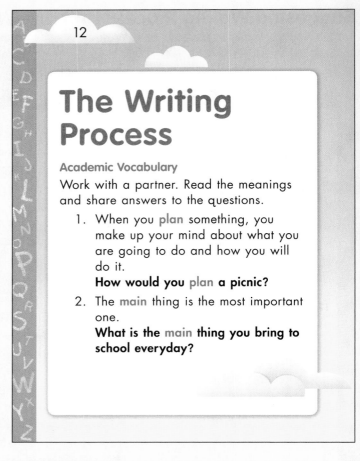

The Writing Process

Academic Vocabulary

Work with a partner. Read the meanings and share answers to the questions.

1. When you **plan** something, you make up your mind about what you are going to do and how you will do it.
   How would you plan a picnic?

2. The **main** thing is the most important one.
   What is the main thing you bring to school everyday?

Minilessons

Thanks, Partner!   Working with a Partner

- **READ** students the following story: "Sandy likes to ride her bike. It is a great bike. She rides it everywhere."

- **ENCOURAGE** partners to think of questions that would bring out missing details. (What color is the bike? When did she get it? What kind of bike is it? Where does she like to ride? When does she like to ride?)

Details = More Interest   Understanding the Writing Traits

- **TELL** a well-known story using the fewest details possible. (Here is an example using "The Three Little Pigs." Three pigs each built a house using different materials. A wolf came along and blew two houses down. The third house stood. The wolf tried to get in, but he fell in hot water and ran away.) **ASK** students what was missing in your story. **MAKE** a list of the details as they are shared. **RETELL** the story, adding the missing elements. **ENCOURAGE** students to use plenty of details in their writing.

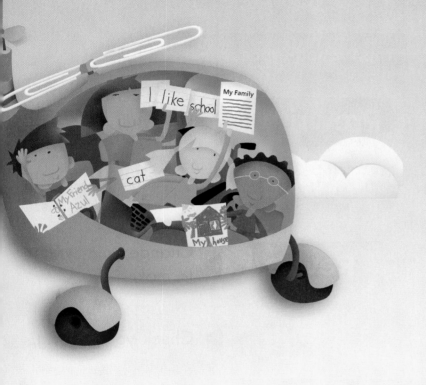

13

There are five steps in the writing process: prewrite, write, revise, edit, and publish. You can use these steps to help you write.

The Writing Process

Introduce the writing process by explaining that a process is a set of steps for doing or making something.

Invite volunteers to talk about a time when they used a process to do or make something (make an art project, play a game, bake cookies). Choose a process students suggest and ask them to help you name the basic steps. For example, for painting a picture . . .

- First, think of an idea for a picture.
- Next, sketch the picture in pencil.
- Then paint the picture.
- Check to be sure you used the paint colors that you want.
- Finally, share your painting with others.

Tell students that there is also a process to follow that will help them when they write. As you explain that this process is called *The Writing Process*, draw a cluster on the board and write *The Writing Process* in the center. Then as you name the steps of the process, write each one on the cluster—*Prewrite, Write, Revise, Edit, Publish*. Explain that the steps depend on each other and that writers often go back and repeat some of the steps before they finish a piece of writing.

Family Connection Letters

As you begin this unit, send home the Writing Process Family Connection letter, which describes what students will be learning.

- Letter in English (TE page 395)
- Letter in Spanish (TE page 404)

Using the Writing Process

> **Objective**
> • identify the five steps in the writing process

Explain that the **writing process** is a series of steps that guide writers. Point out the words on the pencil icons and explain that they name each step in the writing process. Have students point to the pencil icons in their book as you read about each step.

Write the following on the board:
    We prewrite and write,
    And then we revise,
    We edit and publish,
    A writing surprise!

Repeat the rhyme several times, pointing to the writing process words as you say them. Then have students chant the rhyme with you.

Provide photocopies of the reproducible The Writing Process page (TE page 340). Guide students to use their book to help them complete the spelling of each word. Save the graphic for students to use as a cover for a daily journal (Teaching Tip, TE page 17).

14

Using the Writing Process

Kim, Miguel, Emma, and Jake use the writing process to write. They write stories, reports, and poems.

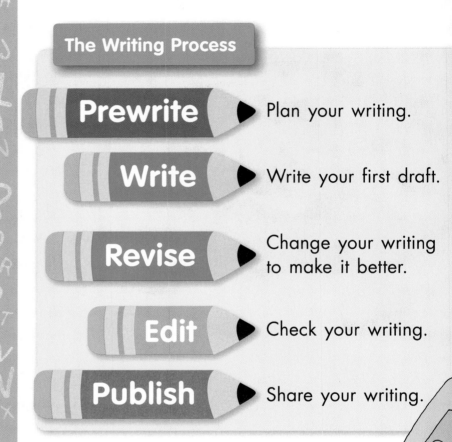

The Writing Process

Prewrite ▶ Plan your writing.

Write ▶ Write your first draft.

Revise ▶ Change your writing to make it better.

Edit ▶ Check your writing.

Publish ▶ Share your writing.

Materials

Black and colored pencils; markers; ink pens; crayons; paper of different textures, sizes, shapes, and colors; envelopes and folders; index cards; self-stick notes; blank books; graph paper, blank flash cards; weather charts, diagrams, photographs (TE p. 15)

Copy Masters

The Writing Process (TE p. 14)

The Writing Process   15

Introduce the children in the illustration as you point to them in a student's book. From left to right they are Kim, Miguel, Emma, and Jake. Explain that the children are learning to use the writing process and that students will learn to use the writing process along with them.

Point out that the children are getting ready to write. Explain that the thought balloons above their heads show that Kim, Miguel, Emma, and Jake are thinking about ideas for their writing. Tell students they will find out more about what Kim is planning to write. Ask students what idea she is thinking of (a butterfly).

Teaching Tip: Writer-Friendly Environment

Create a writing center where three or four students can write comfortably and provide materials such as the following:

Writing Tools

- black and colored pencils
- markers
- ink pens
- crayons

Writing Papers

- paper of different textures, sizes, shapes, and colors
- envelopes and folders
- index cards
- self-stick notes
- blank books

Also be sure to have writing materials handy throughout the classroom for other curriculum activities. For math, students might create graphs and flash cards. For science and social studies, students might write captions for weather charts, diagrams, and photographs; and they might make time lines for life cycles and important events.

One Writer's Process

> **Objective**
> ● follow one writer's progress through the writing process

Prewrite

Focus attention on the pencil icon in students' books. Help them read it aloud. Tell students that when they prewrite, they plan their writing. Talk about what Kim does to plan her writing.

✱ Anytime students need help with choosing topics during prewriting, refer them to the Theme Words, SE pages 298–311.

 Writer's Craft

Process: Many students think of writing as a product (a finished paper) instead of a process (working with words). They want to finish writing and be done with it. If you can make writing fun—*playing* with words rather than *working* with words—you'll help your students become habitual writers. The writing projects in this book are meant to be fun, so students will want to play their way from prewriting to publishing.

16

One Writer's Process

Follow along and see how Kim uses the writing process to write a story about a living thing.

 **Prewrite** ▶

Prewriting is the first step in the writing process. When you **prewrite**, you plan your writing.

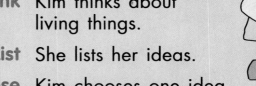

> Here is what Kim does to plan her writing.
>
> **Think** Kim thinks about living things.
>
> **List** She lists her ideas.
>
> **Choose** Kim chooses one idea as her topic.
>
> **Draw** She draws a picture about her topic.

Materials

Construction paper, 11" x 17" (TE p. 17)

Completed copy of reproducible The Writing Process page, glue (TE p. 17)

A few copies of reproducible Daily Journal page (TE p. 17)

Chart paper (TE p. 19)

Drawing materials (TE p. 20)

Pictures (TE pp. 20, 25)

Books (TE p. 24)

Copy Masters

Daily Journal (TE p. 17)

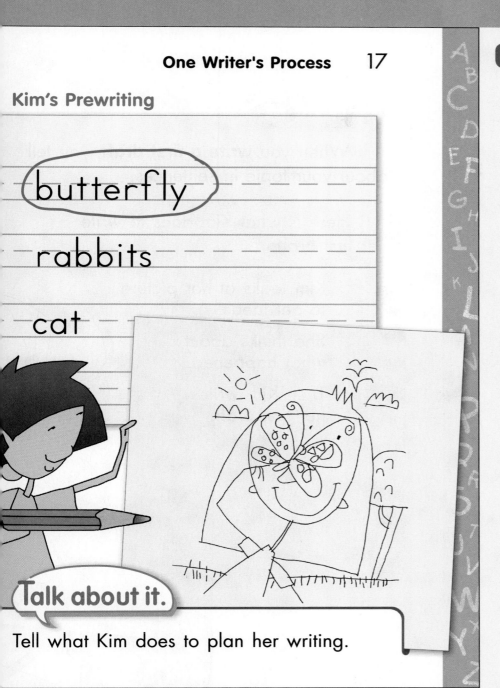

One Writer's Process   17

Kim's Prewriting

Talk about it.

Tell what Kim does to plan her writing.

Kim's Prewriting

Review each red key word on SE page 16 as students discuss what Kim does to plan her writing.

Answers

- **Think** Kim thinks about some living things she might want to write about (butterfly, rabbits, cat).
- **List** Kim writes her ideas in a list.
- **Choose** When Kim chooses one idea for her topic, she circles it (butterfly).
- **Draw** Kim draws a picture about her topic to help her remember details about it.

Explain that a good place to find ideas for writing is in a daily journal. Discuss the basics of **keeping a daily journal** (*see below*).

✱ For more information about daily journals, see SE pages 208–209 and 245.

Teaching Tip: Keeping a Daily Journal

Help students create their own daily journal. Have them fold a piece of 11" x 17" construction paper in half to make a folder and glue their completed copy of the reproducible The Writing Process page (TE page 14) to the front. Help students place a few copies of the reproducible Daily Journal page (TE page 333) inside the cover and staple them together.

Model how you write in your own journal as you guide a shared writing activity about a school happening.

As part of the normal classroom routine, have students write in their journals. The following questions can help them get started.

- What have I seen or heard that I want to remember?
- What have I read lately that was interesting or funny?
- What new things have I tried?

Write

Review the steps Kim took in prewriting (thought of living things, wrote a list of ideas, chose one as a topic, drew a picture). Tell students that now that Kim has thought about a topic, she is ready to write a first draft. Explain that in a first draft a writer writes about his or her topic in sentences.

Focus attention on the red key words in the students' books. Help them read each one aloud with you as you talk about what Kim does to write her first draft.

■ **Look** Call attention to the illustration on SE page 19. Ask why Kim is using binoculars. (She's looking closely at her drawing to remember what happened.)

■ **Think** Ask what Kim might remember about the butterfly when she looks at her drawing. (She is probably thinking about the butterfly's appearance and what it did.)

■ **Write** Stress that when Kim writes her first draft, she gets her ideas down on paper. She doesn't worry about making everything perfect. She knows that she can make corrections later.

18

 **Write** ▶

When you **write a first draft**, you tell about your topic in sentences.

Here is what Kim does to write her first draft.

Look Kim looks at her picture to get ideas.

Think She thinks about what happened.

Write Then Kim writes her first draft.

English Language Learners

Students may enter first grade with minimal English language experience. Their attempts to write in English may, in part, reflect the grammar of their first language. This confusion may produce "errors" in word order, omission of articles, pronouns, and verb tenses.

It is essential that a writing program integrate development of both oral and written language. Students need many and varied opportunities to talk about their ideas before and after they write.

● Sharing before writing allows students to "rehearse" and clarify vocabulary and word order.

● Sharing after writing provides practice using new vocabulary and language patterns.

One Writer's Process   19

Kim's First Draft

I saw a butterfly. the butterfly landed on my nose It tikld me.

Talk about it.

Tell what Kim does to write her first draft.

Kim's First Draft

Throughout this book there are writing samples students can use as models for their own writing. At first, they can follow the models closely, even using the same type of ideas and sentence patterns. Later, they can view each model as an example of how to approach the assignment.

Direct students' attention back to each red key word on SE page 18 as they discuss what Kim does to write her first draft.

Talk about it.

Answers

- **Look** Kim looks at her picture to get ideas.
- **Think** She thinks about what happened.
- **Write** She writes her first draft.

Ask what main detail from her drawing Kim used in her writing (the butterfly landed on her nose).

Briefly acknowledge the errors in Kim's first draft. Emphasize that in this step writers just get their ideas on paper and will correct any mistakes later.

English Language Learners

Turn the **Talk about it** activity into a Think Aloud to model all the steps to produce a first draft. Sketch two class events and share your ideas as you choose your topic before modeling the writing steps. Record your first draft on chart paper for future reference. Help students read the chart together.

Revise

Focus attention on the red key words in students' books. Help them read each one aloud with you as you talk about what Kim does to revise her writing.

Talk about how working with a partner can be helpful in revising.

- A partner can tell you what she or he likes about your writing.
- A partner can ask you questions about your writing.

Mention the question mark under the butterfly in the illustration and explain that Kim's partner, Miguel, has a question about her writing. What might he be asking her? (What color was the butterfly?)

Explain that Kim can change her writing and make it better by adding a word that identifies the color of the butterfly. Adding a color word helps Kim paint a clearer picture in the reader's mind.

20

 **Revise**

When you **revise**, you change your writing to make it better. Sometimes you add words to your writing.

Here is what Kim does to revise her writing.

Read   Kim reads her first draft to a partner.

Listen   She listens to her partner's questions.

Change   Then Kim changes her writing.

English Language Learners

To demonstrate how some words paint clear pictures, set up a Describing Words Game. Create a visual barrier between partners. Give one student a picture and have the second one draw the picture as his or her partner describes it. Compare the pictures. Talk about and list the describing words that "painted the picture."

Struggling Learners

Show how adding describing words makes writing clearer. Write on the board sentence pairs such as the following:

- I have a puppy.
  I have a black puppy.
- I heard a noise.
  I heard a scratching noise.

Read aloud each pair. Ask students which sentence paints the clearest picture in their mind.

One Writer's Process   21

Kim's Revising

yellow

I saw a butterfly.

the butterfly landed

on my nose It tikld me.

yellow

Tell what Kim does to revise her writing.

Direct students' attention back to each red key word on SE page 20 as they discuss what Kim does to revise her writing.

Talk about it.

Answers

- **Read** Kim reads her first draft to a partner.
- **Listen** She listens to her partner's questions.
- **Change** Then Kim changes her writing to make it better.

Read aloud Kim's revision as students follow along in their books. Ask what word Kim added to her first draft (*yellow*). Ask how adding this word made Kim's writing better. (*Yellow* adds an important a detail about the butterfly. It paints a clearer picture in the reader's mind.)

Identify the caret in the sentence. Explain that a caret shows where a word is added. Have students repeat *caret* as they trace the mark with their finger.

Advanced Learners

If students wrote a first draft on TE page 19, invite them to read their draft to a partner.

- Encourage partners to listen carefully and then ask questions about the writing.
- Then have students revise their writing by adding details that will paint a

clearer picture in the reader's mind. Remind students to use a caret to show where they add words.

Have partners take turns reading aloud their revised writing. Then have them save their revised draft for editing (TE page 22).

Edit

Look at the editing checklist in the illustration and explain that it shows how to mark corrections needed in writing.

- Capital letters: Draw three short lines underneath a letter that should be a capital letter.
- End marks: Mark a period and circle it at the end of a sentence that needs a period.
- Spelling: Draw a circle around words that may be spelled wrong.

Have students trace each mark with their finger several times. Then have them practice writing each mark on paper.

✱ Show students that they can find these marks on SE page 298.

22

 **Edit**

When you **edit** your writing, you check for capital letters, end marks, and spelling.

Here is what Kim does to edit her writing.

Read Kim reads her revised writing.

Check She checks her sentences for capital letters, end marks, and spelling.

Correct Kim corrects her sentences.

- ✓ Capital letters ≡
- ✓ End marks ⊙
- ✓ Spelling ◯

English Language Learners

Students may not be ready to edit for all the conventions at one time. For example, editing for end marks requires a natural sense of language fluency. Tell students you will help them whenever they edit their writing. Concentrate on one convention at a time.

Struggling Learners

While writing a first draft, students may naturally use invented or phonic spelling to complete their work. During the editing step, provide feedback and spelling resources to help students correct words that are consistently misspelled.

Advanced Learners

Have students use editing marks during this step (TE page 21). Then have partners exchange writing and use a different color pen or marker to add any editing marks the writer may have missed. Encourage partners to discuss the corrections they think are needed.

One Writer's Process   23

Kim's Editing

yellow

I saw a ∧butterfly. the

butterfly landed on my

tickled

nose. It (tikld) me.

Talk about it.

Tell what Kim does to edit her writing.

Kim's Editing

Direct students' attention back to each red key word on SE page 22 as they discuss what Kim does to edit her writing.

Talk about it.

Answers

- **Read** Kim reads her revised story.
- **Check** She checks for capital letters, end marks, and spelling.
- **Correct** Kim corrects her sentences.

Discuss each correction Kim made.
- A capital letter was added at the beginning of a sentence.
- A period was added at the end of a sentence.
- A spelling mistake was corrected.

✱ For more about using a period and a capital letter, see SE pages 270 and 275–277. For spelling lists students can use to check their spelling, see SE pages 279–283.

Discuss and model some **helpful editing tips** (*see below*).

Teaching Tip: Helpful Editing Tips

Model each of the following editing tips, using Kim's writing on SE page 21.
- *Read your writing aloud.* Sometimes it is easier to find mistakes when you hear them. Read aloud Kim's writing without pausing for the period at the end of the second sentence. Ask why the last part doesn't sound right.

- *Use a paper under each line.* This helps students keep their place and focus.
- *Edit for one thing at a time.* Look at Kim's writing line by line. As you move the paper down, first look for missing end marks, then look for missing capital letters, and last, check for spelling mistakes.

Grammar Connection

Capital Letters
- **Proofreader's Guide** page 275
- **Words** page 222
- *GrammarSnap* Capital Letters
- *SkillsBook* 35–36

ABC Order
- **Proofreader's Guide** pages 281–283
- *SkillsBook* pages 55–56, 57–58, 59–60
- **TE copy masters** pages 387, 388

Publish

Focus attention on the red key words. Help students read each one aloud with you as you talk about what Kim does to publish her writing.

- **Think** Talk about ways of choosing a title. For example, you can use words from the story, or you can think of a clever title. Is *My Butterfly* a good title for Kim's story? Why? Can anyone suggest another title? (Yellow Tickles)
- **Write** Explain that after revising and editing her writing, Kim copies it neatly. Ask why it is important to make a neat final copy (so people can read it easily). Have students compare Kim's writing on SE page 23 and SE page 25. Which is easier to read?
- **Share** Point out students' work that is posted in the room. Anytime students share their writing with others, they are involved in publishing. Be sure students understand that not all writing has to be published.

24

When you **publish** your writing, you share it with others.

Here is what Kim does to publish her writing.

Think Kim thinks of a title for her story.

Write She writes a neat final copy of her story and finishes her picture.

Share Kim shares her writing with her friends.

English Language Learners

Students may have difficulty using previously learned vocabulary in new contexts. For example, they may be confused that *title,* which may refer to the name of a book, may also refer to the name of a piece of their own writing. Before asking them to suggest titles for Kim's story, show students some of the books you have recently read in class.

Hold up one book at a time and ask volunteers to identify the title of each book. Do a Think Aloud to model how titles tell about the stories. For example, *The Three Little Pigs* is about three pigs. Do a Think Aloud to choose a title for the story you wrote to model the writing process (English Language Learners, TE page 19).

Advanced Learners

Have students complete their revised and edited writing (TE page 22) by following the publishing steps Kim followed.

- **Think** Have students think of a title for their writing.
- **Write** Have students write a neat final copy.
- **Share** Have listeners look at SE page 13 while readers share their writing aloud.

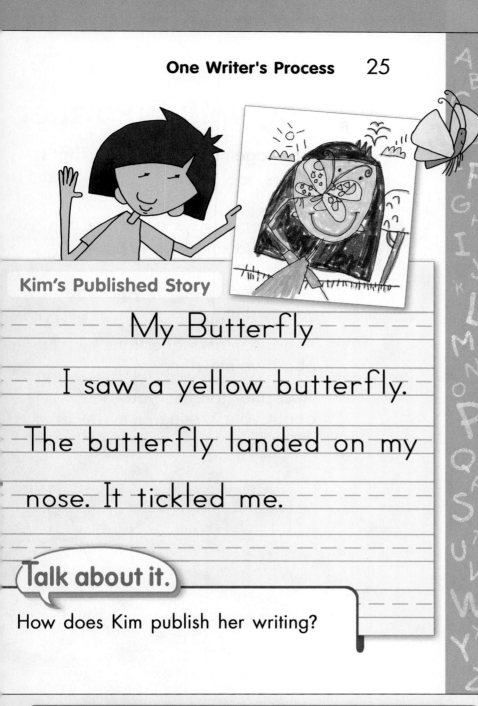

One Writer's Process 25

Kim's Published Story

My Butterfly

I saw a yellow butterfly.

The butterfly landed on my

nose. It tickled me.

Talk about it.

How does Kim publish her writing?

Kim's Published Story

Direct students' attention back to each red key word on SE page 24 as they discuss what Kim does to publish her writing.

Talk about it.

Answers
- **Think** Kim thinks of a title.
- **Write** She writes a neat final copy and finishes her picture.
- **Share** Kim shares her writing.

Read aloud Kim's final copy, and then review what she did to follow the steps in the writing process.
- **Prewrite** Kim listed ideas, chose a topic, and drew a picture.
- **Write** Kim looked at her drawing to get ideas for her writing. She wrote a first draft.
- **Revise** Kim read her writing to a partner. She made her writing better by adding a detail.
- **Edit** Kim edited her writing by checking for capital letters, end marks, and spelling.
- **Publish** Kim added a title and made a neat final copy to share.

Struggling Learners

If students are unsure how to choose a title for a piece of writing, provide practice with pictures. For example, show a picture of a family doing something together. Help them determine what the picture is all about. Ask the following types of questions:
- What do you see in the picture?
- What are the people doing?
- Where is it? When is it?

Help students decide what would be a good title for the picture. If students name very specific details about the picture, help them understand that details tell about parts of the picture, but they may not capture the main idea. If necessary, give students three possible title choices for each picture you display.

English Language Learners

To help students keep track of their papers for each step of the writing process, give them five pieces of colored 11" x 17" construction paper: purple (Prewrite), green (Write), blue (Revise), yellow (Edit), and red (Publish). Help them fold each piece to make and tape a 6-inch pocket on one end, label each pocket with one step, and bind the pocket pages in order.

Working with a Partner

Objective
- learn how partners can help each other

Discuss the importance of having a field trip partner or a swimming buddy. Point out that having a writing partner is important, too. Explain that a writing partner can help make your writing better.

Focus attention on the red key words in the students' books. Help them read each one aloud with you as you talk about working with a partner. Be sure that students understand that one partner reads her or his writing while the other partner listens.

Offer some tips for the readers.
- Read clearly and slowly.
- Pay attention to your partner's comments.

Offer some tips for listeners.
- Look at your partner.
- Listen carefully and don't interrupt.
- Tell your partner what you like about the writing.
- Ask any questions you have.

26

Working with a Partner

Working together can be fun. That's true for writers, too.

Here are some ways a partner can help you make your writing better.

Listen A partner listens as you read your writing.

Ask A partner asks questions about your writing.

Talk A partner talks to you about your writing.

Grammar Connection

Spelling
- **Proofreader's Guide** pages 279–283

Materials

Resource books such as encyclopedias;

nonfiction books about North American desert plants;

a computer with Internet access (TE p. 27)

Copy Masters

Commas in Letters (TE p.27)

Working with a Partner   27

Cactus pears are
yellow, orange, green,
or red. They grow on
a prickly pear cactus.
Some people make salsa
with cactus pears.

How do cactus
pears taste?

Talk about it.

How can partners help each other make
their writing better?

After reading aloud Jake's writing, focus the students' attention on the illustration in the students' books. Explain that the owl is Jake's partner. Read aloud the owl's question, and then ask

- What sentence could Jake add to answer the question and make his writing better?

Discuss the commas in the first sentence. Explain that a comma is used after each word or phrase in a list or series, such as *yellow, orange, green,* or *red.*

✱ For information and a worksheet on commas, see SE pages 272–273 and TE page 379.

Direct the students' attention back to each red key word on SE page 26 as they discuss how partners help each other make their writing better.

Talk about it.

Answers

- **Listen** A partner listens as you read your writing.
- **Ask** A partner asks questions about your writing.
- **Talk** A partner talks to you about your writing.

Struggling Learners

Help students learn to concentrate while listening.

- Provide a quiet environment.
- Model good listening skills. Give the writer your full attention as he or she reads. Smile or nod to indicate that you are listening.
- Be sure that students understand the purpose for listening carefully is to help the partner make his or her writing better.

Advanced Learners

Students may enjoy learning more about the prickly pear cactus. Encourage them to use resource books, nonfiction books about North American desert plants, and the Internet to gather and write notes about this cactus.

Have partners take turns reading their notes and asking questions or making comments.

Understanding the Writing Traits

Writers can't think of everything all at once. They begin with the "big picture"—**ideas**, **organization**, **voice**, especially during prewriting, writing, and the early stages of revising.

Then they slowly sharpen their focus to look at **word choice**, sentence fluency, and **conventions**.

Have students point to each writing trait symbol in their books as you read aloud each description. Then invite volunteers to tell why they think that is a good symbol for the trait.

Writer's Craft

The traits: The six traits give writers a common vocabulary for understanding writing. They help students zero in on specific strengths and weaknesses and help them know how to strengthen their writing.

28

Understanding the Writing Traits

You can use the *six traits* of writing listed below to become a better writer.

 Ideas   Start with great ideas.

 Organization   Make your words and sentences easy to follow.

 Voice   Sound as if you are really interested in your topic.

 Word Choice   Choose the best words.

 **Sentence Fluency**   Use sentences that are fun to read.

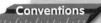 **Conventions**   Follow the rules for writing.

Traits of Writing   29

Use the traits.

Jake knows about the zoo. He writes about something that he saw.

Talk about it.

Tell a partner about something you have seen.

Use the traits.

Repeat the six writing traits and have students follow you as you pantomime them.

- **Ideas** (Point to head.)
- **Organization** (Open a folder. Put a paper inside.)
- **Voice** (Cup hands around mouth.)
- **Word Choice** (Look at open right hand. Look at open left hand.)
- **Sentence Fluency** (Move hands far apart. Move hands closer together.)
- **Conventions** (Check off three rules on a chart or clipboard.)

Guide students to use the illustration in their book to predict what Jake will write about.

Talk about it.

Give students a few minutes to think about something they have seen that they might like to write about. Then have partners take turns telling each other about it.

English Language Learners

Visual aids help students clarify vocabulary and organize their ideas before they tell stories orally.

Modify the **Talk about it** activity to include visual aids.

Have students draw a picture about what they saw before they tell a partner. You draw a picture, too.

Then model telling a partner what you saw as you show your drawing. Also model asking your partner for help with words you need to tell the story.

Pair students with proficient English speakers to maximize the oral language development opportunity.

Ideas

Tell students about things they can do to get ideas for writing topics.

- Students can read stories and articles and write about what happens or about what they learn.
- They can make lists of things they like.
- They can talk to family members and friends.
- They can look through their daily writing journal.

✱ For more information about finding topic ideas, see SE pages 242–247.

Explain that after writers choose a topic, they also think of details about that topic.

Answer

giraffe, leaves

Have students point to Jake's words in their book and read them aloud with you. Then have students look back at the illustration on SE pages 28 and 29 and talk about why Jake wrote those words. (*Giraffe* and *leaves* name what Jake saw. *Green* identifies a detail. *Eating* indicates an action.)

30

Ideas   **Start with great ideas.**

Jake thinks about his trip to the zoo. He writes words about what he saw.

giraffe   leaves   green   eating

Talk about it.

Which words tell you what Jake saw?

Struggling Learners

Display a picture in the writing center. Give students blank word cards. Have them talk about the picture and then write words that tell about it.

Help students edit for correct spelling. Have them make neat final copies of the word cards to display around the picture. Students may use the words to write a sentence about the picture in their journals.

English Language Learners

Research indicates that memories, a source of ideas, are encoded in the language of the experience. Students who want to write about family events may need help with the vocabulary needed to tell their story in English. Have students share their ideas orally before they write. Ask questions and provide vocabulary as needed.

Traits of Writing 31

Organization

Make your words and sentences easy to follow.

Jake organizes his ideas into sentences. He puts the words in an order that makes sense.

Organization

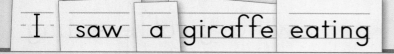

I saw a giraffe eating

Why did Jake put his words in order?

Organization

Using a pocket chart or chalkboard tray, display three or four word cards that form a sentence, but in mixed-up order. Point to each card and have students read the words with you. Ask if the sentence makes sense and why. (No, the words are in the wrong order.)

Rearrange the words so that they form the sentence. Tell students that you put the words in the correct order. After reading the sentence aloud, ask students if the sentence makes sense now. (Yes, the words are in the right order.)

Point out on SE page 30 that Jake's words are not in sentence order. Then point out on SE page 31 how Jake put them in order.

Talk about it.

Answer

Jake put his words in order so that they make sense.

English Language Learners

Limited English proficiency may make it difficult for students to determine what "makes sense." Modify the Struggling Learners activity. Ask students to tell about a shared event such as a recess game. Respond to phrases and sentences that contain errors by modeling correct word order. Have students repeat the corrected sentences as you record them on a language chart. Copy each sentence on word cards and arrange the words in incorrect order. Reinforce correct word order as you help students correct each sentence.

Struggling Learners

Provide practice with arranging words in sentence order. Write several simple sentences on word cards. Place the word cards for each sentence in a separate envelope and leave these sentence puzzles in the writing center for students to use during free time.

Voice

Write the following sentences on the board and read them aloud:

■ It is a big bug.
■ Wow, it's a monster bug!

To help students become aware of a writing voice, ask these questions:

■ Which sentence sounds like the writer is talking to a friend? (*Wow, it's a monster bug!*)
■ Which words make it sound like the writer is talking to a friend? (*Wow, it's,* and *monster*)

As a choral reading, have students read aloud Jake's sentence on SE page 31. Then have them read aloud Jake's sentence on SE page 32. Ask students which one sounds more like Jake would sound if he were talking to a friend (SE page 32).

Answer

The words *and eating* show Jake's writing voice.

Voice **Sound as if you are really interested in your topic.**

Jake adds words that sound as if he really likes his topic.

Voice

I saw a giraffe eating

and eating

Talk about it.

What words did Jake add to show his writing voice?

Help students understand the concept of voice by demonstrating that there are different ways to say the same thing. Provide examples that contrast speaking with teachers (*I can't find my book*) and speaking with friends (*Hey! Where's my book?*). Have students identify which sounds more like talking to a friend. Offer other examples of communicating with an adult. Ask volunteers to suggest how they would tell the same message to a friend.

The concept of voice in writing is difficult for many students to grasp. Have a recording device available, and encourage students to record themselves telling about an event. Then have them listen to their recording and pay close attention to the way they use certain words. Explain that some of these words will capture their writing voice.

Traits of Writing   33

 Word Choice

Choose the best words. They make a clear picture in the reader's mind.

Jake chooses a color word that makes a clear picture in the reader's mind.

Word Choice

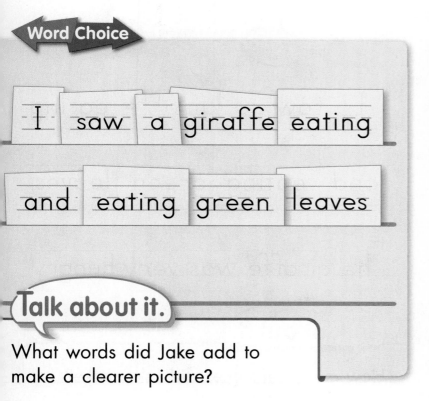

I saw a giraffe eating and eating green leaves

Talk about it.

What words did Jake add to make a clearer picture?

Word Choice

Write the following sentences on the board and read them aloud:

- I ate an apple.
- I ate a juicy, green apple.

Ask students which sentence makes a clearer picture in their mind and why. (The words *juicy* and *green* describe the apple.)

Have students compare and contrast Jake's sentence on SE page 32 with Jake's sentence on SE page 33. Ask these questions: How are the sentences alike? How are they different? Which sentence makes a clearer picture in your mind? (SE page 33)

✱ For information about learning new words to improve word choice, see SE pages 256–259.

Talk about it.

Answer

The words *green leaves* make a clearer picture.

Have students play a version of the Describing Words Game (English Language Learners, TE page 20) to reinforce the value of using specific words in writing. Collect sets of pictures that are similar except for one feature (a dog with a short tail and a dog with a long tail). Challenge a volunteer to use describing words that help the listener pick out the picture being described. Post the sets of pictures with the new describing words under them.

Add new pictures and describing words throughout the year. Encourage students to refer to the word wall whenever they write.

If students have trouble understanding how word choice creates a clearer picture, write this sentence on the board: *I see a pet outside*. Ask students to describe what you see. Then ask what kind of pet it could be, and list answers on the board. Ask where it could be, and list answers. Then rewrite the sentence several times using the answers to show how word choice creates a clearer picture.

Word cards: *The hen sits on the egg to keep it warm a baby chick is inside*

Sentence Fluency

Write this run-on sentence on the board: *I saw a giraffe eating and eating green leaves the giraffe was very hungry*

Explain that Jake added another idea to his writing, but now it is hard to read. Ask what Jake should do to make it easier and more fun to read (make it into two sentences).

Guide students to point in their books to the changes Jake made to his writing. (He added a period after *leaves.* He put a capital letter on *the* and a period after *hungry.*)

Have students read aloud Jake's two sentences with you. Which is longer? Have students count the words in each sentence. Explain that using both long and short sentences can make writing easier to read.

Answer

Jake made two sentences, one long sentence and one short sentence.

34

 **Use sentences that are fun to read.** You might use long and short sentences.

Jake adds another idea, but his writing is hard to read. He makes one long sentence and one short one. Now his writing is fun to read.

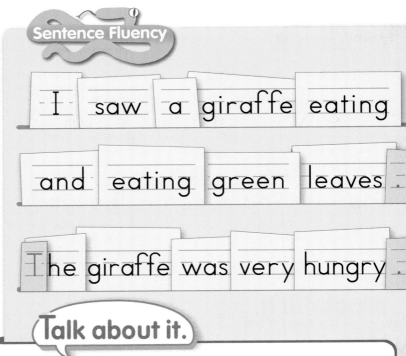

How many sentences did Jake make?

Struggling Learners

To reinforce using long and short sentences, write the following run-on sentence on word cards: *The hen sits on the egg to keep it warm a baby chick is inside.* Read it aloud and ask if it sounds easy to read. Then have students read it with you as you track the words.

Invite volunteers to indicate how to make two sentences out of the run-on. Read aloud and track the two sentences. Guide students to count the words in each sentence. Then have students read the sentences with you as you track them. Is it easier to read the sentences now? Why?

Traits of Writing   35

Conventions   **Follow the rules for writing.**

Jake follows the writing rules and makes a neat copy of his sentences. He uses capital letters and periods.

Conventions

The Zoo

I saw a giraffe eating and eating green leaves. The giraffe was very hungry.

✓ Capital letters ≡

✓ End marks ⊙

✓ Spelling ⬭

Talk about it.

How did Jake follow the writing rules?

Conventions

Talk with students about classroom rules and why it is important for everyone to follow them. Explain that there are writing rules called *conventions* that writers follow.

Focus attention on the clipboard in the illustration in the students' books. Explain that the clipboard shows conventions writers check for in their writing: capital letters, end marks, and spelling.

Discuss the use of a checklist. Point out that the check marks in the boxes mean the writer has checked her or his writing for capital letters, end marks, and spelling.

Be sure students understand that writers check for conventions during the editing step of the writing process. Explain that the clipboard will appear throughout the book to remind them to check for conventions in their writing.

Talk about it.

Answers

Jake followed the rules by adding a capital letter and end marks to his final copy.

English Language Learners

Students' errors in language conventions are often related to translating from their first language to English. When editing, have students, with your help, focus on one convention at a time.

- Look for patterns of errors to determine which writing rules each student should focus on.
- Work on a single convention before moving on.

Advanced Learners

Point out that Jake added a title to his writing. Challenge students to think of other possible titles for Jake's story ("A Hungry Giraffe"). Encourage students to be creative ("Leaves for Lunch").

Grammar Connection

Word Order
- *GrammarSnap* Understanding Sentences
- *SkillsBook* pages 7–8

Plurals
- **Proofreader's Guide** pages 278, 292
- **Words** page 223
- *GrammarSnap* Plural Nouns
- *SkillsBook* pages 71–72

Learning About a Rubric

36

> **Objective**
> ● understand how rubrics can be used to evaluate writing

A rubric helps students distinguish between writing that works and writing that needs revision. The rubric focuses on the traits of good writing, which describe *why* a paper is strong or weak.

Experts recommend using verbal descriptors rather than numerical scores with young writers. In addition, rubrics for young students usually focus on three or four traits, rather than the full six traits.

Demonstrate how to read a rubric.
■ Track and read the verbal descriptors across the top.
■ Next, read the three writing traits down the left side.
■ Point to the ideas symbol. Have students follow along as you read the description for writing that is classified under *Great, Good,* and *Keep Trying*. Repeat for the other two traits.

Learning About a Rubric

A rubric lists the main traits for a form of writing. Jake and his teacher talk about the rubric below. It lists three traits. Now Jake knows what to look for in his writing.

Three Writing Traits

Great!

Ideas — Your writing has one topic and great details.

Organization — Your writing is in an order that makes sense.

Conventions — Your writing follows the writing rules.

English Language Learners

Identify the trait each student needs the most help with. Provide specific examples that demonstrate "Great!," "Good," and "Keep Trying" ratings for the trait. Then point out strategies that can be used to improve the examples that received "Good" or "Keep Trying" ratings. List these strategies on a wall chart.

Learning About a Rubric 37

Jake, you have a great idea!

Good	Keep Trying
our writing has one opic and some details.	Your writing needs one topic and details.
our writing shows ome words and entences in order.	Your writing needs order.
our writing follows ost of the writing rules.	Your writing needs to follow the rules.

Advanced Learners

Challenge students to use the rubric to respond to the following questions:
- How would you improve your writing so it is "Great!" rather than "Good" for *ideas*?
- How would you improve your writing so it is "Great!" rather than "Good" for *organization*?
- How would you improve your writing if it is rated "Keep Trying" for *conventions*?

In the core units (narrative, expository, responding to literature) there are three opportunities to use the rubric to evaluate students' writing.

- First, as students start to revise and edit their work, you can meet with them individually or in small groups to talk about what students can look for during these steps in the process. Begin by focusing on ideas, especially the concept of adding details. Then attend to organization and finally, focus on conventions.
- Second, you can meet with students individually in writing conferences to discuss their final published pieces. Use the rubric to help focus this discussion.
- Third, in the Writing for Assessment lessons, you can work with students as a group to evaluate the sample response in the student edition as well as two additional benchmark papers. Conference notes are provided for your reference.

Writing Workshop

The rubric on this page can help you and students understand how to provide helpful, traits-based feedback when you read and respond to student writing. Always encourage young writers, showing them how they can move up to the next level.

Publishing Your Writing

Objective

• recognize the different ways to publish writing

Remind students that when they publish their writing, they share it with others. Invite volunteers to walk around the classroom and point to an example of published writing on display.

As you read about three different ways to publish writing (Make, Enter, and Post), have students point to an example of it in the illustration on SE page 39.

Emphasize that in order to publish their writing, students need to make a neat final copy.

✳ For information about planning their final copy, refer students to SE pages 262–267.

38

Publishing Your Writing

When you **publish** your writing, you share it with others. Your teacher, friends, and family will enjoy reading about your ideas.

Here are some ways you can share your writing.

Make   You can make a book.

Enter   You can enter your writing on the computer and print a copy or send it by e-mail.

Post   You can post your writing on a wall, door, or bulletin board.

Materials

Magazine photos of children;

sentence strips;

magnetic photo album;

pet-food ads, newsprint,

greeting card covers;

construction paper;

glue (TE p. 39)

Publishing Your Writing   39

Try other ways to publish.

Dear Auntie, I wrote a story about you. Here it is.

Riding the Subway
I went to the subway with my aunt. We waited and waited for the train. Then all the doors opened. We hurried to find seats. The train ride was rocky and squeaky. I want to ride again!

Talk about it.

What ways have you used to publish your writing?

Try other ways to publish.

Call attention to the book in the illustration, *My cat,* that Jake made. Have students talk about the types of books they have made. Include **bookmaking** (*see below*) as an ongoing project in the writing or art center.

Talk about Jake's use of the computer for writing. Discuss other ways to use a computer to publish writing.

- Post the final copy on the school Web site.
- Create a class Web site, or blog, in which students can post their final pieces of writing.
- Insert clip art into a final document or use graphics.

Read aloud Jake's work posted on the chair. Point out areas in the classroom where students' writing is posted.

Talk about it.

Help students recall ways they have published their writing (mailing a thank-you card, sending an e-mail message, posting a list or a drawing at home).

Teaching Tip: Bookmaking

Students will enjoy making their own books. Here are some ideas they can try:

- A photo-essay book

Have student,s cut out magazine photos of children and write captions on sentence strips. Place photos and writing in a photo album.

- A cartoon book

Have students cut out pet-food ads that show pets with funny expressions and glue them on newsprint. Students can add thought balloons and write what the pet is thinking.

- A sequenced story book

Have students choose several greeting card covers and arrange them in a story sequence. Have them glue the cards to separate sheets of construction paper, write sentences below each card, and staple the pages in order.

Using a Portfolio

Objectives
- learn about types of portfolios
- learn how to set up a portfolio

Portfolios are important evaluation tools that show students' progress throughout the year.

Display a file folder with several pieces of writing in it and tell students that this is one type of portfolio. Allow time for students to examine the folder.

Talk about the picture of Jake's portfolio on SE page 41. Then have students decorate the covers of their own portfolio. Their portfolios could be one of the following:
- a construction paper folder
- a plastic container
- a file folder
- a pocket folder
- an accordion file

40

Using a Portfolio

A **portfolio** is a special place to save your writing. You add writing to your portfolio during the year. You can see how your writing is getting better and better.

Keep Use a folder or a box to keep your writing in one place.

Add During the year, add writing to your portfolio.

Look Take time to look at the writing in your portfolio. You can see how your writing is getting better.

Materials

A folder with writing samples in it; materials for making a portfolio, such as construction paper, plastic containers, file folders, pocket folders, and accordion folders; markers; colorful paper; stickers; glue; tape (TE p. 40)

Using a Portfolio   41

Talk about it.

How do you save your writing?

Work with students to decide which writing they should include in their portfolios. For some, if not all the pieces, include prewriting drawings and lists, revised and edited drafts, and final copies.

Add samples on a regular basis and label the writing with the dates students completed them.

Establish a schedule for discussing the portfolios with students. Reviewing their writing samples helps students recall what they have learned during the writing process and helps them see how they have progressed as writers.

Use the portfolio as a basis for **parent conferences** (*see below*) in which you demonstrate and discuss how their child has grown and developed as a writer.

Talk about it.

Help students recall ways they (or their parents or guardians) save their writing (in a box, in a binder notebook, in an electronic file on the computer).

Teaching Tip: Parent Conferences

Saving work throughout the year aids in parent conferences. Portfolios are a hands-on tool that shows growth and development of skills.

• Organize the portfolio.

Arrange the writing samples in chronological order for the designated time period. Be sure each sample is dated.

• Provide background information.

Tell parents why their child wrote about a particular topic. Explain the writing process and how it applies to each piece of writing.

• Discuss student progress.

As you present the writing samples, talk about developmental progress.

For example, point out that at first the child may have ignored spelling errors, but now she uses a picture dictionary to correct spelling during the editing step.

• Encourage writing at home.

Suggest that parents keep a portfolio of writing their child does at home.

Sentences and Paragraphs Overview

Common Core Standards Focus

Writing 5: With guidance and support from adults, focus on a topic, respond to questions and suggestions from peers, and add details to strengthen writing as needed.

Language 1j: Produce and expand complete simple and compound declarative, interrogative, imperative, and exclamatory sentences in response to prompts.

Language 2b: Use end punctuation for sentences.

Language 2d: Use conventional spelling for words with common spelling patterns and for frequently occurring irregular words.

 Technology Connections

 Write Source Online
www.hmheducation.com/writesource

- *Net-text*
- *Bookshelf*
- *GrammarSnap*
- *Portfolio*

- *Writing Network features*
- *File Cabinet*

 Interactive Whiteboard Lessons

Suggested Sentences and Paragraphs Unit (Two Weeks)

Day	Writing and Skills Instruction	Student Edition		Teacher's Edition	SkillsBook	Daily Language Workouts	Write Source Online
		Sentences and Paragraphs Unit	Resource Units*	Grammar Copy Masters			
WEEK 1							
1–3	**Writing a Sentence** (Model)	44–53				14–15	
	Skills Activities:						
	• Sentences		288	341			*GrammarSnap*
	• Sentence order		288	342	5–6		*GrammarSnap*
	• Naming part		229 (+), 288	343	9–10		*GrammarSnap*
	• Telling part		228 (+), 288	344	11–12		*GrammarSnap*
	• Writing sentences		288	345, 346	13–14		*GrammarSnap*
4–5	**Kinds of Sentences**	54–55	290				
	Skills Activities:						
	• Telling sentences		270	347	15–16		*GrammarSnap*
	• Asking sentences		271	348	17–18		*GrammarSnap*
	• Exclamatory sentences		271	349	19–20		*GrammarSnap*
	• Period, question mark, exclamation point		270–271	350, 351, 352			*GrammarSnap*
WEEK 2							
6–7	**Writing a Paragraph**	56–59				16–17	
	Skills Activity:						
	• Spelling		279–283				*GrammarSnap*

* These units are also located in the back of the *Teacher's Edition*. Resource Units include "Words," "A Writer's Resource," "Proofreader's Guide," and "Theme Words."
(+) This activity is located in a different section of the *Write Source Student Edition*. If students have already completed this activity, you may wish to review it at this time.

Teacher's Notes for Sentences and Paragraphs

The overview for sentences and paragraphs includes some specific teaching suggestions for the unit.

Writing a Sentence (pages 44–53)

A sentence is a group of words organized to state a complete thought. Once young writers understand how important it is to have all the words needed in their proper place, they will know how to put their thoughts on paper. The chapter examines the parts of a sentence as well as the way those parts should appear in a sentence to make sense.

Kinds of Sentences (pages 54–55)

Once students learn what a sentence is, they need to know that there are different kinds of sentences. In addition, they will need to know that each kind of sentence has its own end mark.

Writing a Paragraph (pages 56–59)

After learning about sentences, children are ready to learn that paragraphs are made up of sentences about the same topic. One sentence begins the paragraph with the main idea, several sentences add information, and one sentence closes the paragraph with a final thought. A student's visit to the park with his mother is the topic of the sample paragraph, which shows how a paragraph is developed.

Academic Vocabulary

> Read aloud the academic terms, as well as the descriptions and questions. Model for students how to read one question and answer it. Have partners monitor their understanding and seek clarification of the terms by working through the meanings and questions together.

Minilessons

The Spread
Writing a Sentence

- On the board, **WRITE** a sentence modeled after the one on SE page 51. Then **WRITE** the following "sentence":

    dadmadesalad

- **ASK** the children to look at SE page 51 and **TELL** you the three things you need to do to change this list of letters into a sentence.

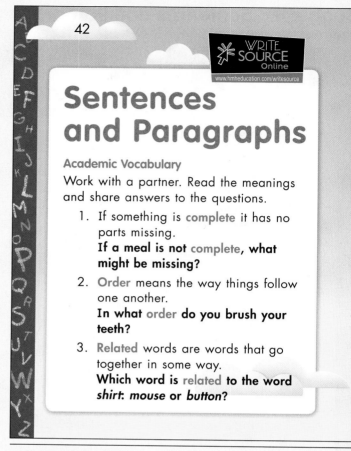

Sentences and Paragraphs

Academic Vocabulary

Work with a partner. Read the meanings and share answers to the questions.

1. If something is **complete** it has no parts missing.
   If a meal is not complete, what might be missing?

2. **Order** means the way things follow one another.
   In what order do you brush your teeth?

3. **Related** words are words that go together in some way.
   Which word is related to the word shirt: mouse or button?

I Like spaghetti. Kinds of Sentences

- **READ** and **DISCUSS** the three different kinds of sentences on SE page 54. **FOCUS** on the asking sentence. **ASK** children to copy the following sentence (question) onto a half piece of paper and then **ANSWER** it with as many words as they can.

    What do you like to eat?

Sentence Variety Kinds of Sentences

- **USE** the list of topics below as a source for sentences. **NAME** the topic and **ASK** the children to **SHARE** one sentence for each of the different kinds of sentences. **WRITE** the sentences on the board. For example, lunch. *It is time for lunch. Do you want to eat lunch? Yea, it is lunchtime!* **ASK** the children what kind of end mark is needed for each sentence.

    Topics: water, school, shoes, book, teacher, weather

Class Act Writing a Paragraph

- **CHOOSE** a recent class activity. **INVITE** the class to join in creating a paragraph on that topic. **HAVE** them figure out a topic sentence, middle sentences, and finally the closing sentence. **WRITE** all the sentences on the board. **HAVE** students **WRITE** the paragraph in their journals with labels for each part.

You think and talk about ideas.
You can also write about your ideas
in sentences. Then you can put the
sentences together to make a paragraph.

43

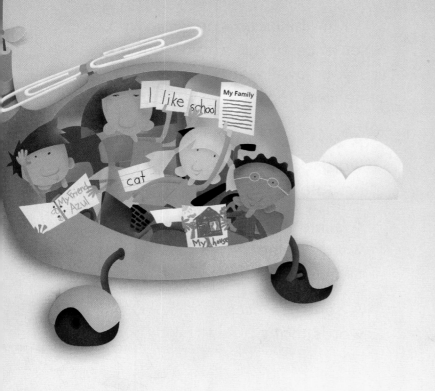

A B C D E F G H I J K L M N O P Q R S T U V W X Y Z

Sentences and Paragraphs

Invite students to think of something interesting or unusual that they saw on their way to school. Ask volunteers to tell how they might share this information. Would they tell someone about it or draw a picture of the scene? Would they write a sentence or a paragraph to tell about it?

Display a familiar picture book and read aloud several paragraphs. Point out that the author uses words to form sentences and groups of sentences to form paragraphs. Tell students that they are going to learn how to write sentences and paragraphs to share their thoughts with others.

Materials

Picture book (TE p. 43)

Writing a Sentence

Objective
- learn that a sentence states a complete thought, has words in the correct order, and uses words that name and tell

 Word cards: *a, fox, I, red, saw, today* .

Define a *complete thought* as "a group of words that makes a clear statement." Explain that if a sentence is missing some words, it won't make sense. To demonstrate this, display word cards for the sentence on SE page 45 in a pocket chart or on the chalkboard tray.

- Explain that a **sentence** is made up of separate words like the words on the cards. Track and read aloud the words with students. Have students count the words in the sentence.
- Then take away the cards for *I* and *fox* and ask if the sentence is still a complete thought. Guide students to see that because words are missing, the sentence does not make sense.

✱ For more information and a worksheet on understanding sentences, see SE page 288 and TE page 341.

44

Writing a Sentence

A **sentence** is a group of related words. It states a complete thought.

Kim thinks of words to write a sentence about a fox. You can use your own words to write sentences, too.

A sentence uses words to state a **complete thought**.

A sentence uses words in the **correct order**.

A sentence uses words that **name** and **tell**.

Materials

Word cards (TE pp. 44, 46, 49, 51)

Drawing paper (TE p. 45)

Chart paper (TE pp. 45, 49)

Crayons (TE pp. 45, 49, 51)

Language chart (TE pp. 46, 50)

Scissors and glue (TE p. 47)

Colored chalk (TE pp. 49, 50, 51)

Sentence strips (TE pp. 51)

Picture cards (TE p. 52)

Copy Masters

Sentences 1 (TE p. 44)

Sentence Order (TE p. 47)

The Naming Part (TE p. 49)

The Telling Part (TE p. 51)

Writing Sentences (TE p. 52)

Sentences 2 (TE p. 52)

Writing a Sentence   45

I saw a red
fox today.

Talk about it.

Use your own words to finish each sentence.

1. The ant _____.

2. _____ digs holes.

Focus attention on the thought balloon that crosses over from SE page 44 to the top of SE page 45. Make sure students understand that it shows what Kim is thinking.

■ After reading aloud what Kim wrote, ask if her sentence tells a **complete thought** (*see below*).

■ Discuss with students how they can tell that this sentence states a complete thought. (It has all the words it needs to make sense to the reader.)

Talk about it.

Possible answers:
1. is carrying a leaf
2. My new puppy

**Teaching Tip:
Complete Thoughts**

To illustrate that sentences express complete thoughts, distribute drawing paper and crayons and have students draw something they saw on the way to school. Have them display their picture and share a sentence about it with the class. Have students tell if the sentence tells a complete thought about the picture.

Struggling Learners

Listen for articles and word order as students describe their drawing (Teaching Tip). If possible, model the sentence pattern *I saw a/the _____,* and have them use it for their own sentence. Record their sentences on chart paper. Track and read chorally the sentences. Save this language chart.

English Language Learners

Listen for articles and word order as students describe their drawing (Teaching Tip). Model the sentence pattern *I saw a/the _____* as you echo students, and have them repeat your models. Record their sentences on chart paper. Track and read chorally the sentences. Save this language chart (English Language Learners, TE page 46).

Put your words in order.

 Word cards: *a, bushy, fox, has, tail, The, .*

Ask volunteers to hold up the word cards. Arrange students so that the words are out of order, as above. Point to the words and guide students in reading them aloud.

- Ask if the words make sense in this order and have students explain why or why not.
- Explain that when words are not written in the correct order, they do not make sense.
- Have students holding the cards rearrange themselves so that the words form the sentence *The fox has a bushy tail*. Point to each word as you guide students in reading aloud the sentence.

After reading aloud the page, be sure students understand the **concept of order** (*see below*). Have them explain what it means when words are in the correct order. (It means that the words are in an order that makes sense.)

46

Put your words in order.

The words in a sentence must be in the **correct order** to make sense.

These words are not in the correct order. They do not make sense.

fox A lives

woods the in

Grammar Connection

Sentences

- **Proofreader's Guide** page 288
- *GrammarSnap* Understanding Sentences
- **TE copy master** page 341

Sentence order

- **Proofreader's Guide** page 288
- *GrammarSnap* Understanding Sentences
- *SkillsBook* pages 5–6
- **TE copy master** page 342

Teaching Tip: Concept of Order

Explain that to order things means "to arrange things in a certain way." Have volunteers suggest short sentences. Give each student a word and have them line up in correct order for their sentence and say their word. Are the words in an order that makes sense? Emphasize that in writing, the words must be "lined up" in an order that makes sense.

English Language Learners

To reinforce correct word order, use the students' own sentences from the language chart (English Language Learners, TE page 45). Have each student copy the words from his or her sentence on word cards. Arrange each set of word cards in incorrect order and read them aloud. Then read the original sentence from the language chart. Help students rearrange the out-of-order sentences.

Writing a Sentence   47

These words are in the correct order. They make sense.

A fox lives in the woods.

Talk about it.

Read each group of words. Tell which one makes sense.

1. Eyes has green cat the.
2. The cat has green eyes.

Have students point to each word as you read aloud the sentence about the fox. Ask if the words are now in the correct order and how students can tell (because the sentence makes sense).

Use the board to model how to put the words in sentences 1 and 2 in correct order. Then distribute photocopies of the reproducible Sentence Order page (TE page 342). Ask a volunteer to read aloud the words in the first box. Help students order the words so that the sentence makes sense. Have them check the order by asking: *Does this sentence make sense?* Then have them write the sentence on their paper. Repeat for number 2.

Distribute scissors and glue and have students cut out the words. After students arrange the words on their paper, write their responses on the board so they can check their work before gluing the words in place.

Talk about it.

Answer
The second sentence makes sense.

Find the naming part.

Write the following sentence frame on the board: _____ *jumps.*

- Ask one student to act out this action.
- Ask "Who jumps?" and write the student's name in the blank to complete the sentence. Point out that this part of the sentence completes the sentence and tells *who* the sentence is about. Explain that this part of the sentence is called the naming part.
- Then rewrite the sentence and substitute an article and a common noun *(a fox)* in the blank to show that the naming part can also tell *what* the sentence is about.

Focus attention on the illustration and ask students what animal is pictured (a fox). Tell students they will read another sentence about the fox on the next page.

48

Find the naming part.

Every sentence has a naming part. The **naming part** tells who or what the sentence is about.

Grammar Connection

Naming part
- **Proofreader's Guide** page 288
- **Words** page 229 (+)
- *GrammarSnap* Understanding Sentences
- *SkillsBook* pages 9–10
- **TE copy master** page 343

Struggling Learners

If students have difficulty understanding why a naming part can tell either who or what, explain that we use the word *who* to refer to people and the word *what* to refer to animals and nonliving things.

Draw a T-chart on the board with the headings *Who* and *What*. Say the following nouns and have students identify whether they tell *who* or *what:* *brother, puppy, Grandpa, Susan, kite, kitten, pan,* and *friend.* Write the words under the appropriate heading on the T-chart as students identify them.

Guide students in reading the chart.

Writing a Sentence 49

Naming Part

A fox lives in the woods.

Talk about it.

What is the **naming part** of each sentence?
1. My cat climbs the tree.
2. I jump up and down.
3. Mom looks up in the tree.
4. Dad gets a ladder.

Point out the tinted box above the words *A fox*. Focus attention on the label *Naming Part* and help students read it aloud. Explain that both words in the tinted box, *A fox*, make up the naming part of the sentence.

- Ask students whether this naming part tells who or what is doing the action (it tells *what*).
- Invite students to suggest other naming parts that could be substituted into this sentence. Write these suggestions as complete sentences on the board. Then ask students to identify the naming part in each sentence. Use colored chalk to box and label the naming part.

Talk about it.

Distribute photocopies of the reproducible Naming Part page (TE page 343). As students identify each naming part, write their responses on the board. Have students use crayons to circle and lightly shade the naming part on their paper.

Answers
1. My cat
2. I
3. Mom
4. Dad

English Language Learners

Use the word cards from the English Language Learners activity on TE page 46 to reinforce the naming part of sentences. Have students tell something about the people and objects as they point to the word cards. Model complete sentences and record students' sentences on a language chart. After students read the chart chorally, ask *who* and *what* questions. Circle the naming words on the chart as students respond, taking care to include the articles. Reinforce the concept orally by saying, "Yes, *the book* answers the question *what*. *The book* is the naming part of this sentence." Save the chart (English Language Learners, TE page 50).

Advanced Learners

Have students reread the **Talk about it** sentences and identify whether the naming part tells *who* or *what*. Challenge students to rewrite the first sentence so that the naming part tells *who*, and the next two sentences so that the naming part tells *what*.

Find the telling part.

List three students' names on the board. Then take the three students aside and tell each one to hop, skip, or jump.

- As students, one at a time, act out the actions, ask the class to identify what each student does. Record these responses next to the students' names to make sentences.
- Help students read these sentences aloud. Then ask them to identify what each student did (the telling part of the sentence).
- Use colored chalk to box the predicate (the telling part) of each sentence. Point out that the telling part (one or more than one word) says something about the naming part.

After reading aloud the page, focus students' attention on the picture. Ask them to come up with a sentence that tells about Mr. Fox. Write the sentences on the board and have students identify the telling part. Use colored chalk to box and label the telling part.

50

Find the telling part.

Every sentence has a telling part. The **telling part** says something about the **naming part**.

Grammar Connection

Telling part
- **Proofreader's Guide** page 288
- **Words** page 228 (+)
- *GrammarSnap* Understanding Sentences
- *SkillsBook* pages 11–12
- **TE copy master** page 344

English Language Learners

To introduce the concept that a part of every sentence *tells about* the naming part, review sentences on the language chart (English Language Learners, TE page 49). Track and read, then cover the naming part of one sentence. Read chorally the words that *tell about the naming part* and then draw a box around them. Repeat for all the sentences.

Writing a Sentence 51

Telling Part

A fox lives in the woods.

Talk about it.

What is the **telling part** of each sentence?
1. I throw a ball to Sadie.
2. She is our new puppy.
3. We play together.

Have students use a finger to track the text in their book as you read aloud the sentence on this page.

- Focus attention on the shaded part of the sentence and help students read it aloud with you. Point out the label *Telling Part* and explain that all the words in the shaded part make up the **telling part** (*see below*) of the sentence.
- Invite students to suggest other telling parts that could be substituted into this sentence. Write these suggestions on the board as complete sentences.
- As students identify the telling part in each sentence, have volunteers use colored chalk to box these words. Then as students observe, label both parts (naming and telling).

Talk about it.

Distribute crayons and photocopies of the reproducible Telling Part page (TE page 344). As students identify the telling part of each sentence, write the sentence on the board and circle each telling part. Have students use crayons to circle and lightly shade the telling part of each sentence on their paper.

Answers
1. throw a ball to Sadie
2. is our new puppy
3. play together

Teaching Tip: Telling Part

To help students identify the telling part, point out that where words are in a sentence is a clue that can help them. Explain that the telling part usually follows the naming part.

Struggling Learners

To help students understand the difference between the naming and telling parts, write the following sentence frames on sentence strips:

The children _____.
The animals _____.

Explain that each pair of words is the naming part of a sentence.

Have students brainstorm some action words, and write each word on a word card. Help students read the words. Explain that these words could be used as the telling part in sentences. Have students take turns slotting the word cards in the blanks to complete each sentence. Help students read the sentences aloud to make sure that they express complete thoughts.

Write complete sentences.

Remind students that a sentence states a complete thought. Sentences must have a **naming part** and a **telling part**.

Have students point to each sentence part in their book as you ask these questions:

- What does the naming part of the sentence do? (It says *who* or *what*.) Which words are in the naming part? (*the fox*)
- What does the telling part of the sentence do? (It says something about the naming part.) Which word is the telling part? (*hides*)

Point out the addition symbol between the two labels. Have students tell what it means. (The two parts are added together.)

Model the process of writing sentences. Then distribute photocopies of the reproducible Writing Sentences and Sentences 2 pages (TE pages 345 and 346) and work as a class to complete the pages.

✳ For more information on writing sentences, see SE page 288.

52

Write complete sentences.

Remember that every sentence has a **naming part** and a **telling part**. See how these two parts go together.

Naming Part + **Telling Part**

The naming part tells who or what.

The telling part says something about the naming part.

the fox

hides

Grammar Connection

Writing sentences

- **Proofreader's Guide** page 288
- *GrammarSnap* Understanding Sentences
- *SkillsBook* pages 13–14
- **TE copy masters** page 345, 346

English Language Learners

Gather picture cards that can represent naming and telling parts of a sentence. Have partners pair a naming picture with a telling picture to form a complete thought and "read" the cards aloud.

Sentence

The naming part and telling part make a sentence. The sentence states a **complete thought**.

The fox hides.

Begin each sentence with a capital letter. Finish each sentence with an end mark.

Teaching Tip: Capital Letters

Point to a classroom alphabet chart or use the list that begins on SE page 279. Remind students that each letter has two forms—an uppercase form, called a capital letter, and a lowercase form, called a small letter. Have students point to all the capital letters on the page in their book.

Focus attention on the taped-together parts in the illustration and explain that it shows the naming part and the telling part (SE page 52) put together to make a complete thought.

- Point to the equal sign and discuss its meaning. Inform students that when the naming and the telling parts are "added," or joined together, they "equal" a complete sentence.

Focus attention on Mr. Fox's speech balloon at the bottom of the page as you read aloud the text.

- Have students point to the **capital letter** *(see below)* at the beginning of each sentence in the speech balloon in their book. Then have them point to the period at the end of each sentence.
- Emphasize that every sentence must begin with a capital letter and end with an end mark.

✳ For information on capital letters, see SE page 275.

Kinds of Sentences

Objectives
- identify telling, asking, and exclamatory sentences
- use appropriate end marks at the end of sentences

Show students an illustration in a familiar picture book and ask a volunteer to tell about it in one sentence. Record this sentence on the board and identify it as a telling sentence. Have another volunteer ask a question about the picture. Then share an exclamatory sentence of your own about it. Record both of these sentences.

Tell students that the word *exclamatory* comes from the word *exclaim*, which means "to speak out loudly and suddenly in great surprise." Provide several examples of exclamatory sentences and have students dramatize "exclaiming" them.

✳ For more information and worksheets on different kinds of sentences, see SE page 290 and TE pages 347–349.

54

Kinds of Sentences

Here are different kinds of sentences.

Telling Sentence

A **telling sentence** tells about something or someone.

A bird sits in the tree.

Asking Sentence

An **asking sentence** asks a question.

Do you see the bird?

Exclamatory Sentence

An **exclamatory sentence** shows surprise or strong feeling.

It has a huge bill!

Grammar Connection

Telling sentences
- **Proofreader's Guide** page 270
- *GrammarSnap* Kinds of Sentences
- **SkillsBook** pages 15–16
- **TE copy master** page 347

Asking sentences
- **Proofreader's Guide** page 271
- *GrammarSnap* Kinds of Sentences

- **SkillsBook** pages 17–18
- **TE copy master** page 348

Exclamatory sentences
- **Proofreader's Guide** page 271
- *GrammarSnap* Kinds of Sentences
- **SkillsBook** pages 19–20
- **TE copy master** page 349

Materials/Copy Masters

Picture book (TE p. 54)

Telling Sentences (TE p. 54)

Asking Sentences (TE p. 54)

Exclamatory Sentences (TE p. 54)

Crayons, index cards (TE p. 55)

Use a Period (TE p. 55)

Use a Question Mark (TE p. 55)

Use an Exclamation Point (TE p. 55)

Kinds of Sentences 55

Use end marks.

Every sentence needs an **end mark**.

Period .

Use a **period** at the end of a telling sentence.

Question Mark ?

Use a **question mark** at the end of an asking sentence.

Exclamation Point !

Use an **exclamation point** at the end of an exclamatory sentence.

Talk about it.

Which **end mark** should you use?

1. I see a tiny bird ____
2. It is flying backward ____
3. Do you know its name ____

Use end marks.

Explain that each type of sentence ends with a different **end mark** *(see below)*. Have students point to each end mark in their book as you read aloud its rule. Then ask these questions:

■ What end mark do you use at the end of a telling sentence? (a period)

■ What end mark do you use at the end of an asking sentence? (a question mark)

■ What end mark do you use at the end of an exclamatory sentence? (an exclamation point)

✱ For more information and worksheets on using punctuation, see SE pages 270–271 and TE pages 350–352.

Talk about it.

Answers

1. period
2. exclamation point
3. question mark

Teaching Tip: End Marks

Distribute a crayon and three index cards to each student. Have them make a large copy of each end mark, one on each card.

As you name each mark, ask students to hold up the appropriate card.

Then share example sentences and have students display the card that shows the end mark that belongs at the end of each one. Once students understand the activity, call on volunteers to share sentences of their own for the class to punctuate.

Grammar Connection

Period, question mark, exclamation point

■ **Proofreader's Guide** pages 270–271

■ *GrammarSnap* End Marks Overview

■ **TE copy masters** pages 350, 351, 352

Writing a Paragraph

Remind students that a sentence is made up of words that state a complete thought. Then explain that a paragraph is made up of sentences that tell about the same topic.

As you read aloud the information about the three parts of a paragraph, share the following additional information:

- The **main idea** *(see below)* of a paragraph is what the paragraph is all about.
- Details provide more information about the paragraph's main idea.
- The ending sentence often shares the writer's feelings about the topic.

56

Writing a Paragraph

A **paragraph** is a group of sentences about the same topic.

Miguel uses sentences to write a paragraph. Here are some important points to remember when you write a paragraph.

A paragraph has a beginning sentence that tells the main idea.

A paragraph has middle sentences that tell more about the main idea. These sentences share details.

A paragraph has an ending sentence that adds one last thought.

Writing a Paragraph   *57*

A paragraph begins in a special way. You **indent**, or leave space, at the beginning of the paragraph.

The Park

Indent

One day, Mom took Elsa and me to the park. We climbed the jungle gym. Then we slid down the biggest slide. Finally, we played tag with friends. Wow! We had lots of fun at the park.

Have students use a finger to point out how each tinted section on the page in their book connects to one of the parts of the paragraph described on SE page 56.

- Focus attention on the sentence in the green section and read it aloud. Have students identify the main idea. (Miguel's mom took Miguel and Elsa to the park.)
- Have students identify details in the orange section. (They climbed the jungle gym, slid down the slide, and played tag.)
- Have students identify the final thought in the blue section of the paragraph. (They had fun.)

Frame the word *we* and have students count how many times it appears (four). Explain that *we* takes the place of naming words. Help students identify who *we* stands for.

✳ For information about using the word *we*, see SE page 226.

Read aloud the speech balloon at the top of the page. Have a volunteer point to where Miguel **indents** (*see below*) his paragraph.

Point out that each word in the title of the paragraph begins with a capital letter.

Teaching Tip: Indenting

A quick and easy way for students to tell how much space to indent is to place the edge of their thumb on the left margin of their paper. They should then begin the first sentence on the other side of their thumb. Left-handed students will find it easier to use a flat eraser instead of their thumb.

Advanced Learners

Point out that including different types of sentences in a paragraph can make it more interesting to read. Have students identify the two types of sentences that Miguel uses in his paragraph (telling and exclamatory). Then challenge students to write an asking sentence that Miguel might have included in his paragraph.

Miguel writes a paragraph.

Read the pencil icons on this page and the next aloud and ask students what they recall about each step in the writing process. Explain that Miguel followed these steps when writing his paragraph.

- Direct attention to Miguel's list. Have students tell what topics he thought of and which one he chose to write about.
- Point out that Miguel's numbered drawings are a story map. Explain that writers use a story map to gather details and plan their writing. Discuss what each drawing shows and have students explain why they think Miguel numbered them. (He numbered the drawings to show the order in which they did things.) Explain that Miguel follows the order of his story map when he writes his paragraph.

After reading SE pages 58 and 59, use a **shared-writing experience** to practice writing a paragraph.

✳ For spelling lists students can use to check their spelling, see SE pages 279–283.

58

Miguel writes a paragraph.

Miguel uses the writing process to write his paragraph. This is how you can write a paragraph, too.

park

swimming pool

ball game

Name: _Miguel_

1. Mom Me Elsa
2. jungle gym
3. big slide
4. tag

Prewrite

Choose a topic and gather details.

Teaching Tip: Shared-Writing Experience

Begin by having students brainstorm topics about recent classroom events, such as a class trip, a guest speaker, a class play, and so on. Write their ideas on the board and help the class choose one topic to write about.

Distribute crayons and photocopies of the reproducible Story Map (TE page 335). Have each student draw pictures showing in the correct order what happened during the event.

After you discuss the steps on SE pages 58–59, have students refer to their drawings and share their ideas for a paragraph. Record their ideas on chart paper.

Use different colored markers to show any revising and editing that you do.

Write the final copy and then lead the class in reading it aloud.

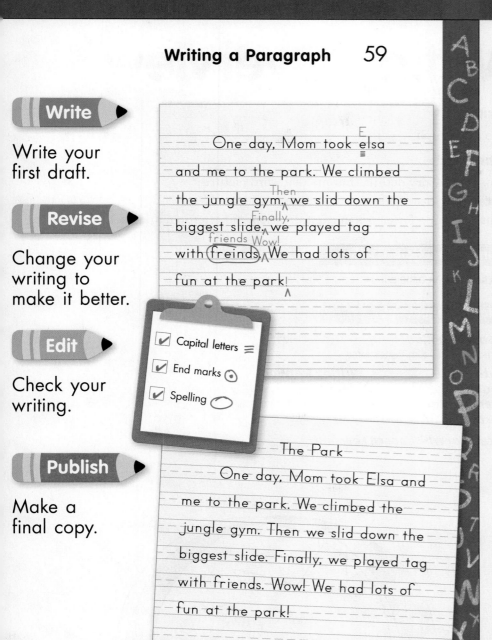

Write

Write your first draft.

Revise

Change your writing to make it better.

Edit

Check your writing.

Checklist:
- ☑ Capital letters ≡
- ☑ End marks ⊙
- ☑ Spelling ◯

Publish

Make a final copy.

Writing a Paragraph   59

One day, Mom took Elsa (E)
and me to the park. We climbed
the jungle gym, (Then) we slid down the
biggest slide, (Finally,) we played tag
with (freinds) friends Wow! We had lots of
fun at the park!

The Park
One day, Mom took Elsa and
me to the park. We climbed the
jungle gym. Then we slid down the
biggest slide. Finally, we played tag
with friends. Wow! We had lots of
fun at the park!

Focus attention on the samples of Miguel's writing.

■ Point out that when Miguel writes his first draft, his goal is to get his ideas down on paper. He doesn't worry about end punctuation and spelling. Ask students how they can tell that Miguel referred to his drawing while he was writing. (His first draft follows the order of his drawings.)

■ Ask students to identify each change Miguel made when he revised (in blue) and edited (in red) his first draft. Have them identify what words he added, what word he capitalized, where he added an end mark, and the spelling correction he made.

■ Discuss the purpose of the editing checklist by pointing out that it helps Miguel know what changes he might need to make.

■ Ask how Miguel could share the final copy of his paragraph with others.

English Language Learners

Since students with limited English vocabulary will have difficulty writing first drafts, provide them with oral rehearsal opportunities. Have students tell you about their illustration during the **prewrite** step. Supply words for them to use when they write.

Struggling Learners

To help students understand the function of transition words, model Miguel's thoughts by sharing a Think Aloud. For example, say Miguel might have thought the following: I want readers to know what we did first, what we did next, and what we did last, so I'll add the words *Then* and *Finally* to make the order clear.

Advanced Learners

Explain that time order words tell when something happened. Have students locate the two time order words that Miguel added (*Then, Finally*). Explain that words such as *first, next,* and *last* are also time order words. Challenge students to determine if any of these words could be added to the paragraph (Possible answer: First, we climbed the jungle gym.)

Descriptive Writing Overview

Common Core Standards Focus

Writing 5: With guidance and support from adults, focus on a topic, respond to questions and suggestions from peers, and add details to strengthen writing as needed.

Language 2: Demonstrate command of the conventions of standard English capitalization, punctuation, and spelling when writing.

Writing Form

■ descriptive paragraph

Focus on the Traits

■ **Ideas** Choosing sensory details that make a word picture
■ **Word Choice** Using describing words
■ **Conventions** Checking for errors in capitalization, punctuation, and spelling

 Literature Connections

• **"Beaks Eat"** (an article in Harcourt *Storytown*)

 Technology Connections

 Write Source Online
www.hmheducation.com/writesource

- • **Net-text**
- • **Bookshelf**
- • **GrammarSnap**
- • **Portfolio**
- • **Writing Network features**
- • **File Cabinet**

 Interactive Whiteboard Lessons

Suggested Descriptive Writing Unit (Three Weeks)

Day	Writing and Skills Instruction	Student Edition		Teacher's Edition	SkillsBook	Daily Language Workouts	Write Source Online
		Descriptive Writing Unit	Resource Units*	Grammar Copy Masters			
1–2	**Descriptive Start-Up** ⓛ Literature Connections "Beaks Eat"	61–63				18–19	
	Skills Activity: • Adjectives		238, 297				*GrammarSnap*
3–5	**Descriptive Paragraph** (Model, Prewriting)	64–69					*Interactive Whiteboard Lessons, Net-text*
6–10	**Descriptive Paragraph** *(cont.)* (Writing, Revising, Editing)	70–75	238 (+), 239, 297		83	20–21	*Net-text*
	Skills Activities: • Verbs		228, 229, 294	353–354	75–76, 79–80		*GrammarSnap*
	• Verb tenses		230 (+), 231 (+), 232, 233, 295, 296	355–356	77–78		*GrammarSnap*
	Working with a Partner	26–27					
11–13	**Descriptive Paragraph** *(cont.)* (Publishing)	76–79				22–23	*Portfolio, Net-text*
	Publishing Your Writing	38–39					
14–15	**Across the Curriculum**	80–81			92–93		
	Skills Activities: • Pronouns		224, 293		73–74		*GrammarSnap*
	• Using the right word		285	390	63–64		

(Week 1: Days 1–5; Week 2: Days 6–10; Week 3: Days 11–15)

* These units are also located in the back of the *Teacher's Edition*. Resource Units include "Words," "A Writer's Resource," "Proofreader's Guide," and "Theme Words."
(+) This activity is located in a different section of the *Write Source Student Edition*. If students have already completed this activity, you may wish to review it at this time.

Teacher's Notes for Descriptive Writing

The overview for descriptive writing includes some specific teaching suggestions for the unit.

Descriptive Start-Up (pages 62–63)

When students write a description, they must rely on their five senses. Before writing a descriptive sentence or paragraph about something, they should write down what they can see, hear, smell, taste, or feel. As they learn to observe carefully, through their senses, students will find the words they need for writing.

Descriptive Paragraph (pages 64–79)

In this chapter, the model paragraph shows how sentences with descriptive words can describe something such as a tire swing. The steps used to write the paragraph are included. Students should use each step to write their own descriptive paragraphs. You can either have students write about the same object, or you can have them write about something at home.

Across the Curriculum (pages 80–81)

There are many opportunities for students to do descriptive writing in different subject areas. For example, this chapter includes a student's description of a triangle. Experimenting with different objects discussed in other subjects is a good way for students to practice descriptive writing.

Academic Vocabulary

> Read aloud the academic terms, as well as the descriptions and questions. Model for students how to read one question and answer it. Have partners monitor their understanding and seek clarification of the terms by working through the meanings and questions together.

Minilessons

The Five Senses
Descriptive Start-Up

- **HELP** students get a feel for describing by having them **USE** their five senses to talk about the following things. **MAKE** a cluster for each noun on the board or on chart paper.

    banana, fire, thunderstorm, grass, flowers, noun of choice

- **WRITE** students' descriptive words (adjectives) for each cluster.

Think Again!
Descriptive Paragraph

- **ASK** students to **DESCRIBE** each object as if they were the creatures in the following situations:

    a bird describing a rocket ship
    an ant describing a truck
    a snail describing a fish

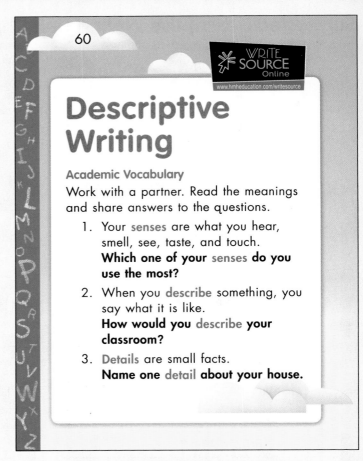

- Then **HAVE** students **WRITE** one of their own descriptions.

What Am I?
Descriptive Paragraph

- **PLAY** a guessing game. **TELL** students to pick something in or around the school and, without naming it, **DESCRIBE** it. **WRITE** the following starters to help students use their senses.

    It looks _____.
    It sounds _____.
    It feels _____.
    It tastes _____.
    It smells _____.

- **TRY** this game in groups of 6 to 8 students. After a student describes something, the rest of the group must guess the object.

What Is It?
Across the Curriculum

- **LIST** objects from math and science. **HAVE** each student **CHOOSE** an object to describe without naming it. **ASK** for a volunteer who would like to have you read her or his paragraph. **HAVE** the class **GUESS** what object is being described. (Objects could be circle, rectangle, snake, ball, tree, thermometer, ruler, bear, and so on.)

61

In **descriptive writing**, you use the five senses to create a picture in the reader's mind. You tell what something looks like, sounds like, smells like, feels like, or tastes like.

 Literature Connections: You can find an example of descriptive writing in the article "Beaks Eat."

Descriptive Writing

Write *See, Hear, Smell, Taste, Touch* on the board and read them aloud. Explain that in **descriptive writing**, writers use some or all of these senses to describe people, places, and things. Tell students that when a writer uses different senses in descriptive writing, he or she "paints a picture in the reader's mind." Describing words help the reader picture a descriptive topic in his or her mind.

Display a picture that shows children participating in an activity. Have students imagine themselves in the scene.
- What would you see?
- What sounds would you hear?
- What might you smell?
- Would there be something to taste?
- What things could you touch?

Encourage students to suggest describing words for what they imagine. List the words under the appropriate heading on the board and read them aloud. Then have students close their eyes as you describe the picture using words from the lists. Can students picture the scene in their mind? Did you paint a picture in their mind?

 Literature Connections

The nonfiction article "Beaks Eat" describes beaks and how birds use them. Point out some of the words that describe beaks, such as *tough, strong,* and *sensitive.* Then review the labeled bird illustrations and encourage students to describe the different beaks they see.

This descriptive article can be found in Harcourt *Storytown.* For additional descriptive models, see the Reading-Writing Connections beginning on page TE-36.

Family Connection Letters

As you begin this unit, send home the Descriptive Writing Family Connection letter, which describes what students will be learning.

- Letter in English (TE page 397)
- Letter in Spanish (TE page 406)

Materials

Picture or photo of children participating in an activity (TE p. 61)

Descriptive Start-Up

Objectives

- understand the content and structure of a descriptive paragraph
- choose a topic (one thing to describe) to write about
- plan, draft, revise, and edit a descriptive paragraph

As you read aloud each sense word in item 2, have students point to the cue picture in their book and then to their own eyes, ears, nose, mouth, and fingers.

Discuss the three reminders on SE page 62.

- Remind students that the *topic* is what the writing is about.
- Explain that sometimes not all of the senses are appropriate for what is being described.
- Tell students that a describing word tells about a person, place, or thing.

62

Descriptive Start-Up

In **descriptive writing**, you write sentences about what you see, hear, smell, taste, and touch.

Jake describes a tire swing.

Jake uses his senses to think of words that tell how the swing looks, sounds, and feels.

Remember these three points when you write a description.

1. You think about your topic.

2. You use your senses to get ideas.

see   hear   smell   taste   touch

3. You write describing words.

Materials

Various objects (TE p. 63)

Word cards (TE pp. 63, 65)

Removable tape (TE p. 63)

Sentence strips (TE p. 65)

Construction paper, 11" x 17" (TE p. 66)

Chart paper (TE pp. 67, 71, 77)

Shared writing topic list (TE p. 69)

Drawing materials (TE pp. 69, 78)

Shared writing sensory chart (TE pp. 71, 73)

Shared writing first draft (TE p. 73)

Shared writing revised draft, colored pencils (TE p. 75)

Shared writing edited draft (TE pp. 76, 77)

Shared writing final copy (TE pp. 78, 79)

Copy Masters

Verbs 1 (TE p. 64)

Verbs 2 (TE p. 64)

Action Verb Tenses (TE p. 64)

Linking Verb Tenses (TE p. 64)

Choose a Topic (TE p. 67)

Sensory Chart (TE pp. 69, 81)

Editing Checklist (TE p. 75)

Thinking About Your Writing (TE p. 79)

Suggested Narrative Writing Unit (Four Weeks)

Day	Writing and Skills Instruction	Student Edition		Teacher's Edition	SkillsBook	Daily Language Workouts	Write Source Online
		Narrative Writing Unit	Resource Units*	Grammar Copy Masters			
1–2	**Narrative Start-Up** ⓘLiterature Connections *Our Sled Club*	83–85				24–25	
	Skills Activity: • Capital letters		275, 276	360, 380, 381			*GrammarSnap*
opt.	*Speaking to Others*	202–203					
3–5	**Narrative Paragraph** (Prewriting)	86–91					*Interactive Whiteboard Lessons, Net-text*
6–10	**Narrative Paragraph** *(cont.)* (Writing, Revising, Editing)	92–97				26–27	*Net-text*
	Skills Activities: • Pronouns		224, 293				*GrammarSnap*
	• Verbs		232 (+), 233 (+), 294, 296		81–82		*GrammarSnap*
	Working with a Partner	26–27					
11–15	**Narrative Paragraph** *(cont.)* (Publishing)	98–101				28–29	*Portfolio, Net-text*
	Speaking to Others	202–203					
	Learning to Listen	204–205					
16–20	**Across the Curriculum**	102–103			94–95	30–31	
	Skills Activity: • Pronouns		226, 227, 293 (+)				*GrammarSnap*
	Writing for Assessment	104–105					
	Skills Activities: • Using the right word		286	391	65		

* These units are also located in the back of the *Teacher's Edition*. Resource Units include "Words," "A Writer's Resource," "Proofreader's Guide," and "Theme Words."
(+) This activity is located in a different section of the *Write Source Student Edition*. If students have already completed this activity, you may wish to review it at this time.

Week 1 / Week 2 / Week 3 / Week 4

Teacher's Notes for Narrative Writing

The overview for narrative writing includes some specific teaching suggestions for the unit.

Narrative Start-Up (pages 84–85)

Telling stories comes very naturally to most young children. With guidance, they can write these stories down and enjoy them for a long time. Personal experience provides a natural starting point for young storywriters. To get started, have your students think about a happy day. Then share a very happy experience you have had. Invite students to help you create a cluster about your experience. At another time, do a shared writing using the cluster.

Narrative Paragraph (pages 86–101)

With the topic sentence written, your students can move to the next step, which is the narrative paragraph. Following the directions of this chapter, they will add sentences giving information about their experience. A story map can help them.

Across the Curriculum (pages 102–103)

Students may use narrative writing in many subject areas. In this chapter, the narrative about a powwow and its music provides one such example. The letter to an author is yet another example. Tell students that if they write a personal narrative in a letter to an author, the story they share should relate to the theme of the book they have read.

Writing for Assessment (pages 104–105)

A narrative prompt may come from the teacher or be part of a state or district assessment exam. Regardless of the source, this chapter shows students how to respond to a prompt.

Academic Vocabulary

Read aloud the academic terms, as well as the descriptions and questions. Model for students how to read one question and answer it. Have partners monitor their understanding and seek clarification of the terms by working through the meanings and questions together.

Minilessons

Special Times   Narrative Start-Up

- **READ** or **TELL** about a special time. **ASK** children what they do with their families—how they help, play, and work together at home. **INVITE** students to **SHARE** special activities they enjoy. **LIST** these on a chart in the classroom.

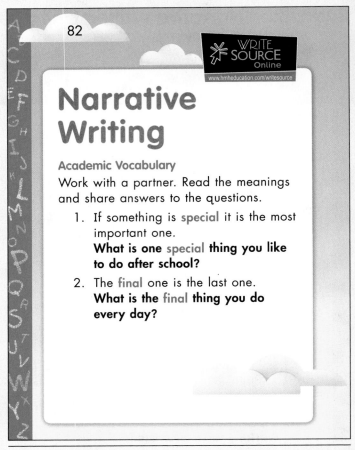

Narrative Writing

Academic Vocabulary

Work with a partner. Read the meanings and share answers to the questions.

1. If something is special it is the most important one.
   What is one special thing you like to do after school?

2. The final one is the last one.
   What is the final thing you do every day?

Something for You   Narrative Paragraph

- **SUPPLY** the children with materials to **MAKE** a keepsake poster or greeting card, based on their finished personal narratives.

Authors' Stories   Narrative Paragraph

- **READ** autobiographical stories like Patricia Polacco's *Thundercake* or Tomie dePaola's *The Art Lesson* to spark a discussion about ideas to use for story writing.

Map It!   Writing for Assessment

- **TELL** students to think of a time when they really laughed loudly. Once they **RECALL** that moment, have them **DRAW** a story map. **TELL** them to **SAVE** the story map for a future assignment.

In **narrative writing**, you share a story about something that really happened. It can be about you or someone else. In this chapter, you will learn how to write about a special time.

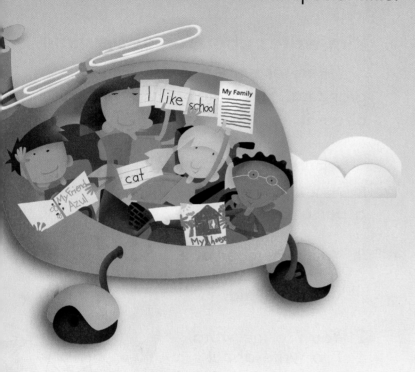

 Literature Connections: You can find an example of narrative writing in *Our Sled Club* by Beatrice Wolfe.

Narrative Writing

Invite volunteers to share stories about things that happened to them. They could tell about
- what they did on the first day of school,
- a time they made a new friend, or
- something funny that happened to them.

After volunteers have shared their stories, point out that these stories are called *personal narratives*. Explain that a narrative is a story, and that a personal narrative is a true story about something that happened to the person telling the story.

Talk about the differences between a true story and a fictional story. Display a personal narrative, such as *In My Family* by Carmen Lomas Garza, and a fictional story, such as *Hog-Eye* by Susan Meddaugh. Read aloud passages from each book and ask whether the author is telling a story that is true or a story that is make-believe (fiction). Ask how students can tell true stories from made-up stories. Guide students in identifying the characteristics of each book.

Literature Connections

The narrative *Our Sled Club* by Beatrice Wolfe tells the story of three children who each pull a different sled to the top of Block Hill.

Encourage students to use time-order words to retell the story. Then ask students to predict what will happen next. For additional narrative models, see the Reading-Writing Connections beginning on page TE-36.

Family Connection Letters

As you begin this unit, send home the Narrative Writing Family Connection letter, which describes what students will be learning.

- Letter in English (TE page 398)
- Letter in Spanish (TE page 407)

Materials

Picture books (TE p. 83)

Narrative Start-Up

Objectives
- understand the content and structure of a narrative paragraph
- choose a topic (a special time) to write about
- plan, draft, revise, and edit a narrative paragraph

Write the term *personal narrative* on the board. Underline the word *person* in *personal*. Explain that a **personal narrative** is a true story about the *person* who wrote it.

Discuss the concept of writing to an audience. Point out that whenever students write, they are writing for someone.

Focus attention on item 2 and have students point to the word *I* in their book. Remind students that *I* is always written as a capital letter.

✷ For more about using the word *I*, see SE page 225.

Distribute photocopies of Capital Letters 1 (TE page 360). On the board, model how to edit the first sentence. Tell students that they will be editing four sentences.

Grammar Connection

Capital Letters
- **Proofreader's Guide** pages 275, 276
- *GrammarSnap* Capital Letters
- **TE copy masters** pages 360, 380, 381

A B C D E F G H I J K L M N O P Q R S T U V W X Y Z

84

Narrative Start-Up

In a **personal narrative**, you write a story about something you did.

Kim writes about a special time.

Kim remembers a day with her grandma. She writes a first sentence about it.

Here are two points to remember when you write a personal narrative.

1. You remember one special time and what you did.

2. You use the word *I* to write about yourself.

Materials

Chart paper (TE pp. 85, 87, 89, 95)

Blank picture cards (TE p. 91)

Recording device (TE p. 92)

Picture dictionaries (TE p. 97)

Nonfiction picture books (TE p. 98)

Drawing supplies (TE p. 100)

Recordings of music (TE p. 103)

Pictures of objects (TE p. 105)

Copy Masters

Capital Letters 1 (TE p. 84)

Sentence Starters (TE p. 89)

Story Map (TE pp. 91, 104)

Editing Checklist (TE p. 97)

Thinking About Your Writing (TE p. 101)

Friendly Letter (TE p. 102)

Conference Notes (TE p. 105)

Narrative Start-Up 85

One day, I
had lunch
with Grandma.

Talk about it.

Tell a partner about one special
time that you remember.

Have students focus on the thought balloon that crosses over from SE page 84 to the top of SE page 85. Ask them what Kim is thinking about (a special day she spent with her grandma).

- Then focus attention on Kim's sentence.
- Call on a volunteer to read aloud the sentence.
- Reread the two points listed at the bottom of SE page 84. Ask whether Kim remembered these points when she wrote her sentence. (Yes, the sentence tells about a special time and what she did. Kim used the word *I* in her sentence.)
- Call attention to the comma in the sentence and model how to pause after the comma.

Talk about it.

Remind students to talk about only *one* special time. Encourage them to **ask questions** (*see below*) to learn more details about what their partner did.

Teaching Tip: Ask Questions

Write the following questions on chart paper or on the board:

- Who was with you?
- What did you do first?
- What did you do after that?
- How did you do it?
- What part did you like best?

Track and read aloud the questions with students. Encourage them to use these questions to learn more details about their partner's special time.

English Language Learners

If students lack the proper vocabulary to tell a partner about a special time, ask them first to draw a picture of the special time (refer to the drawing of the thought balloon). Then have them describe their drawing to their partner with as many words as they can. Have students keep this drawing for future reference to help them plan and write their narrative.

Narrative Paragraph

Point out that Kim wrote more sentences in order to form a paragraph. Review the parts of a paragraph by having students point to the parts in their book as you ask the following questions:

- What is the title of Kim's paragraph? (Noodles)
- What does Kim do to start her paragraph? (She indents the first line.)
- Can you find and read the sentence that tells the main idea of the paragraph? (the first sentence)
- Which sentences give details, or tell more, about the main idea? (the second, third, and fourth sentences)
- Which sentence adds one last thought to end the paragraph? (the last sentence)
- What does the word *we* stand for in the paragraph? (Grandma and Kim)

 Technology Connections

Use this unit's Interactive Whiteboard Lesson to introduce narrative writing.

 Interactive Whiteboard Lessons

86

Narrative Paragraph

Kim wrote more sentences about the special time with her grandma. Then she put her sentences together to form a paragraph.

> Noodles
> One day, I had lunch with Grandma. We made noodles. I put some noodles in the soup. Then I ate them. I like cooking with Grandma.

Struggling Learners

Remind students that writing different types of sentences in their paragraph can make it more interesting to read. Challenge students to suggest an exclamatory sentence that Kim could add to her paragraph, such as *I love noodles!* or *They were yummy!*

Narrative Paragraph   87

Understand your writing goal.

The three traits listed below will help you write a narrative paragraph.

Ideas   Choose **one special time** to write about.

Organization   Use **time-order words**.

Conventions   Follow the **writing rules**.

Talk about it.

1. What one special time does Kim share?
2. Find one writing rule that Kim follows.

Understand your writing goal.

As you read about the three traits for writing a narrative paragraph, review with students what they already know about these traits:

- Ideas are their thoughts and questions about a topic.
- Organization means putting thoughts and sentences in the best order.
- Conventions are writing rules, such as beginning a sentence with a capital letter and ending it with an end mark.

Explain that time-order words can help writers organize their sentences in a clear way. Help students find time-order words in Kim's paragraph (*One day, Then*). Ask how the time-order words are helpful. (They tell when Kim had lunch with her grandma and when she ate the noodles.)

Answers

1. her lunch with Grandma
2. Possible responses: Kim uses capital letters to begin sentences, for the word *I*, and for special names; she uses periods and a comma; she spells words correctly.

Struggling Learners

Give students more experience with time-order words so they will feel more confident about using them in their writing.

- Ask them to describe events that are part of their daily routine, using the words *first, next,* and *last*: First, I eat dinner. Next, I read a book. Last, I go to bed.

- Write their sentences on chart paper and read them aloud. Do the time-order words make the order clear?

Prewrite Choose your topic.

Before reading aloud the page, ask students to share what they know about the Prewrite step of the writing process.

Then call attention to the three things Miguel does to choose a writing topic.

- **Think** Ask students why the first thing Miguel does is *think*. Help students understand that writers often get their best ideas when they sit quietly and think, and this step is very important. Point out that some writers also like to *talk* about their ideas with others and then *think* about them some more.
- **Finish** Point out that Miguel is making a list of his ideas by finishing some sentence starters.
- **Choose** Have students tell whether they think this step is easy or hard. Point out that it can be hard to choose a topic when you have more than one good idea!

Technology Connections

Students can use the added features of the Net-text as they explore this stage of the writing process.

✳ *Write Source Online* **Net-text**

88

Prewrite ▶ Choose your topic.

When you **prewrite**, you plan your writing. To get started, choose a topic.

Here is what Miguel does to choose his topic.

Think Miguel thinks about some special times.

Finish He finishes some sentence starters to get ideas.

Choose Miguel chooses his favorite idea as his topic.

Narrative Paragraph   89

Miguel's Topic Ideas

Sentence Starters

1. One summer, **I went to Texas.**

2. One day, **I lost Azul at school.**

3. One night, **I saw an owl!**

Prewrite

Choose your topic.

1. **Think** of some special times.
2. **Finish** each sentence starter with one idea.
3. **Choose** your topic and circle it.

Miguel's Topic Ideas

Ask which topic idea Miguel chose to write about (number 2). Then invite students to guess who or what Azul might be. (Azul is the lizard pictured next to Miguel on SE page 88 and on the front cover of the text.)

Distribute photocopies of the reproducible Sentence Starters page (TE page 361) for students to use for choosing a topic.

- Ask students to think about special times they have enjoyed.
- Have students finish each sentence starter with a different idea. If students wish to change a sentence starter (*One summer* to *One winter*), encourage them to do so.
- Provide suggestions for students who have difficulty thinking of **topic ideas** (*see below*).
- Finally, have students choose the topic idea they want to write about and circle it.

Teaching Tip: Topic Ideas

Write the following topic ideas on chart paper and post the list in the classroom. Throughout the school year, continue to add to the list and encourage students to add their own ideas as well.

- a favorite place to visit
- a special parade
- a friend sleeps over
- a special day at school
- the day I learned how to . . .

English Language Learners

If students are working independently and have difficulty accessing vocabulary to complete each sentence starter, have them begin by writing one word that reminds them of their idea. Then have them dictate their ideas to you or a class helper who can write the idea in correct sentence form. Make sure that students understand the sentences.

Struggling Learners

To help students complete the sentence starters, point out that the next word should be *I*. Explain that *I* is the naming part of the sentence, and review that the naming part tells who or what the sentence is about. Remind students that the last part of the sentence is the telling part, and they should finish the sentence by telling what they did.

Prewrite Gather your details.

Have students recall the topic Miguel chose to write about (losing Azul). Point out that now Miguel is ready to gather details about his topic. Remind students that details tell interesting information about the topic.

Call attention to the three things Miguel does to gather details.

■ **Draw** Guide students to understand that Miguel draws pictures to show what happened in the correct order. Explain that this is how he plans what to write.

■ **Write** Review with students that words that tell *who* tell about people (or pets), words that tell *what* tell what people (or pets) do, and words that tell *where* tell about places.

■ **Tell** Ask students why working with a partner can help make their writing better. Point out that partners listen to each other's writing and talk about it. These things can help make their writing better.

90

Prewrite ▶ Gather your details.

Gathering details about your topic is the next part of prewriting. **Details** tell more about your topic.

Here is what Miguel does to gather his details.

Draw Miguel draws pictures on a story map.

Write He writes words that tell *who, what,* and *where.*

Tell Miguel tells his story to a partner.

Miguel's Story Map

Narrative Paragraph   91

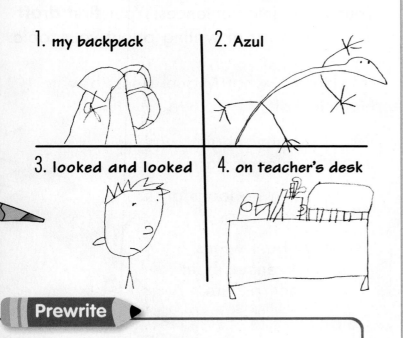

1. my backpack	2. Azul
3. looked and looked	4. on teacher's desk

Prewrite

Gather your details.

1. **Draw** a story map that shows what happened.

2. **Write** words that tell *who, what,* and *where.*

3. **Tell** your story to a partner using your story map.

Miguel's Story Map

Help students find the *who, what,* and *where* in Miguel's story map. Then ask why the drawings are numbered (to show the order of events).

✱ For another example of a story map, see SE page 251.

On the board, **make a story map** *(see below)* of a familiar story as a shared writing experience.

Then distribute photocopies of the reproducible Story Map (TE page 335). Before students start to draw, have them refer to their sentence starters with the topic idea they circled (TE page 89). Then have them close their eyes and think about their special time.

Circulate and check students' work as they draw and label their story map. Help them write the words that tell *who, what,* and *where* on their map.

Remind students to listen carefully to their partner's story and ask questions if they don't understand something or if the events seem out of order.

Teaching Tip: Make a Story Map

Choose a familiar story, such as "The Three Billy Goats Gruff." Have students tell the main events as volunteers draw pictures: 1. The troll sits under a bridge. 2. Little Billy Goat crosses the bridge. 3. Bigger Billy Goat crosses the bridge. 4. Biggest Billy Goat kicks the troll in the air. Guide students to label the pictures with words that tell *who, what,* and *where.*

English Language Learners

Check in with students after they make their drawings and give them any necessary vocabulary they need in order to write words that tell *who, what,* and *where* on their story map. Create a booklet or a section in students' writing notebooks for new vocabulary and ask them to write any new words in it for future use.

Struggling Learners

If students have difficulty ordering events on their story map, have them use four blank cards to draw pictures of what happened. Then as they tell you the story, have them put the cards in order and number them. Help them write words that tell *who, what,* and *where* on their cards. Then staple or tape the cards onto their story map.

Write **Write your first draft.**

Explain that in a first draft, the writer puts ideas into sentences for the first time. Point out that a first draft does not have to be perfect because writers can go back later to make changes and corrections during the revising and editing steps.

Call attention to the three things Miguel does to write his first draft, and ask the following questions:

■ What two things does Miguel need in order to write his first draft? (his sentence starter and story map)

■ How does Miguel use these two things? (He begins his first draft with his sentence starter. Then he writes a sentence about each picture in his story map.)

 Literature Connections

Mentor texts: Pull out some favorite narratives about a special time, such as *My Day in the Garden* by Miela Ford and Anita Lobel or *The Day I Had To Play With My Sister* by Crosby Bonsall. Read portions of these books to show students how professional writers tell their stories. Ask, "What was most special about this time?" Take suggestions. Then ask, "How did the author(s) make you feel that this time was special?" Encourage students to write in the same way.

 Technology Connections

Students can use the added features of the Net-text as they explore this stage of the writing process.

☀ *Write Source Online* **Net-text**

92

Write ▶ **Write your first draft.**

When you write a first draft, you put your ideas into sentences. Your **first draft** is your first try at writing about your topic.

Here is what Miguel does to write his first draft.

Begin   Miguel begins with his sentence starter.

Look   Then he looks at his story map.

Write   Miguel writes a sentence about each picture.

English Language Learners

Even after you emphasize that a first draft does not have to be perfect, students may be shy about writing if they believe that their written English is not very good. Provide support by giving students an opportunity to orally "rehearse" writing their first draft.

● Have students tell their sentence for each picture on their story map using a recording device. Offer assistance by providing necessary vocabulary.

● When it's time to write their sentences (SE page 93), students can listen to their recording as a guide to writing.

Narrative Paragraph   93

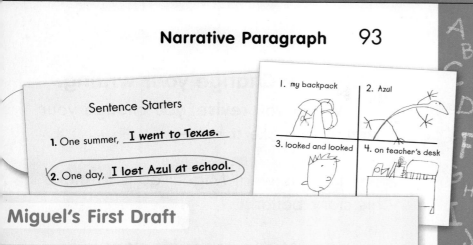

Sentence Starters

1. One summer, <u>I went to Texas.</u>

2. One day, <u>I lost Azul at school.</u>

1. my backpack   2. Azul

3. looked and looked   4. on teacher's desk

Miguel's First Draft

One day, I lost Azul at school.

I opened my backpack.

Azul jumt out.

I looked and looked

he was on my teacher's desk!

Write

Write your first draft.

1. **Begin** with your sentence starter.
2. **Look** at your story map.
3. **Write** a sentence for each picture.

Miguel's First Draft

Talk about how Miguel used his sentence starter and story map to write his first draft.

- How did Miguel begin his first draft? (He began with the sentence starter he circled.)
- How can you tell that Miguel wrote a sentence about each picture? (His first draft includes the events shown in his pictures in the same order.)
- What did Miguel do with the words on his story map? (He used the words to form the sentences of his first draft.)

Point out to students that Miguel made a few mistakes writing his sentences, but that it is not important now because it is his first draft. He will fix them later.

English Language Learners

Students learn the names of concrete objects before other words, such as verbs and connectors. If this is the case, help students by telling them the necessary words to complete their ideas and let them write them down without worrying about correct spelling.

Struggling Learners

Work individually with students to help them construct sentences about the pictures on their story map. After students write their sentence starters, have them use the words they wrote on their story map for the first picture to form a complete oral sentence. Have them write down the sentence before moving on to the next picture.

Advanced Learners

Suggest that as students look at their story map, they might think of additional details to include in their first draft. To demonstrate this, have students look at Miguel's story map and suggest other details he could have included. For example, he could have described what Azul looks like or the places where he looked for Azul.

Revise Change your writing.

Review the steps in the writing process that students have completed so far. Then focus on what Miguel does to **revise his writing** *(see below)*:

- **Read** Point out that when Miguel reads aloud his story, he can hear how it sounds. Remind students that their writing should sound as if they are really interested in their topics. Explain that as they revise their draft, they can change or add words to improve their writing.
- **Talk** Remind students that partners help each other make their stories better by talking about the writing and asking questions.
- **Change** Explain that writers use a caret to show where they want to add information. Help students read the list of time-order words.

✱ For more time-order words, see SE page 260.

Technology Connections

Have students use the Writing Network features of the Net-text to comment on each other's drafts.

✸ *Write Source Online* **Net-text**

94

Revise ▶ Change your writing.

When you **revise**, you change your writing to make it better.

Here is what Miguel does to make his story better.

Read Miguel reads his story to a partner.

Talk They talk about the story. Miguel's partner asks a question.

Change Miguel uses carets (∧) to show where he wants to add words. He answers his partner's question and adds a time-order word.

Time-order words tell when something happens.

Time-Order Words

then	soon
first	later
next	now

Narrative Paragraph   95

Miguel's Revising

Organization

Azul is my pet lizard.

One day, I lost Azul at school. ∧

   I opened my backpack.

Then

∧Azul jumt out.

   I looked and looked

   he was on my teacher's desk!

Revise

Change your writing to make it better.

1. **Read** your writing to a partner.
2. **Talk** about your story.
3. **Change** your writing to make it better.

Struggling Learners

Work one-on-one or with a small group to help students know what to look for as they revise. Write the following questions on chart paper:

- Does your first sentence name your topic?
- Are your events in order?
- Does your writing sound as if you are talking to a friend?
- Did you add time-order words?

Read aloud each question, pausing to help students check their writing for these questions.

Miguel's Revising

Explain that the blue markings are the changes Miguel made to his writing.

- Point out that Miguel added another sentence after the first sentence. Remind students that Miguel's partner asked him questions about his first draft. What question might his partner have asked that made Miguel add this sentence? (Who is Azul?) How did Miguel show where he was adding the sentence? (He used a caret.)
- Why did Miguel add the time-order word *then*? (This word makes it clear that Azul jumped out of his backpack *after* Miguel opened it.)

Discuss whether Miguel's paragraph sounds as if he is telling the story to a friend. Ask students to point out sentences that give the paragraph a narrative voice. (The sentences *I looked and looked* and *He was on my teacher's desk!* make it sound as if Miguel is telling the story to a friend.)

✳ During the revising and editing steps, work with students to improve their writing by asking the questions in the Teaching Tip on TE page 100.

Edit Check your writing.

Discuss with students why it makes sense to edit *after* they write and revise. Point out that once they are happy with their ideas, they should check for conventions.

Share the following hints to help students with the editing process:

- **Read** the sentences silently first and then aloud to catch any mistakes that need to be fixed.
- **Check** for one writing rule at a time.
- **Mark** the changes with a different color pencil. That will make it easy to see the corrections you make.

Writer's Craft

Conventions: The reason to wait until the end to correct errors is that if students focus first on conventions, they are unlikely to make any changes that improve their ideas. Conventions have one main purpose—to help communicate the great ideas in writing.

Technology Connections

Students can use the added features of the Net-text as they explore this stage of the writing process.

Write Source Online **Net-text**

96

Edit ▶ Check your writing.

When you **edit**, you check your writing for conventions. You check for capital letters, end marks, and spelling.

Here is what Miguel does to check his writing.

Read Miguel reads his sentences.

Check He checks for capital letters, end marks, and spelling.

Mark He marks the changes he needs to make.

Grammar Connection

Pronouns
- **Proofreader's Guide** page 293
- **Words** page 224
- *GrammarSnap* Pronouns

Verbs
- **Proofreader's Guide** pages 294, 296
- **Words** pages 232 (+), 233 (+)
- *GrammarSnap* Verbs
- *SkillsBook* pages 81–82

English Language Learners

If possible, work one-on-one with students to help them find errors. If students' language skills are very basic, focus on only one or two spelling or grammar concepts to correct, such as adding -*s* and -*es* to plurals or -*ed* to past tense verbs.

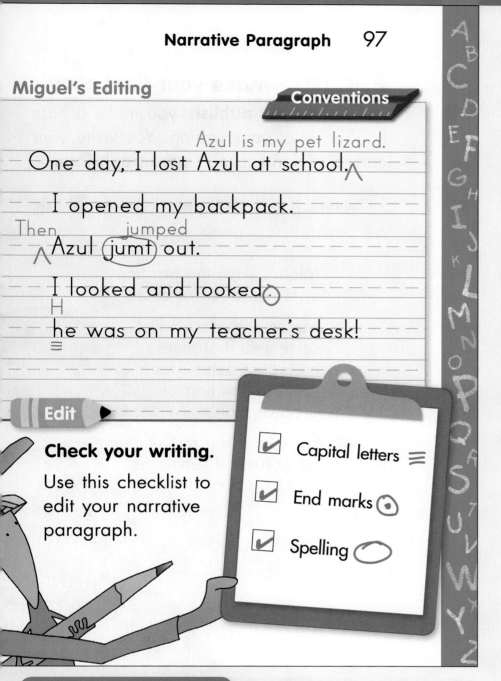

Narrative Paragraph 97

Miguel's Editing

Conventions

Azul is my pet lizard.

One day, I lost Azul at school.

I opened my backpack.

Then
jumped
Azul (jumt) out.

I looked and looked.

H
he was on my teacher's desk!

Edit

Check your writing.

Use this checklist to edit your narrative paragraph.

☑ Capital letters ≡

☑ End marks ⊙

☑ Spelling ◯

Miguel's Editing

Remind students that the blue markings are the changes Miguel makes during the revising step. Explain that the red markings are the corrections Miguel makes as he edits his writing.

Point out that Miguel made corrections using the three editing marks that are shown on the checklist. Have students point to the editing mark in Miguel's writing as you call out each editing convention on the checklist.

Provide photocopies of the reproducible Editing Checklist (TE page 358) for students to use as they edit their writing.

- Remind students to check for one convention at a time.
- Tell them to put a check mark next to each item only after they have carefully checked their writing for that type of error and made any necessary corrections.

✱ To help students check their spelling, have them refer to the ABC list of words on SE pages 279–283. Encourage students to use picture dictionaries, as well.

Struggling Learners

Double-check students' editing checklists against their writing to make sure all corrections have been made. If an error has been overlooked, play a game of "I Spy" with the student. You could tell a student, for example, "I spy a sentence without an end mark." Then have the student track down the error.

Publish Make your final copy.

Remind students that publishing is the last step in the writing process. Point out that the word *final* means "last," and they should make their final copy the best that it can be.

Then call attention to what Miguel does to make his final copy.

- **Skip** Point out that Miguel's story does not have a title yet. When the writing is complete, it is a good time to **create a title** *(see below)*.
- **Indent** Point out that the first sentence of a paragraph is always indented.
- **Copy** If they are not using a computer, remind students that they should use their best handwriting to make a neat copy of the story.

Whenever students prepare a neat final copy, stress that proper spacing between letters, words, and sentences is important in making a document easy to read.

Technology Connections

Remind students that they can use the Writing Network features of the Portfolio to share their work with peers.

 *Write Source Online* **Portfolio**

Write Source Online **Net-text**

98

Publish ▶ Make your final copy.

When you **publish**, you make a neat final copy of your writing. You write your corrected sentences in paragraph form.

> Here is what Miguel does to publish his paragraph.
>
> **Skip** Miguel skips the first line to leave room for a title.
>
> **Indent** Miguel indents his first sentence. That means he leaves extra space at the beginning of a paragraph.
>
> **Copy** He copies the rest of his corrected sentences in paragraph form.

Teaching Tip: Create a Title

To give students practice creating titles, display a few nonfiction picture books such as *My Visit to the Dinosaurs* by Aliki and *Wolves* by Seymour Simon. Ask students to think of alternative titles for the books as they keep the following points in mind:

- The title should name or describe the topic.
- There can be more than one good title for a story.
- A creative or funny title may be a good way to get a reader's attention.

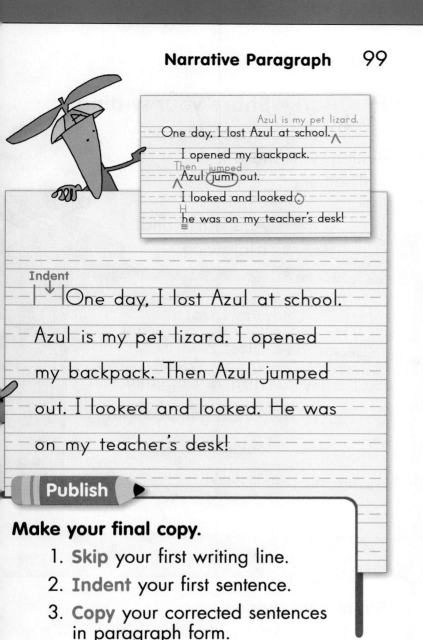

Narrative Paragraph 99

Azul is my pet lizard.
One day, I lost Azul at school. ∧

I opened my backpack.
Then jumped
∧Azul jumt out.

I looked and looked.
H
he was on my teacher's desk!

Indent
↓
One day, I lost Azul at school.

Azul is my pet lizard. I opened

my backpack. Then Azul jumped

out. I looked and looked. He was

on my teacher's desk!

Publish

Make your final copy.

1. **Skip** your first writing line.
2. **Indent** your first sentence.
3. **Copy** your corrected sentences in paragraph form.

Help students compare Miguel's final copy with his revised and edited first draft. Point out the places in his final copy where he includes his revisions and edits.

Then have students check to see whether Miguel
- skipped the first line to leave room for a title,
- indented his first sentence, and
- copied all of his corrected sentences in paragraph form.

Remind students to write their final copy using their best handwriting. Encourage students to have a partner check their final copies.

English Language Learners

After students finish copying their corrected paragraphs, ask them to read aloud their final copies to you or to a small group. This will reinforce their understanding of any new vocabulary and grammar rules.

Struggling Learners

Work individually with students to make sure they are copying their edited sentences correctly. Some students may need to have you check their work as they write one sentence at a time.
- Help students understand how to incorporate their revisions and edits as they write their final copy.

- For students who have difficulty with small motor skills, if possible, help them use a computer to make their final copy.

Publish Share your writing.

Call on a volunteer to read aloud Miguel's speech balloon to find out what he needs to do before sharing his writing.

- Ask students what they think of the title Miguel chose for his paragraph. How does it compare to another title, for example, *My Pet Lizard*? Which title do students like better? Which title is livelier and more interesting? Encourage students to think of a title that is interesting and will get a reader's attention. Point out that each word in the title begins with a capital letter.

- Have students draw a picture of their special time. Encourage them to show *who* took part in the experience, *what* happened, and *where* it took place.

Set aside enough time for students to share their writing with the class. Then over the next few days, hold a **writing conference** *(see below)* with each student to assess her or his final copy, using the rubric on SE pages 36–37.

100

Publish ▶ Share your writing.

When you publish your writing, you share it with others.

Add a title and a drawing.

Leaping Lizard

One day, I lost Azul at school. Azul is my pet lizard. I opened my backpack. Then Azul jumped out. I looked and looked. He was on my teacher's desk!

Publish

Share your writing.

Read your narrative to someone.

Teaching Tip: Writing Conference

The writing conference should be a relaxed, informal dialogue between you and the student. The goal of the conference is to give the student positive reinforcement for those traits that show some mastery and to point out traits that need improvement.

Focus the conference on the writing goals for the assignment (SE page 87).

- **Ideas** Is your topic about one special time? Did you write sentences that tell *who, what,* and *where*?
- **Organization** Did you use time-order words to show the order of events?
- **Conventions** Did you follow the writing rules for capital letters, end marks, and spelling?

Narrative Paragraph 101

Reflect on your writing.

Miguel thinks about his writing. He tells how he feels about his narrative paragraph.

Thinking About Your Writing

1. I picked this topic because

   Azul always surprises me.

2. The best thing about my writing is

   the happy ending.

Reflect

Think about your writing. On your own paper, finish the two sentences above.

Reflect on your writing.

Point out to students that when they *reflect on* their writing, they think about it. Have volunteers read aloud the two sentences that tell what Miguel thinks about his writing.

Provide photocopies of the reproducible Thinking About Your Writing page (TE page 359) for students to complete.

■ Have students complete the first sentence starter to tell why they picked their topic.

■ To complete the second sentence starter, have students think about what they liked best about their writing. Students can also think about comments they received from partners and classmates during sharing times and from you during a writing conference.

Have students write the date on their completed reflection page and clip it to their narratives. Before placing the pages in their writing portfolios, have students take both pages home to share with their families.

✻ For more about student portfolios, see SE pages 40–41.

English Language Learners

Students may feel self-conscious about their writing and may not think anything about it is "best." To help students complete the second sentence, have them compare this assignment with their previous assignments and find some way that they have improved.

Struggling Learners

Some students may find it difficult to express how they feel about their writing. Encourage them to talk to you about the sentence starters on the Thinking About Your Writing page. Write down words and phrases students use orally so they can refer to them as they complete the sentence starters in writing.

Advanced Learners

Have students complete another sentence starter: *One thing I learned while writing my personal narrative is _____.*

Point out that they should focus on what they learned about this writing form or the process. For example, students might write that *making a story map helps me to write my story.*

Across the Curriculum

Reading

Explain that sometimes readers write letters to favorite authors to share stories related to their books.

Talk about the main parts of a letter: date, greeting, message, and closing. Point out that a comma is used in the date to separate the day from the year, and after the greeting and the closing parts.

✱ For another example of a friendly letter, see SE page 273.

Model the process of writing a letter to an author who is popular with your students. Ask students to contribute sentences to the message of the letter. Then provide photocopies of the reproducible Friendly Letter (TE page 336) for students to use as a template to practice writing their own letter to an author. If you will be mailing the letters, have students either copy their letter onto plain lined paper or use a computer.

102

Across the Curriculum

You may be asked to do narrative writing for some of your school subjects.

Reading

Nola writes a letter to an author, Mercer Mayer. She shares a story related to his book.

October 5, 2011

Dear Mr. Mayer,
    I read the story <u>You're the Scaredy Cat</u>. Once I tried to camp in my yard. It rained. I had to go inside, too. I love your books! I want to read all of them.
                    Your fan,
                    Nola

Struggling Learners

Students who have difficulty writing a letter on their own can copy your model letter, change the closing, and write their name. Encourage them to add a sentence or two of their own to the letter.

Grammar Connection

Pronouns

- **Proofreader's Guide** page 293 (+)
- **Words** pages 226, 227
- *GrammarSnap* Pronouns

Suggested Expository Writing Unit (Three Weeks)

Day	Writing and Skills Instruction	Student Edition		Teacher's Edition	SkillsBook	Daily Language Workouts	Write Source Online
		Expository Writing Unit	Resource Units*	Grammar Copy Masters			
1–2	**Expository Start-Up** ⓛ Literature Connections "Drums"	107–109				32–33	
	Skills Activities: • Nouns		220–221, 291–292		67–68		*GrammarSnap*
opt.	*Speaking to Others*	202–203					
3–5	**Expository Paragraph** (Model, Prewriting)	110–115			96–97		*Interactive Whiteboard Lessons, Net-text*
6–10	**Expository Paragraph** *(cont.)* (Writing, Revising, Editing)	116–121				34–35	*Net-text*
	Skills Activities: • Time-order words	260					
	• Plurals		223 (+), 278, 292		43–44		*GrammarSnap*
	• End marks		270–271, 290		25–26		*GrammarSnap*
	Working with a Partner	26–27					
11	**Expository Paragraph** *(cont.)* (Publishing)	122–125				36–37	*Portfolio, Net-text*
12–15	**Across the Curriculum**	126–127					
	Skills Activities: • Proper nouns		222, 291		69–70		*GrammarSnap*
	• Capital letters		276		37–38		*GrammarSnap*
	• Using the right word		284	389	61–62		
	Writing for Assessment	128–129					
	Skills Activity: • Sentences		288–289		21–22		*GrammarSnap*

* These units are also located in the back of the *Teacher's Edition*. Resource Units include "Words," "A Writer's Resource," "Proofreader's Guide," and "Theme Words."
(+) This activity is located in a different section of the *Write Source Student Edition*. If students have already completed this activity, you may wish to review it at this time.

Teacher's Notes for Expository Writing

The overview for expository writing includes some specific teaching suggestions for the unit.

Expository Start-Up (pages 108–109)

Writing directions is an excellent way for students to learn how to order information in a step-by-step sequence. Students can identify the steps required to do a familiar task, a useful skill in all future writing tasks.

Expository Paragraph (pages 110–125)

When writing the paragraph, each step must be placed in order. By following the steps in the writing process, children can write a good how-to paragraph. The model for this chapter is about making green paint using blue and yellow paint.

Across the Curriculum (pages 126–127)

Sharing information about a topic does have application in other subject areas. For example, in this chapter, one student writes about a math problem while another student tells about an Indian tribe. Each writer provides information that explains the topic.

Writing for Assessment (pages 128–129)

Expository prompts are a common form of assessment. Students should learn that the key to writing a good response is understanding the prompt, so they can organize their information and write their response.

Academic Vocabulary

Read aloud the academic terms, as well as the descriptions and questions. Model for students how to read one question and answer it. Have partners monitor their understanding and seek clarification of the terms by working through the meanings and questions together.

Minilessons

I Can Do That! — Expository Start-Up

■ **HAVE** students write the numbers 1 to 10 on a piece of paper. Next, **READ** off 10 how-to topics. As you **READ** each one, have students **WRITE** "yes" if they know how to do it or "no" if they don't. **CHOOSE** things like build a real car, tie a shoe, button a shirt, throw a ball, perform heart surgery, and so on. **WRITE** the numbers on the board and then find out how many could do a particular action. **EXPLAIN** that unless you know how to do something, you can't explain it to someone else.

106

Expository Writing

Academic Vocabulary

Work with a partner. Read the meanings and share answers to the questions.

1. To **share** something with others means to tell them your ideas or feelings.
   What would you like to share with a friend?

2. If you **gather** things you collect them together.
   What kinds of things can you gather in a park?

Everyday Stuff — Expository Paragraph

■ **WRITE** directions on the board or chart paper with input from the class. **USE** a familiar task, like tying shoes or brushing teeth. **ASK** one student to pantomime the activity. **STOP** after each significant step and **WRITE** what has happened. For example, (1) Put water on the toothbrush. Revise as needed.

This Way — Expository Paragraph

■ **TELL** students that you are going to wash a glass. **PUT** water in a plastic tub. Then **THROW** the water out. Next, **PUT** a dirty glass in the tub and **USE** a dry cloth to try to wash the glass. Then **SET** the glass on your desk. Finally, **PUT** soap in the tub. **ASK** the students what went wrong. **EMPHASIZE** why the proper order matters. Afterward, **ASK** them to **WRITE** a paragraph about how to brush teeth.

Just What's Needed . . . — Across the Curriculum

■ **WRITE** a paragraph about whales. **INCLUDE** in the paragraph that elephants are big and that some mice are grey. **ASK** students to read the paragraph and **FIND** the sentences that don't fit. **POINT OUT** that those sentences don't provide information about whales. Those sentences are distracting.

Expository Paragraph   117

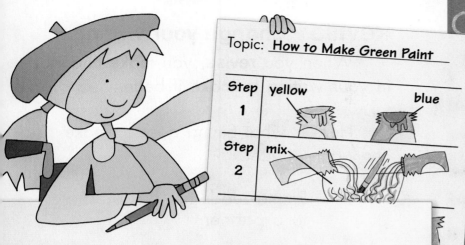

Topic: How to Make Green Paint

Step 1	yellow	blue
Step 2	mix	

You can make green paint.

First, get yellow paint and blue paint

Then mix both of the paints togethr.

now, the two colors make green paint.

▸ Write

Write your first draft.

1. **Start** with a **You can** sentence.
2. **Write** a sentence for each of your steps.
3. **Use** a time-order word for each step.

Show students how Emma used her order chart to write her sentences. Have students turn back to SE page 115 and point at each picture as you read aloud the sentence Emma wrote for it.

Point out Emma's use of the homophones *blue* and *two*. Ask students for other words that sound the same as *blue* and *two* but have different spellings and meanings (*blew; to, too*). Explain that thinking about the meaning of each word helps Emma choose the correct spelling. But emphasize again that students shouldn't worry about spelling at this point. They can check it later.

✴ For information and worksheets on using the right word, see SE pages 284–286 and TE pages 389–391.

As students write their first draft, remind them to skip a line between sentences.

After students write their first draft, have them check to be sure they have **followed the writing steps** *(see below)*.

Teaching Tip: Follow the Writing Steps

To help students check that they have followed the steps to write a first draft, give them three colored pencils. Have students (1) circle the words *You can* in their first sentence with one color, (2) underline each sentence that describes a step from their order chart with a second color, and (3) circle all time-order words with a third color. Is anything missing?

English Language Learners

Provide visual support to clarify the homophone examples. Have volunteers sketch or pantomime actions to make the meanings of the suggested homophones obvious as you spell the words on the board.

Struggling Learners

Help students write their steps in the correct order. Provide photocopies of the reproducible Order Chart (TE page 363). Have students refer to the order chart they made during **Prewrite** and write on the blank order chart one sentence that describes each step. Have them write a *You can* sentence next to *Topic*. Help students replace step numbers with time-order words.

Revise Change your writing.

Discuss why reading aloud the first draft to a partner during the revising step is a good idea. Make the point that it is important to check for understanding because a how-to paragraph tells how to do something. If a partner cannot understand the steps, then the writing is not clear, and the writer needs to add or rearrange something.

Write a caret on the board. Remind students that this mark shows where added words belong in the paragraph. Model how to use a caret. Write a sentence on the board. Insert a caret and a word to add.

Remind students that adding to or changing words can help create *voice*, which is an important writing trait. Point out that Emma wants her word choices to sound as if she is really interested in her topic.

✳ For an example of expository voice, see SE page 255.

Technology Connections

Have students use the Writing Network features of the Net-text to comment on each other's drafts.

✳ *Write Source Online* **Net-text**

118

Revise ▶ Change your writing.

When you **revise**, you make changes in your writing to make it better.

Here is what Emma does to make her writing better.

Read   Emma reads her first draft to a partner.

Listen   Emma wants her how-to paragraph to be clear. She listens to her partner's ideas.

Change   She uses carets (∧) to show where she wants to add to her writing. She adds a missing detail and a feeling word.

English Language Learners

After students read their first draft to a proficient English speaker, have them listen as that partner reads their paragraph back to them before they discuss, ask, and answer questions.

Expository Paragraph   119

Emma's Revising

You can make green paint.

First, get yellow paint and blue paint

Then ⌃ mix both of the paints togethr.
 use a paintbrush to

now, the two colors make green paint. ⌃
                                  Wow!

> You could add an exciting word.

 Revise

Change your writing to make it better.

1. **Read** your sentences to a partner.
2. **Listen** to your partner's ideas.
3. **Change** your writing to make it better.

Struggling Learners

Students who find writing challenging may feel bad if their partner suggests too many changes. For now, working with you, the teacher, might be a better choice. Introduce one revision at a time. When students gain more confidence, they can be paired with a partner to work on revising.

Advanced Learners

Remind students that one of the writing traits is word choice—choosing the best words to make a clear picture in the reader's mind. Circle one or two words in their writing that could be improved with better word choice. Show students how to use a children's thesaurus to find better words.

Emma's Revising

Explain that the blue markings show the revisions Emma made. Have students point to the places where Emma used a caret to make changes to her writing.

Discuss the details Emma added (a missing detail, *use a paintbrush to*; and an exclamatory word, *Wow!*). Point out that in the illustration, Emma is listening to her partner Miguel. Read aloud Miguel's speech balloon and explain that Emma listened to Miguel's suggestion and added the word *Wow!* Ask students why they think Emma added the information about the paintbrush. (Miguel probably asked what she used to mix the paints together.)

Remind students of the role of a partner:
- A partner listens carefully as the writer reads the writing.
- A partner asks questions about things that aren't clear.
- A partner makes suggestions about changing the writing to make it better.

Emphasize that writers should consider a partner's suggestions, but they don't have to act on all of them.

✱ During the revising and editing steps, work with students to improve their writing by asking the questions in the Teaching Tip on TE page 124.

Edit Check your writing.

Remind students that *conventions* are the rules writers follow to make sure that their writing is correct and easy to read. Explain that when you edit, you check to make sure you followed the rules. Point out that this means checking for capital letters, end marks, and spelling.

Review conventions by asking these questions:

- How can Emma tell if she has used capital letters correctly? (She should check the first word of each sentence.)
- What end mark should Emma use at the end of a telling sentence? (a period)
- What end mark should Emma use at the end of an exclamatory sentence? (an exclamation point)
- How can Emma check words she thinks might be spelled wrong? (look in a dictionary, ask the teacher, refer to the Proofreader's Guide)

Technology Connections

Students can use the added features of the Net-text as they explore this stage of the writing process.

Write Source Online **Net-text**

Grammar Connection

Plurals

- **Proofreader's Guide** pages 278, 292
- **Words** page 223 (+)
- *GrammarSnap* Plural Nouns
- *SkillsBook* pages 43–44

End Marks

- **Proofreader's Guide** pages 270–271, 290
- *GrammarSnap* End Marks Overview
- *SkillsBook* pages 25–26

120

Edit ▸ Check your writing.

When you **edit**, you check your writing for conventions. You check for capital letters, end marks, and spelling.

Here is what Emma does to check her writing.

Read Emma reads her sentences.

Check She checks for capital letters, end marks, and spelling.

Mark Emma marks the changes she needs to make.

English Language Learners

Writing in the language students are still learning to speak requires considerable effort. To make editing a little easier, modify the order of checking for conventions.

- In one-on-one conferences, have students listen and identify when each sentence ends as you read aloud their paragraph.

- Help them check their written sentences for end punctuation before helping them edit for capital letters.

Inserting missing end punctuation first will help students see where capital letters are needed.

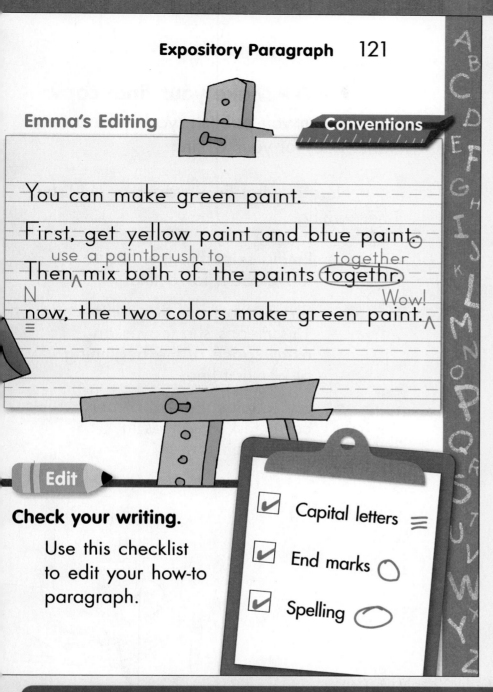

Expository Paragraph 121

Emma's Editing

Conventions

You can make green paint.

First, get yellow paint and blue paint.

use a paintbrush to   together
Then mix both of the paints togethr.
N
now, the two colors make green paint.
≡   Wow!

Edit

Check your writing.

Use this checklist
to edit your how-to
paragraph.

✓ Capital letters ≡

✓ End marks ◯

✓ Spelling ◯

Emma's Editing

Remind students that the blue markings are the revisions Emma made. Explain that the red markings are Emma's edits. Point out her corrections and ask these questions:

- What does the circled period mean? (Emma adds an end mark.) Why does she do this? (A telling sentence ends with a period.)
- What do the three lines under the *n* mean? (to capitalize the *n*) Why does she do this? (*Now* is the first word in a sentence.)
- What spelling change does Emma make? (She changes the spelling of *together*.)

Provide photocopies of the reproducible Editing Checklist (TE page 358). Guide students to use the checklist to edit their writing for one convention at a time. Tell students to first check their writing for capital letters and make any corrections. Then have them check off the capital letters box on their checklist. Repeat for end marks and spelling.

Some students may be ready to use a beginner's dictionary for spelling.

- Tell students that words in a dictionary are listed in alphabetical (ABC) order. Point out that students can refer to the classroom alphabet chart to check where the first letter of a word comes in the alphabet.
- Use a beginner's dictionary to model the use of guide words at the top of the page. Point out that the words on the page come between these two words because the words are in alphabetical order.
- Tell students that if they use what they know about sounds and letters to spell the word, they will often come up with a spelling that is close enough to help them find the word.

- Remind students that some words are not spelled the way they sound. Explain that checking spelling lists or asking a spelling partner for help may be necessary.

✱ For lists of words that first-grade writers use and homophones, see SE pages 279–286.

Publish **Make your final copy.**

Remind students that publishing is the final step in the writing process. Explain that published writing is writing that is shared with others. Point out that before they can share their writing, they have to make a neat final copy of their revised and edited first draft. Ask students why this is important (because the marked-up first draft is now hard to read).

Talk about the red key words.

- **Skip** If students already have a title in mind, they can write it on the first line instead of skipping the line.
- **Indent** Teach students the "rule of thumb" so they know how much space to indent. Tell them they can place the edge of their thumb on the left margin of their paper. They should then begin the first sentence on the other side of their thumb.
- **Copy** Point out that it is important to make sure that all changes and corrections made during revising and editing are included in the final copy.

Whenever students prepare a neat final copy, stress that proper spacing between letters, words, and sentences is important in making a document easy to read.

Technology Connections

Remind students that they can use the Writing Network features of the Portfolio to share their work with peers.

✦ *Write Source Online* **Portfolio**

✦ *Write Source Online* **Net-text**

122

Publish ▶ **Make your final copy.**

When you **publish**, you make a neat final copy of your writing.

Here is what Emma does to publish her writing.

Skip   Emma skips the first line to leave room for a title.

Indent   She indents her first sentence. This means she leaves an extra space at the beginning of her first line.

Copy   She copies the rest of her corrected sentences in paragraph form.

English Language Learners

If you plan to meet with students in individual writing conferences (Teaching Tip, TE page 124), take some time now to modify your approach with students who are not English-proficient. Use your knowledge of students' oral language proficiencies to identify the one trait each student is most ready to work on improving.

- Focus on discussing that one trait during the conference.
- Offer specific suggestions to help students improve their writing (for example, we will talk more before you write).

Expository Paragraph 123

You can make green paint.

First, get yellow paint and blue paint.

Then ∧ mix both of the paints (togethr)

use a paintbrush to

together

N

now, the two colors make green paint. ∧

Wow!

Indent

↓ You can make green
paint. First, get yellow paint
and blue paint. Then use a
paintbrush to mix both of the
paints together. Now, the two
colors make green paint. Wow!

Publish ▶

Write your paragraph.

1. **Skip** the first writing line.

2. **Indent** your first sentence.

3. **Copy** your corrected sentences in paragraph form.

Review how Emma used her first draft and followed the publishing steps in order to write her final copy.

■ Have students point to the line that Emma skipped on her final copy. Ask them to explain what will go there (a title).

■ Have students try the "rule of thumb" and place their thumb in the space where Emma indented. Remind them that an indent is used to show the beginning of a paragraph.

■ Help students compare Emma's edited first draft to the final copy. Guide them to see that she copied all her sentences in order and included all her revisions and corrections. Point out that the sentences in her first draft were written on separate lines, but in her final copy they are written one after the other, in paragraph form.

As students write their final copy, circulate and make sure they are including all their revisions and edits.

English Language Learners

Students who are learning a new language are often uncomfortable sharing in a large group. Before asking students to read their paragraph and show their drawing to the entire class (TE page 124), have them share with an individual.

Advanced Learners

After students write their final copies, guide them in brainstorming additional ways to share their how-to paragraphs. Possibilities include making an audiotape of an oral reading, an interactive computer report, or a videotape demonstrating each step of the paragraph as it is read aloud.

Publish Share your writing.

Have students point to the title of Emma's how-to paragraph.

- Call on a volunteer to read the title aloud.
- Ask students if Emma's title fits her paragraph, and have them give reasons explaining their answer. (Yes, it tells what the paragraph is all about.)
- Point out that each important word in a title begins with a capital letter. Have students point to and name each capital letter.

Give students time to think of a title. Distribute crayons and have students add a drawing to their paragraph.

Hold a **writing conference** (*see below*) with each student to assess his or her final copy.

If time allows, have each student read aloud his or her paragraph and show the drawing. Encourage students to share their writing with someone at home.

124

Publish ▶ Share your writing.

When you publish, you share your writing.

Add a title and a drawing.

Make Green Paint

You can make green paint. First, get yellow paint and blue paint. Then use a paintbrush to mix both of the paints together. Now, the two colors make green paint. Wow!

Publish

Share your writing.

Read your how-to paragraph to someon

Advanced Learners

Depending on the skill level of individual students, explore additional traits during the writing conference. Refer only to traits that you have explicitly discussed in connection with writing a how-to paragraph, such as Voice and Word Choice.

Teaching Tip: Writing Conference

The writing conference should be a relaxed, informal dialogue between you and the student. The goal is to give the student positive reinforcement for those traits that show some mastery and to point out traits that need improvement.

Focus on the writing goals for the assignment (SE page 111).

- **Ideas** Is your topic something you can explain well? Did you include enough details to make your writing clear?
- **Organization** Did you write the steps in the correct order using time-order words?
- **Conventions** Did you follow the writing rules for capital letters, end marks, and spelling?

Expository Paragraph   125

Reflect on your writing.

Emma thinks about her writing. She tells how she feels about her how-to paragraph.

Thinking About Your Writing

1. I picked this topic because

I like to paint pictures.

_____

2. The best thing about my writing is

my steps are in the

correct order.

Reflect

Think about your writing. On your own paper, finish the two sentences above.

English Language Learners

Students often learn it is easier to copy models verbatim than to think of how to communicate their own ideas. Review reflections students have done in other chapters to determine if they copied the model or attempted to tell their own feelings about their writing.

- Have students who tended to copy now tell and *show* you the best thing about their writing before they complete the Thinking About Your Writing page.
- Provide necessary vocabulary and spellings of new words.
- If you choose to take dictation, write on a separate piece of paper and then choral read it with the student. Have students copy their dictated ideas on their own reflection sheet.

Reflect on your writing.

By the time students are ready to reflect on their writing, they have received comments from a partner during the revising step and from you during an individual writing conference. Suggest that students keep these comments in mind as they think about their writing.

Provide photocopies of the reproducible Thinking About Your Writing page (TE page 359).

While most students will be able to write about why they picked their topic, some may find it challenging to identify what they think is the best thing about their writing. Explain that there are no right or wrong answers to this question. Help students focus their thinking about the best thing by asking these questions:

- What did you do to make your writing clear and easy to understand?
- What are your favorite words or sentences?
- How did you help readers understand the order of your steps?

Across the Curriculum

Math

Review the goals of expository writing:
- to explain how to do something
- to write steps in order

Talk about Tyler's writing.
- What topic does Tyler choose? (how to add two numbers)
- What steps does Tyler include in his paragraph? (draw dots to stand for each number; count the dots and draw that number; write the number sentence) Are the steps in the right order? (yes)
- What time-order words does Tyler use? (*first, then, finally*)
- How is this paragraph like Emma's? (It begins with the words *You can*. It tells step-by-step how to do something. It has time-order words.)

Using Tyler's how-to paragraph as a model, guide students through a shared-writing activity in which the class dictates sentences for a math how-to paragraph. Write these sentences on chart paper.

126

Across the Curriculum

You may be asked to do expository writing for different school subjects. You share information about what you learn.

Math

Tyler writes about a math problem. He draws a picture. It helps him explain addition.

2 + 3 = 5

Adding Numbers

You can add 2 + 3. First, draw dots. Make a set of two dots. Then make a set of three dots. Finally, count all of the dots. Make five dots. You can see that 2 + 3 = 5.

Writing in Math and Social Studies   127

Social Studies

Maya learns about the Havasupai Indian tribe. They live in Arizona. She writes a paragraph about them.

Collar Makers

Indian tribes live in Arizona. One tribe lives at the bottom of the Grand Canyon. They are the people of the blue and green waters. They make collars with tiny beads. Can you guess what color beads they like to use?

Across the Curriculum

Social Studies

Ask students to summarize what Maya explained about her topic, the Havasupai Indian tribe, in her paragraph (where they live, what they make).

Discuss how Maya's paragraph differs from those of Emma and Tyler. (It doesn't tell how to make something. It doesn't list steps in order. It doesn't use time-order words. It ends with a question.)

Guide students in a shared-writing activity about a topic the class has studied in social studies. As students dictate, write their sentences on chart paper. Encourage them to follow the order and pattern of sentences in Maya's paragraph.

Grammar Connection

Proper Nouns
- **Proofreader's Guide** page 291
- **Words** page 222
- *GrammarSnap* Proper Nouns
- *SkillsBook* pages 69–70

Capital Letters
- **Proofreader's Guide** page 276
- *GrammarSnap* Capital Letters
- *SkillsBook* pages 37–38

Using the Right Word
- **Proofreader's Guide** page 284
- *SkillsBook* pages 61–62
- **TE copy master** page 389

Advanced Learners

Invite curious students to find out what the *blue and green waters* are. Display a map of the United States and help students locate Arizona and the Grand Canyon. Then have students go to the Havasupai Tribe Web site (www.havasupaitribe.com) and click on *Waterfalls*. Ask students to write about the blue and green waters and share what they learn.

Writing for Assessment

Explain that a writing prompt is a set of directions that tells the students what to write about. They need to read it very carefully before they write a response to it.

Point out that before Alano begins to write, he chooses a topic and makes a cluster in which he quickly writes down details.

If you wish to give students exposure to timed, test-taking situations, you can assign the prompt as an informal or formal assessment either before or after you evaluate Alano's response on SE page 129.

Before students **respond to the prompt** *(see below)*, distribute photocopies of the reproducible Cluster (TE page 337) and have them write details about the topic they choose.

128

Writing for Assessment

Alano's teacher gives him an expository **prompt** to write about. Alano reads the prompt, makes a cluster, and writes a paragraph.

Writing Prompt

In a paragraph, explain something new you have learned.

Alano's Cluster

old coins

come from many countries

collecting coins

new coins

silver, gold, copper

Grammar Connection

Sentences

■ **Proofreader's Guide** pages 288–289

■ *GrammarSnap* Understanding Sentences

■ *SkillsBook* pages 21–22

Teaching Tip: Respond to the Prompt

Provide regular opportunities to respond to prompts in a fixed amount of time. Tell students to

● read the prompt several times,

● then make a cluster; drawing, or list to plan their response; and

● allow time at the end to review their writing and correct any mistakes.

Struggling Learners

Some students may benefit from brainstorming with others to complete the cluster. Help this group choose a topic. Then draw a cluster on the board and use it as you guide a brainstorming session. As students mention details to include, write them on the cluster. Encourage students to use these details when they write their response.

Alano's Writing

Writing for Assessment 129

Alano's Writing

Coins

Collecting coins is an interesting hobby. Coins can be silver, gold, or copper. They come from many countries. Some coins are very old. It is easier to find new coins.

Using the rubric on SE pages 36–37 and a photocopy of the Conference Notes on TE page 322, work with students to evaluate Alano's paragraph. Two additional paragraphs are available in copy master form (see **Benchmark Papers** box below). Conference notes are provided for each benchmark paper.

If you have asked students to respond to the prompt, schedule a writing conference with individual students to help them do a self-assessment of their own writing. The rubric on TE pages 36–37 provides a framework for the discussion.

English Language Learners

Some students may not have the experiences we assume to be universal (having a hobby). Explain that a *hobby* is something people do for fun. Give examples of hobbies, specifically those that involve collecting items.

Benchmark Papers

Fun with Beads (good)
● TE pp. 323–324

Draw (poor)
● TE pp. 325–326

Persuasive Writing Overview

Common Core Standards Focus

Writing 1: Write opinion pieces in which they introduce the topic or name the book they are writing about, state an opinion, supply a reason for the opinion, and provide some sense of closure.

Language 2: Demonstrate command of the conventions of standard English capitalization, punctuation, and spelling when writing.

Writing Form

- persuasive paragraph

Focus on the Traits

- **Ideas** Expressing an opinion and supporting it with reasons
- **Voice** Using strong words that convince the reader
- **Conventions** Checking for errors in capitalization, punctuation, and spelling

 Literature Connections

- **"Three Reasons Why Pets Are Great"** (an article in Harcourt *Storytown*)

 Technology Connections

 Write Source Online
www.hmheducation.com/writesource

- *Net-text*
- *Bookshelf*
- *GrammarSnap*
- *Portfolio*
- *Writing Network features*
- *File Cabinet*

Interactive Whiteboard Lessons

Suggested Persuasive Writing Unit (Four Weeks)

Day	Writing and Skills Instruction	Student Edition		Teacher's Edition	SkillsBook	Daily Language Workouts	Write Source Online
		Persuasive Writing Unit	Resource Units*	Grammar Copy Masters			
1–2	**Persuasive Start-Up** ⓛ Literature Connections "Three Reasons Why Pets Are Great"	131–133				38–41	
	Skills Activities: • Opposites		287	392	66		
opt.	*Speaking to Others*	202–203					
3–5	**Being a Smart Viewer**	212–213					
6–10	**Persuasive Paragraph** (Model, Prewriting, Writing)	134–135				42–43, 83	*Interactive Whiteboard Lessons, Net-text*
11–15	**Persuasive Paragraph** *(cont.)* (Revising, Editing)	136–137				44–45, 84	*Net-text*
	Skills Activity: • End marks		270–271, 290	393			*GrammarSnap*
	Working with a Partner	26–27					
16–20	**Persuasive Paragraph** *(cont.)* (Publishing)	138				46–47, 85	*Portfolio, Net-text*
	Across the Curriculum	139			90		
	Skills Activity: • Commas in a series		272–273		29–30		*GrammarSnap*

* These units are also located in the back of the *Teacher's Edition.* Resource Units include "Words," "A Writer's Resource," "Proofreader's Guide," and "Theme Words."
(+) This activity is located in a different section of the *Write Source Student Edition.* If students have already completed this activity, you may wish to review it at this time.

Teacher's Notes for Persuasive Writing

The overview for persuasive writing includes some specific teaching suggestions for the unit.

Persuasive Start-Up (pages 132–133)

In persuasive writing, the writer expresses an opinion and tries to persuade others to agree. For example, supporters of public transportation might write to discourage the use of private cars for each individual or at the very least, encourage car-pooling where public transportation is not available. The example in the book is meant to convince fellow students to walk in the halls. A poster is the writer's form of publishing.

Persuasive Paragraph (pages 134–138)

A poster is one way to persuade others, but posters can only say so much. A persuasive paragraph can explain why the reader should change or adopt the idea the writer presents. The chapter explains each step students need to take in order to write a convincing persuasive paragraph. The model features the argument for walking in the halls at school for safety.

Across the Curriculum (page 139)

Persuasive writing in other disciplines may not be as common as descriptive, narrative, or expository. In this chapter, a student has learned about food groups in health class and wants to get his mother to make pizza because it is full of good ingredients.

Academic Vocabulary

Read aloud the academic terms, as well as the descriptions and questions. Model for students how to read one question and answer it. Have partners monitor their understanding and seek clarification of the terms by working through the meanings and questions together.

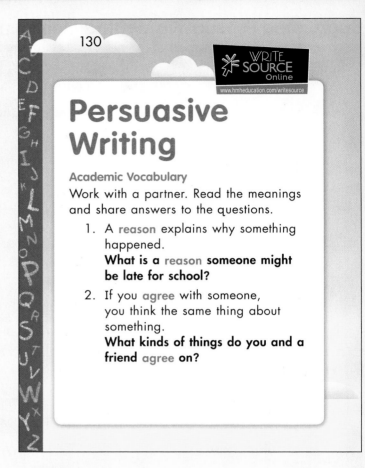

130

Persuasive Writing

Academic Vocabulary

Work with a partner. Read the meanings and share answers to the questions.

1. A **reason** explains why something happened.
   What is a reason someone might be late for school?

2. If you **agree** with someone, you think the same thing about something.
   What kinds of things do you and a friend agree on?

Minilessons

Rules Rule   Persuasive Start-Up

- After reviewing pages 132–133, **TALK** with your students about laws for pedestrians (walking on the side of the road facing traffic when there are no sidewalks, crossing only at intersections, waiting for stop lights to change, and so on). Afterward, have students **CHOOSE** which law they think is most important.

Hear, Ye! Hear, Ye!   Persuasive Paragraph

- **ASK** your students to **CHOOSE** a storybook that they enjoyed reading. (There may be as many books as students.) **HAVE** them each **WRITE** a persuasive paragraph so that others in the class will want to read the book.

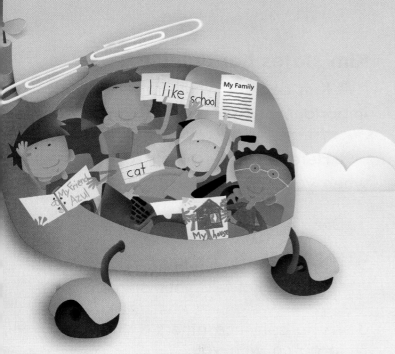

131

In **persuasive writing,** you share your opinion. You give reasons why others should agree with you.

 Literature Connections: You can find an example of persuasive ideas in the article "Three Reasons Why Pets are Great."

Family Connection Letters

As you begin this unit, send home the Persuasive Writing Family Connection letter, which describes what students will be learning.

- Letter in English (TE page 400)
- Letter in Spanish (TE page 409)

Persuasive Writing

Invite volunteers to tell about their favorite playground activity. Ask them to share reasons why they think their classmates also enjoy this activity.

- Point out that when students tell about the activity they think is best, they are expressing their opinion. Explain that an opinion is what someone believes, thinks, or feels about a topic.
- Then explain that when students try to convince others to agree with their opinion, they are being persuasive.
- Ask students if the word *persuasive* makes them think of any other word. Talk about the meaning of *persuade*.

Invite volunteers to tell about times when they have tried to persuade their friends or family members to agree with them. How successful were they at being persuasive?

 Literature Connections

The article *Three Reasons Why Pets are Great* describes the joys of owning a pet. Explain that this article is a good example of persuasive writing because detailed reasons support the writer's opinions.

This persuasive text is a student model from Harcourt *Storytown.* For additional persuasive models, see the Reading-Writing Connections beginning on page TE-36.

Mentor texts: Use a book, such as the ones listed on page TE-40, to discuss persuasion. After reading the book out loud to the class, ask students questions such as these: "Who is doing the persuading?" (It might be the author or a character in a story.) "What is the person trying to convince others to do? Would you be persuaded?"

Persuasive Start-Up

Objectives

- understand the content and structure of a persuasive paragraph
- choose a topic (a safety rule) to write about
- plan, draft, revise, and edit a persuasive paragraph

Ask students to recall what an opinion is (what someone thinks, believes, or feels about something). Explain that in **persuasive writing,** the writer tells her or his opinion and tries to persuade others to agree with this opinion.

Have students point to each numbered point in their book as you read it aloud. Discuss why posters are used to persuade people. (Many people see them. They are big enough for a picture and a message.)

Have students summarize the page by having them tell in their own words what they should remember when they write to persuade someone of their opinion. (Tell your opinion. Use *should* when telling the opinion. Give reasons to persuade others to agree with you.)

132

Persuasive Start-Up

In **persuasive writing,** you write sentences that tell your opinion. An **opinion** tells how you feel about something.

Kim states her opinion.

Kim decides which rule is the most important. She makes a poster about it.

Here are three points to remember when you write to persuade.

1. Decide what your opinion is.

2. Use the word *should* in a sentence that tells your opinion.

3. Try to convince others to agree with you.

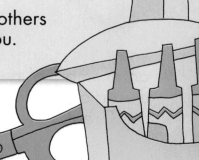

Materials

Drawing materials (TE p. 133)

Chart paper (TE pp. 133, 135, 136, 139)

Copy Masters

List (TE pp. 134)

Editing Checklist (TE p. 137)

Note (TE p. 139)

Persuasive Start-Up   133

School Rules

<u>In the Halls</u>
- Walk in the halls.
- Wait quietly in line.

<u>On the Playground</u>
- Take turns.

We should walk in the halls.

Talk about it.

1. Talk about your school rules.
2. Decide which rule is most important.
3. Use the word *should* in a sentence that tells your opinion.

Discuss Kim's thought bubble at the top of the page. After reading aloud the text, point out that these are the topics that Kim thinks about when deciding what school rule is most important in her opinion.

Then focus attention on Kim's finished poster.
- Ask students to describe the picture. Then call on a volunteer to read the message.
- Review the three points listed at the bottom of SE page 132. Ask if Kim followed each point when making her poster. (She selected her opinion; she used the word *should*; her picture and message try to convince others of her opinion.)

Talk about it.

Lead a discussion of your classroom and/or school rules. Then have each student **select a topic** *(see below)* by sharing his or her opinion about which rule is most important. Point out that students may have differing opinions. Remind students to state their opinion using the words *We should* to show that they feel strongly about it.

Teaching Tip: Select a Topic

If students have difficulty choosing a topic, suggest that they use one from the list in Kim's thought balloon. After students talk about their topic, distribute drawing materials and have them make a poster like Kim's. Have them save their poster to refer to when they write their persuasive paragraph (TE page 135).

English Language Learners

During the **Talk about it** activity, emphasize that *should* tells people what they *need to do*. Model use of *should* as you respond to their opinions. Have them repeat the modeled sentences and write them on chart paper as a language chart.

Grammar Connection

Opposites
- **Proofreader's Guide** page 287
- *SkillsBook* page 66
- **TE copy master** page 392

Persuasive Paragraph

Have students recall Kim's poster and the steps she followed to create it. (She selected her topic. She told her opinion about it using *should*. She made a poster to convince others.)

Explain that now Kim is going to write a paragraph to go with her poster. Before she begins to write, Kim makes a list of reasons to plan her writing. Ask a volunteer to read the list aloud. Discuss whether Kim's reasons (details) support her opinion.

✻ For another example of a list, see SE page 248.

To model the **Prewrite** activity, give an example of a rule, such as raising hands in class, and invite volunteers to tell why students should follow it. Record students' reasons on a list. Distribute photocopies of the reproducible List page (TE page 338). Circulate to provide assistance as students **list reasons** to support the opinion they illustrated on their poster.

 Technology Connections

Use this unit's Interactive Whiteboard Lesson to introduce persuasive writing.

 Interactive Whiteboard Lessons

 Technology Connections

Students can use the added features of the Net-text as they explore this stage of the writing process.

 Write Source Online **Net-text**

134

Persuasive Paragraph

Kim looks at her poster. She writes some sentences about why the rule is important. Then she puts them together in a paragraph.

Prewrite ▶ Gather your reasons.

When you **prewrite**, you make a list to gather reasons for your opinion.

Kim lists three reasons to follow the rule.

We should walk in the halls.

My Reasons
1. to be quiet
2. to see where we are going
3. to stay safe

Prewrite

Gather your reasons.

List reasons to follow the rule.

Teaching Tip: List Reasons

Customize the reproducible list. Change the heading *Details* to *My Reasons* and write *1., 2., 3* down the left-hand side. Change *Topic* to *Opinion*.

● Have students write their opinion sentence from their poster next to the heading *Opinion*. Reasons can be phrases like Kim's.

● Pair students who have difficulty thinking up reasons and have them brainstorm ideas.

English Language Learners

To help students think of reasons for their opinion, explain that *reasons* answer *why* questions. Have students work with partners to ask and answer *why* questions about their own poster. Help students put their reasons into words, and encourage them to share orally before they begin writing their list of reasons.

Persuasive Paragraph   135

Write ▶ Write your first draft.

When you write a **first draft**, you put your reasons into sentences.

Kim starts with her opinion sentence. Then she writes a sentence for each reason. Her last sentence repeats the rule.

> We should walk in the halls it
> helps us be quiet. We can see where
> we are going. Walking helps everyone
> stay safe. Always walk in the halls.

Write ▶

Write your first draft.

1. **Start** with your opinion sentence.
2. **Write** a sentence for each reason.
3. **Repeat** the rule in a new way.

Write Write your first draft.

Have students point to the appropriate sentences in Kim's first draft in their books as you discuss the **persuasive paragraph's structure** (see below).

Model how to repeat the rule in a new way. On the board, write an opinion sentence, such as *You should raise your hand before you speak in class.* Track and read it aloud. Below it, repeat the rule in a new way, such as *Be sure to raise your hand before you speak in class.* Track and read it aloud, and then point out the differences between the two sentences. Can students think of other ways to rewrite this opinion sentence?

As students write their first draft, remind them to begin with their opinion sentence, follow it with reasons from their lists, and end with a sentence repeating the rule in a new way.

Technology Connections

Students can use the added features of the Net-text as they explore this stage of the writing process.

Write Source Online **Net-text**

Teaching Tip: Persuasive Paragraph's Structure

To help students understand the structure of a persuasive paragraph, copy Kim's final paragraph from SE page 138 onto chart paper. Use three colors of markers to highlight the first sentence, the middle sentences, and the last sentence. Point to each section as you discuss its function. Ask these questions:

- What is the purpose of the first sentence of a persuasive paragraph? (to state an opinion using *should*)
- What is the purpose of the sentences in the middle of a persuasive paragraph? (to give reasons in support of the opinion sentence)
- What is the purpose of the last sentence? (to repeat the opinion in a new way)

Struggling Learners

Guide students to see that Kim used her list to write the middle sentences in her paragraph. Discuss how she added words to turn each reason in her list into a complete sentence. Before students write, provide oral practice by having them turn the reasons in their lists into complete sentences.

Revise Change your writing.

As students revise their drafts, they can change or add words to create a strong voice that will persuade readers to follow the school rule. Discuss how the words Kim added in blue make her writing more persuasive. (The words *be sure* make her sound more confident.)

✱ For another example of persuasive voice, see SE page 255.

Review how a partner can help a writer improve her or his writing (SE page 26).

Remind students to use a caret to show where they want to add words. Model this by writing a sentence on the board and adding words with a caret.

Hold one-on-one writing conferences with students after they have finished **revising** *(see below)*. Review the changes marked and make other suggestions for improvements.

Technology Connections

Have students use the Writing Network features of the Net-text to comment on each other's drafts.

🖈 *Write Source Online* **Net-text**

136

Revise ▶ Change your writing.

When you **revise**, you make changes in your writing. You add words that will get the reader to do something.

Kim reads her writing and talks about it with a partner. Then she adds another idea.

> We should walk in the halls it
>
> helps us be quiet. We can see where
>
> we are going. Walking helps everyone
>
> Be sure you
> stay safe. ∧ Always walk in the halls.

Revise

Change your writing to make it better.

1. **Read** your writing.
2. **Talk** about your writing with a partner.
3. **Make** changes to help the reader.

English Language Learners

Modify the Working with a Partner steps (SE page 26). Instead of having the partner listen as the writer reads aloud his or her writing, have the partner read aloud the writer's writing so the writer can hear how it sounds.

Teaching Tip: Revising

Point out that when revising a persuasive paragraph, the focus should be on making the reasons that support the opinion even stronger. Write the following phrases on the board:

● *Be sure you*
● *Don't forget to*
● *Always remember to*

Explain that these phrases can make a student sound more persuasive.

Struggling Learners

To help students recall what to look for as they revise, write this checklist on chart paper:

__ **1.** Did you begin with your opinion?

__ **2.** Did you give reasons?

__ **3.** Did you repeat your opinion in a new way?

Track and read aloud one item at a time, and guide students to check their writing for each item.

Reviewing a Fiction Book 147

Revise ▶ Change your writing.

When you revise, you change your writing to make it better.

Read Emma reads her first draft to a partner.

Add Emma adds two new details.

I read <u>Yoko</u> by Rosemary Wells. The story is about ^a cat named^ Yoko. She likes to eat sushi for lunch the problem is that the other animals think her sushi is strang. I like this book because ^it has a happy ending.^ Yoko makes a new friend.

Revise ▶

Change your writing to make it better.

1. **Read** your first draft to a partner.
2. **Add** more details to your writing.

Revise Change your writing.

Explain that the blue additions are Emma's revisions. Point to the caret symbol and have students name it. Remind students that writers use a caret when they want to add a letter, a word, or words.

As you read aloud Emma's revised first draft, pause to discuss the two new details she adds. Have students talk about how these additions make Emma's writing better.

Display the first draft of the class model book review (TE page 146). Track and read it aloud. Then ask if there's anything that isn't clear. Invite students to suggest more details to add. Make the necessary changes. Save the revised draft for editing (TE page 148).

Before students read their first drafts to a partner, remind everyone that partners should listen carefully and then ask questions about anything that isn't clear. Also remind writers to think about their partner's suggestions for adding more details and decide if the suggestions would make the writing better.

✳ During the revising and editing steps, work with students to improve their writing by asking the questions in the Teaching Tip on TE page 149.

Technology Connections

Have students use the Writing Network features of the Net-text to comment on each other's drafts.

✳ *Write Source Online **Net-text***

English Language Learners

Prepare partners who will be working with students who are not yet fully English-proficient.

● Have partners read the book that is being reviewed to better understand the vocabulary and plot line of the story so that they can more effectively suggest revisions for the writing.

● Tell partners to help students make their writing sound more like speaking. Partners' suggestions might include adding or deleting words to help the sentences flow better.

Grammar Connection

Nouns
- **Proofreader's Guide** page 291
- **Words** page 222 (+)
- *GrammarSnap* Nouns
- **TE copy masters** pages 364, 365, 366

Capital Letters
- **Proofreader's Guide** page 276
- **Words** page 225 (+)
- *GrammarSnap* Capital Letters
- **TE copy master** page 367

Edit **Check your writing.**

The blue markings are Emma's revisions, and the red markings are her edits. Discuss each correction.

- A period was added at the end of a sentence.
- A capital letter was added at the beginning of a sentence.
- A spelling mistake was corrected.

Provide photocopies of the reproducible Editing Checklist (TE page 358). Model how to use the checklist as you edit the revised class model book review (TE page 147). Save the edited draft for publishing (TE page 149). Then have students use the editing checklist to edit their own book reviews.

Students may check for one convention at a time by placing a sheet of paper under a line of text and moving it down looking for missing capital letters, then end marks, and finally spelling errors.

✱ For a worksheet on capital letters, see TE page 367.

Technology Connections

Students can use the added features of the Net-text as they explore this stage of the writing process.

Write Source Online **Net-text**

Grammar Connection

Spelling
- **Proofreader's Guide** pages 279–283

148

Edit ▶ Check your writing.

When you edit, you check your writing for conventions. You check for capital letters, end marks, and spelling.

Here is what Emma does to edit her writing.

> I read <u>Yoko</u> by Rosemary Wells.
> The story is about ∧ a cat named Yoko. She likes to
> eat sushi for lunch. the problem is that
> the other animals think her sushi is
> ~~strang~~ strange. I like this book because ∧ Yoko
> makes a new friend. it has a happy ending.

Edit ▶

Check your writing.

Use this checklist to edit your book review.

- ✔ Capital letters
- ✔ End marks
- ✔ Spelling

Struggling Learners

As students use the checklist to edit their writing, circulate and offer support on what to look for.

- Do all important words in the title begin with capital letters? Is the title underlined?
- Does each sentence begin with a capital letter?
- Do proper nouns and the word *I* begin with capital letters?

- Is there a period at the end of each telling sentence, a question mark at the end of each question, and an exclamation point at the end of each exclamatory sentence?
- Are the words spelled correctly? How can you check?

Reviewing a Fiction Book   149

Publish ▶ Share your writing.

When you publish, you make a neat final copy of your review to share.

> Sushi Cat
>
> I read <u>Yoko</u> by Rosemary Wells. The story is about a cat named Yoko. She likes to eat sushi for lunch. The problem is that the other animals think her sushi is strange. I like this book because it has a happy ending. Yoko makes a new friend.

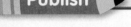

Share your writing.

1. **Make** a neat final copy.
2. **Read** it to the class.

Publish Share your writing.

Have students compare and contrast Emma's edited copy with her published copy. How is the published copy different from the edited copy? How is it the same?

Use the edited class book review (TE page 148) to model how to make a neat final copy. Work with students to write the final copy on another sheet of chart paper.

- Add a title.
- Guide students in how to incorporate the revisions and edits.
- Have volunteers point out where to begin the first sentence.
- Have individuals identify places where capital letters and end marks are needed.

Post the final copy of the book review on a bulletin board in the classroom or in the school library.

Have students make neat final copies of their own book reviews, complete with titles. Hold a **writing conference** *(see below)* with each student to assess her or his final copy.

Technology Connections

Remind students that they can use the Writing Network features of the Portfolio to share their work with peers.

※ *Write Source Online* **Portfolio**

※ *Write Source Online* **Net-text**

Teaching Tip: Writing Conference

The writing conference should be a relaxed, informal dialogue between you and the student. The goal is to give the student positive reinforcement for those traits that show some mastery and to point out traits of writing that need improvement.

Focus the conference on the points for writing a fiction book review (SE page 142) and on conventions.

- **Beginning** Did you tell the title and author of the book?
- **Middle** Did you tell what the book is about and give the main problem?
- **Ending** Did you tell why you like the book?
- **Conventions** Did you follow the writing rules for capital letters, end marks, and spelling?

Advanced Learners

Invite students to use what they have learned about writing book reviews to write a review about:

- a school play,
- a school concert,
- a family movie, or
- a community event.

Have students give the review a title and share it with the class.

Reviewing a Nonfiction Book

Objectives
- understand the content and form of a nonfiction book review
- choose a book to review
- plan, draft, revise, and edit a book review

Display a familiar nonfiction book. Explain that books that tell facts, or things that are known to be true, are called nonfiction. Remind students that books that tell make-believe stories are called fiction.

Explain that when you write a review of a nonfiction book, you tell what the book is about, share interesting facts, and tell why you like the book.

Have students point to the words *Beginning, Middle,* and *Ending* in their books as you read aloud the information.

ABCDEFGHIJKLMNOPQRSTUVWXYZ

150

Reviewing a Nonfiction Book

Books about real facts are called **nonfiction**.

Linda writes a book review.

In her review, Linda shares the most interesting facts from *I Want to Be an Astronaut* by Byron Barton.

Remember these points when you write a nonfiction book review.

The Beginning names the title and the author.

The Middle tells what the book is about and shares interesting facts.

The Ending tells why you like the book.

Materials

Familiar nonfiction book (TE p. 150)

I Want to Be an Astronaut by Byron Barton (TE p. 151)

Nonfiction books (TE p. 152)

Chart paper (TE pp. 154, 157)

First draft of class model book review (TE p. 155)

Revision of class model book review (TE p. 156)

Edited class model book review (TE p. 157)

Photos of people bowling, plastic bowling set (TE p. 158)

Copy Masters

Pronouns (TE p. 151)

Nonfiction Fact Sheet (TE pp. 153, 154)

Editing Checklist (TE p. 156)

Poetry Details Sheet (TE p. 158)

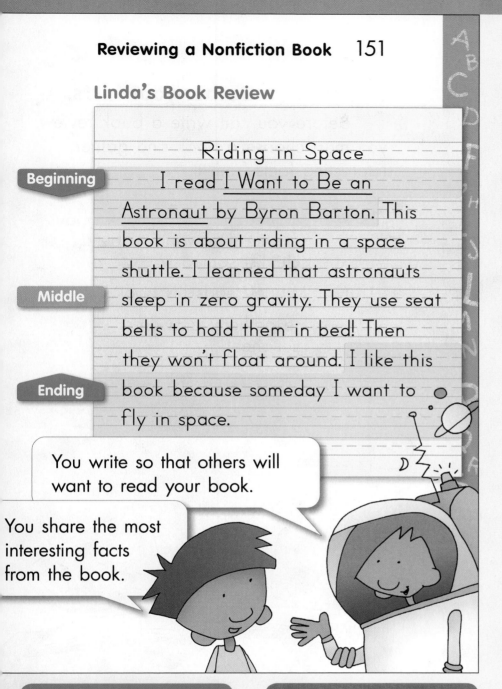

Reviewing a Nonfiction Book   151

Linda's Book Review

Riding in Space

Beginning

I read <u>I Want to Be an Astronaut</u> by Byron Barton. This book is about riding in a space shuttle. I learned that astronauts

Middle

sleep in zero gravity. They use seat belts to hold them in bed! Then they won't float around. I like this

Ending

book because someday I want to fly in space.

You write so that others will want to read your book.

You share the most interesting facts from the book.

Linda's Book Review

Have students point to the beginning, middle, and ending labels as you read aloud Linda's book review.

Reinforce the difference between **fiction and nonfiction books** *(see below)* by asking students how they know that this is a nonfiction book review. (It is about a book that tells facts. It is not about a make-believe story.) Does the book review make you want to read the book? Why?

Read aloud *I Want to Be an Astronaut* by Byron Barton. Then ask these questions: Would you have included different facts? Which ones?

Use the model review to explore pronouns and the nouns they refer to. (I-Linda; they-astronauts)

✱ For information and a worksheet on pronouns, see SE pages 224–227 and 293; and TE page 369.

Teaching Tip: Fiction and Nonfiction Books

Remind students that fiction books tell about people and things that are make-believe. Nonfiction books tell facts about a topic. To illustrate the difference, ask the following questions.

- What kind of book tells about a talking lizard on Mars? (fiction)
- What kind of book tells facts about Mars? (nonfiction)

English Language Learners

Define the following words before reading the model review:

- astronaut (a person who travels in outer space)
- space shuttle (vehicle that takes people to outer space)
- zero gravity (no force, which makes people stay in place on the ground)
- float (move around in the air)

Prewrite **Gather your facts.**

Work with students to choose a nonfiction book to review as a class. Begin by having students discuss topics they have been studying in science, math, health, music, and social studies classes. List the topics they mention on the board. Then schedule class library time and share the topics list with the librarian so she or he is prepared to help students locate books.

■ Have students look for books about the listed topics.

■ Have students also browse the nonfiction shelves for books on interesting topics that are not on the class list.

Help each student select two books from the library, one for the class to vote on for the class book review, and one on his or her own reading level to review independently.

Discuss the class nonfiction books. Have students vote to choose one book as the topic of a class book review. Read the book aloud.

Have students read the book they chose to use for their own nonfiction book review. Offer help as needed.

Technology Connections

Students can use the added features of the Net-text as they explore this stage of the writing process.

✴ *Write Source Online* **Net-text**

152

Prewrite ▶ Gather your facts.

Before you can write a book review, you must choose a book and gather interesting facts from it.

Choose   Miguel chooses a book about science. He wants to be a scientist someday.

Read   Miguel reads his book.

Gather   He gathers facts on a fact sheet.

Grammar Connection

Pronouns
■ **Proofreader's Guide** page 293
■ *GrammarSnap* Pronouns
■ **TE copy master** page 369

English Language Learners

Allow students to read several books with an English-proficient partner who can help them understand any difficult vocabulary or concepts. Include books that are about topics students are studying in school so that they can understand the vocabulary more easily. Then have students choose the book that they find most interesting and that they thoroughly understand.

Miguel's Fact Sheet

Reviewing a Nonfiction Book   153

Fact Sheet

1. I read <u>What Is a Scientist?</u>
by <u>Barbara Lehn.</u>

2. The book is about <u>what scientists do.</u>

3. I learned that <u>scientists ask a lot</u>
<u>of questions. They do exparaments.</u>
<u>Sometimes they keep trying again</u>
<u>and again.</u>

4. I like this book because <u>science is my</u>
<u>best subject.</u>

Prewrite ▶

Choose your book and gather facts.

1. **Choose** a nonfiction book to review.
2. **Read** your book.
3. **Gather** facts from your book on a fact sheet.

Miguel's Fact Sheet

Explain that after Miguel reads his book, he gathers details by writing interesting facts from the book on a fact sheet.

Read aloud each sentence starter and have volunteers read aloud how Miguel completes each one. Point out that Miguel writes three facts about scientists. Ask students where Miguel writes these facts (after the sentence starter *I learned that*).

On the board, write the four sentence starters for a Nonfiction Fact Sheet, as on SE page 153. Then work with students to complete the sentences, modeling how to gather facts for the nonfiction book chosen for the class book review. Make sure students understand that it is important to write facts accurately. Save the responses for writing the class first draft (TE page 154).

Provide photocopies of the reproducible Nonfiction Fact Sheet (TE page 370) for students to use as they gather details for their own nonfiction book review. Remind them to double-check each fact they list by revisiting the page in the book where it is mentioned. Remind students to write their facts after the sentence starter *I learned that*. Circulate and assist students who need help finding facts.

English Language Learners

If students have difficulty understanding nonfiction texts, have them complete the sentence starter *I learned that* by writing definitions of words they learned while reading. For example, "I learned that a scientist is a person who does experiments."

Help students understand any new vocabulary in their book by relating new words to words they already know, such as *scientist* to *science*. This often helps students learning English to have better overall comprehension of texts.

Write **Write your first draft.**

Remind students that in the writing step, writers get their ideas down on paper.

On chart paper, work with students to write a first draft for the class book review. Model how to use the fact sheet that the class completed (TE page 153). Demonstrate how to recheck facts and how to leave space for revising and editing changes. Save the class first draft for revising (TE page 155).

Have students use their own completed fact sheets to write their first drafts. As students write their draft, suggest that they look back at their fact sheets often so they remember what they want to include. Remind students to skip a line between each line of text to leave room for revising and editing.

 Writer's Craft

Writing freely: The writing step of the process should be done freely, without worrying too much about spelling and punctuation. Instead of focusing on getting everything just right, students should focus on communicating. They should write as if they were telling the details to a friend. The opportunity to revise and edit later frees up writers to create an easy first draft.

 Technology Connections

Students can use the added features of the Net-text as they explore this stage of the writing process.

※ *Write Source Online* **Net-text**

154

Write ▶ Write your first draft.

When you write, you put your ideas into sentences.

Write Miguel writes the sentences from his fact sheet to tell about his book.

> I read <u>What Is a Scientist?</u> by Barbara Lehn. The book is about what scientists do. I learned that scientists ask a lot of questions. They also do exparaments. Sometimes they keep trying again and again I like this book because science is my best subject.

Write ▶

Write your first draft.

Write the sentences from your fact sheet.

Reviewing a Nonfiction Book   155

Revise ▶ Change your writing.

When you revise, you change your writing to make it better.

Read   Miguel reads his first draft to a partner.

Add   He adds a detail.

> I read <u>What Is a Scientist?</u> by Barbara Lehn. The book is about what scientists do. I learned that scientists ask a lot of questions. They also do
> to solve problems
> exparaments. Sometimes they keep trying again and again I like this book because science is my best subject.

Revise

Change your writing to make it better.

1. **Read** your first draft to a partner.
2. **Add** a detail or two to your writing.

Revise Change your writing.

Have students compare Miguel's book review on this page with his copy on SE page 154. What is different? Explain that the blue markings show where he added a detail. Remind students that a caret shows where something is being added.

Have students work together to revise the class first draft (TE page 154). Ask a volunteer to mark the suggested changes by putting a caret in the proper place on the draft. Save the revised draft for editing (TE page 156).

Before students begin the revising step on their own first draft, talk about **helpful peer feedback** *(see below)*.

✳ During the revising and editing steps, work with students to improve their writing by asking the questions in the Teaching Tip on TE page 157.

Technology Connections

Have students use the Writing Network features of the Net-text to comment on each other's drafts.

Write Source Online ***Net-text***

**Teaching Tip:
Helpful Peer Feedback**

Create a positive atmosphere by offering ways to give constructive comments during revising sessions.

- Encourage students to begin by telling their partner what they like about their writing.
- Encourage students to ask questions politely: "Would you please tell me more about this idea?"

English Language Learners

Remind revision partners that they should not revise students' work for language issues unless they cannot understand what students are trying to express in their writing. Ask partners to focus only on adding details, and explain that grammar will be corrected during editing.

Edit Check your writing.

Remind students that the blue markings show the detail that Miguel added during the revising step.

Point out and discuss the editing corrections Miguel made in red.

■ A spelling mistake was corrected.
■ A period was added at the end of a sentence.

Provide photocopies of the reproducible Editing Checklist (TE page 358). Use one copy to work with students to edit the revised class book review (TE page 155). Edit for one convention at a time. Save the edited book review for publishing (TE page 157).

Have students use a copy of the checklist to edit their own book reviews. Encourage students to use the book they reviewed to check for correct spelling of words.

Explain that a writing partner can help catch mistakes the writer has missed. Have partners exchange their book reviews and check for conventions.

Technology Connections

Students can use the added features of the Net-text as they explore this stage of the writing process.

✴ *Write Source Online* **Net-text**

Grammar Connection

End Marks
■ *Proofreader's Guide* pages 270–271
■ *GrammarSnap* End Marks Overview
■ *SkillsBook* pages 23–26

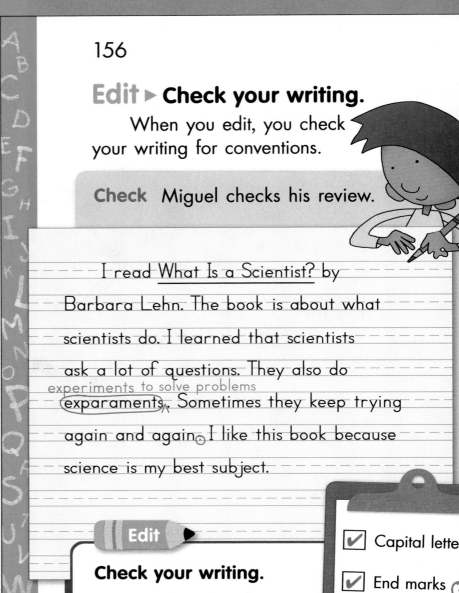

156

Edit ▶ Check your writing.

When you edit, you check your writing for conventions.

Check Miguel checks his review.

> I read <u>What Is a Scientist?</u> by Barbara Lehn. The book is about what scientists do. I learned that scientists ask a lot of questions. They also do ~~exparaments~~ experiments to solve problems. Sometimes they keep trying again and again. I like this book because science is my best subject.

Edit

Check your writing.

Use this checklist to edit your book review.

☑ Capital letters
☑ End marks ⊙
☑ Spelling ◯

English Language Learners

If students often repeat a noun describing the topic of their books (for example, *scientists*), teach a minilesson about how to use pronouns.

● Encourage students to vary their writing by using a combination of pronouns and nouns so that their paragraph is not repetitive.

● You may want to focus only on third-person pronouns (he, she, it, they), and teach students the correct verb agreement for each pronoun.

✴ For more information on pronouns, see SE pages 224–227 and page 293.

Reviewing a Nonfiction Book 157

Publish ▶ Share your writing.

When you publish your review, you make a neat final copy.

Scientists

I read <u>What Is a Scientist?</u> by Barbara Lehn. The book is about what scientists do. I learned that scientists ask a lot of questions. They do experiments to solve problems. Sometimes they keep trying again and again. I like this book because science is my best subject.

Publish

Share your writing.

Read your book review to the class.

Publish **Share your writing.**

Invite students to suggest ways Miguel could publish or share his neat final copy. Write their suggestions on the board. Also add some of your own suggestions.

- Make a colorful poster with the final copy.
- Put the final copy at the center of a mobile.
- Read the final copy to younger children.
- Include it in a class writing book.

Display the edited class book review (TE page 156) and write a neat final copy on another sheet of chart paper. Have students use the list on the board to vote on a way to publish the class book review.

Guide students to use their own edited first draft to make a neat final copy. Circulate and make sure students include their revisions and edits as they copy their sentences. Remind students to write their reviews in paragraph form.

Whenever students prepare a neat final copy, stress that proper spacing between letters, words, and sentences is important in making a document easy to read.

Hold a **writing conference** *(see below)* with each student to assess his or her final copy.

◈ Technology Connections

Remind students that they can use the Writing Network features of the Portfolio to share their work with peers.

✳ *Write Source Online* **Portfolio**

✳ *Write Source Online* **Net-text**

Teaching Tip: Writing Conference

The writing conference should be a relaxed, informal dialogue between you and the student. The goal is to give the student positive reinforcement for those traits that show some mastery and to point out traits of writing that need improvement.

Focus the conference on the key points for writing a nonfiction book review (SE page 150) and on conventions.

- **Beginning** Did you tell the title and author of the book?
- **Middle** Did you tell what the book is about and share interesting facts?
- **Ending** Did you tell why you like the book?
- **Conventions** Did you follow the writing rules for capital letters, end marks, and spelling?

Writing for Assessment

Explain that a writing prompt is a set of directions that tells a student what to write about. They need to read it carefully before they respond to it.

Discuss the sample prompt. Guide students to understand that it asks them to do three things.
- Tell what the poem is about.
- Choose their favorite part.
- Tell how their favorite part makes them feel.

Point out that before Shane begins to write, he fills out a details sheet to organize his writing.

If you wish to give students exposure to timed, test-taking situations, you can assign the prompt before or after you evaluate Shane's response on SE page 159.

Before students respond to the prompt, show photographs of people bowling. Talk about the goal of bowling (to get points by knocking over pins with a bowling ball) and the role the gutter plays. (If the ball rolls into the gutter, it can't knock over pins.)

Then distribute copies of the Poetry Details Sheet (TE page 371) for students to use to plan their response.

158

Writing for Assessment

Shane's teacher gives the class a responding-to-literature **prompt** to write about. Shane finishes a details sheet and writes his paragraph.

Writing Prompt

Tell what the poem "Gutter Ball" is about. Choose your favorite part and tell how it makes you feel.

Gutter Ball

I went bowling yesterday.
My ball went down the gutter.
I almost went along with it.
My feet slid, like on butter.

My fingers stuck inside the holes.
The big ball weighed a ton.
I wonder when I'm big someday,
If bowling will be fun.

—J.R. Taylor

Grammar Connection

Irregular Plurals
- **Proofreader's Guide** page 278
- *GrammarSnap* Irregular Plurals
- *SkillsBook* pages 45–46

English Language Learners

Define the following words before reading the poem:
- gutter (scooped-out edge of the bowling alley)
- bowling (an indoor sport played by rolling a ball to knock over pins at the end of an alley)
- slid (slipped)
- ton (very heavy)

For better comprehension of the poem, show pictures of bowling.

Writing for Assessment 159

Shane's Details Sheet

1. What is the poem about?

   bowling

2. What is your favorite line or part?

   feet sliding like on butter

3. Why do you like this line or part?

   It makes me think of sliding on
   my kitchen floor.

Shane's Paragraph

"Gutter Ball"

The poem is about bowling. I like the part about the feet sliding like on butter. It makes me think of sliding on my kitchen floor.

Using the rubric on SE pages 36–37 and a photocopy of the Conference Notes on TE page 327, work with students to evaluate Shane's paragraph. Two additional paragraphs are available in copy master form (see **Benchmark Papers** box below). Conference notes are provided for each benchmark paper.

If you have asked students to respond to the prompt, schedule a writing conference with individual students to help them do a self-assessment of their own writing. The rubric on TE pages 36–37 provides a framework for the discussion.

English Language Learners

If you ask students to write a response to the prompt, ensure that they understand the prompt and the poem by asking simple comprehension questions before they begin writing. Provide necessary vocabulary as they answer the questions, and have them write down those words to use in their writing.

Benchmark Papers

Bowling (good)
- TE pp. 328–329

Bowl (poor)
- TE pp. 330–331

Creative Writing Overview

Common Core Standards Focus.

Writing 3: Write narratives in which they recount two or more appropriately sequenced events, include some details regarding what happened, use temporal words to signal event order, and provide some sense of closure.

Language 2: Demonstrate command of the conventions of standard English capitalization, punctuation, and spelling when writing.

Writing Forms

- stories
- poems

Focus on the Traits

- **Ideas** Creating a main character with a problem
- **Organization** Writing a beginning that names the main character, the setting, and the problem; a middle that tells how the main character tries to solve the problem; and an ending that tells how the problem is solved
- **Conventions** Checking for errors in capitalization, punctuation, and spelling

 Literature Connections

- ***A Cupcake Party*** by David McPhail

 Technology Connections

 Write Source Online
www.hmheducation.com/writesource

- *Net-text*
- *Bookshelf*
- *GrammarSnap*
- *Portfolio*
- *Writing Network features*
- *File Cabinet*

 Interactive Whiteboard Lessons

Suggested Stories Unit (Three Weeks)

Day	Writing and Skills Instruction	Student Edition		Teacher's Edition	SkillsBook	Daily Language Workouts	Write Source Online
		Creative Writing Unit	Resource Units*	Grammar Copy Masters			
WEEK 1 1–5	**Writing Stories** (Model, Prewriting) ⓘ Literature Connections *A Cupcake Party*	161–166				56–57, 90	*Interactive Whiteboard Lessons, Net-text*
	Skills Activity: • Apostrophes		236–237, 274	372	31–32		*GrammarSnap*
WEEK 2 6–10	**Stories** *(cont.)* (Writing, Revising, Editing)	167–168				58–59, 91	*Net-text*
	Skills Activity: • Kinds of sentences		290				
WEEK 3 11–15	**Working with a Partner**	26–27				60–61, 92	
	Skills Activity: • Spelling		279–283				
	Stories *(cont.)* (Publishing)	169					*Portfolio, Net-text*
opt.	*Speaking to others*	202–203					

Suggested Poems Unit (Two Weeks)

Day	Writing and Skills Instruction	Student Edition		Teacher's Edition	SkillsBook	Daily Language Workouts	Write Source Online
		Creative Writing Unit	Resource Units*	Grammar Copy Masters			
WEEK 1 1	**Writing Poems** (Model, Prewriting)	170–173				62–63, 93	*Net-text*
	Skills Activity: • Adjectives		238–239 (+), 297	373, 374	83–84		*GrammarSnap*
2–3	(Writing)	174					*Net-text*
	Working with a Partner	26–27					
4–5	(Revising, Editing, Publishing)	175–176					*Net-text, Portfolio*
	Skills Activities: • Parts of speech		220–239 (+), 291–297		85–86		*GrammarSnap*
opt.	*Speaking with Others*	202–203					
WEEK 2 6–10	**Poems** *(cont.)* (ABC poem, rhyming poem)	177				64–65, 94	
	Working with a Partner	26–27					
	Skills Activities: • Spelling		279–283				
opt.	*Speaking to others*	202–203					

* These units are also located in the back of the *Teacher's Edition*. Resource Units include "Words," "A Writer's Resource," "Proofreader's Guide," and "Theme Words."
(+) This activity is located in a different section of the *Write Source Student Edition*. If students have already completed this activity, you may wish to review it at this time.

Teacher's Notes for Creative Writing

The overview for creative writing includes some specific teaching suggestions for the unit.

Writing Stories (pages 162–169)

Earlier in the book, the focus of telling stories was on the student writer's own experiences. Later, students learned how to write a review of a fiction book. In this chapter, they will have the chance to write their own fiction freely using their imaginations.

Children know the simplest elements of the stories they've heard—there are characters, and something happens. Stories have a beginning, a middle, and an ending. When children tell stories, they naturally include these elements. Storytelling can lead students to draw pictures and write down their stories in words. Young writers can also use their oral language and artistic abilities to plan their stories.

Writing Poems (pages 170–177)

Short poems offer a starting point for beginning readers and writers. Help students understand that poets use words like a painter uses paint to create a picture—a word picture. Writing poems encourages careful word choice. The simple list-poem style makes it possible for your students to try creating their own poems without worrying about rhyme or trying to understand rhythm.

Academic Vocabulary

Read aloud the academic terms, as well as the descriptions and questions. Model for students how to read one question and answer it. Have partners monitor their understanding and seek clarification of the terms by working through the meanings and questions together.

Minilessons

New Endings
Writing Stories

■ **READ** a familiar or favorite story to students. **RECALL** the sequence of events and **STRESS** the beginning, middle, and ending. Then **ASK** "what if" questions and have students **FORM** small groups to **MAKE UP** different endings. (This exercise helps make students aware of the beginning-middle-ending elements in stories.)

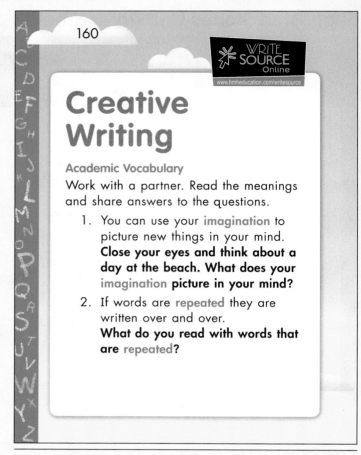

160

Creative Writing

Academic Vocabulary

Work with a partner. Read the meanings and share answers to the questions.

1. You can use your imagination to picture new things in your mind. **Close your eyes and think about a day at the beach. What does your imagination picture in your mind?**

2. If words are repeated they are written over and over. **What do you read with words that are repeated?**

The Storyteller
Writing Stories

■ **ASK** students to **NAME** their favorite kinds of stories (for example, stories about animals, outer space, cars, and so on). On a sheet of paper, have them **LIST** the characters who would be part of their favorite kind of story. **HAVE** them **SAVE** the list for future assignments.

Color Poems
Writing Poems

■ **NAME** a color. **HAVE** students **MAKE UP** short sentences about the color, beginning each sentence with the name of the color. Each line should **DEFINE** (Red is hot!), or **DESCRIBE** (Red is Sarah's mittens), and so on. **BEGIN** and **END** the group of lines with the color (Red) to create a list poem. (Students can write their own color poems at another time.)

ABC Poems
Writing Poems

■ **READ** a variety of alphabet books to your class. **HAVE** students **CHOOSE** a topic and **WRITE** a list poem. **ENCOURAGE** them to **DECORATE** the page.

161

In **creative writing,** you use words and your imagination to write stories and poems.

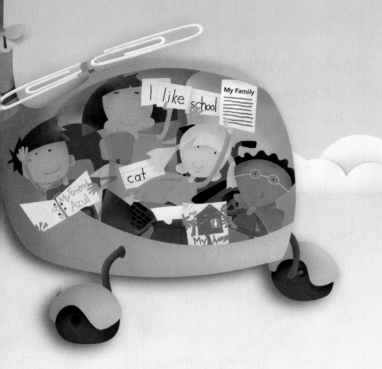

 Literature Connections: You can find an example of creative writing in *A Cupcake Party* by David McPhail.

Creative Writing

Invite students to share the titles of their favorite stories. Ask them where they think the authors got their ideas for their stories. Explain that make-believe (fiction) stories and poems come from the authors' imaginations.

Ask students to close their eyes and imagine a purple cat riding a yellow bicycle. Point out that the picture in their minds comes from their imaginations. Call on volunteers to use their imaginations to describe more about the purple cat (Is it wearing clothes? What do they look like?) and other make-believe things that it might do.

Explain that students can take imaginary ideas and turn them into stories and poems. Tell students that this kind of writing is called **creative writing** *(see below)*.

Literature Connections

In *A Cupcake Party* by David McPhail, the main character, a chipmunk named Fritz, misses his furry friends so he invites them to a big party.

Discuss elements of this story that capture the reader's imagination, such as the animal characters speaking and interacting like people. For additional creative models, see the Reading-Writing Connections beginning on page TE-36.

Family Connection Letters

As you begin this unit, send home the Creative Writing Family Connection letter, which describes what students will be learning.

- Letter in English (TE page 402)
- Letter in Spanish (TE page 411)

Teaching Tip: Creative Writing

Point out that creative writing includes fairy tales and stories about animals that act like people. Creative writing can also be a make-believe story that is about real life. The characters can be like people they know, and the things that happen in the story can be things that happen in everyday life.

Work with students to list examples of each kind of creative writing. On the board, make a T-chart with the headings *Could Happen* and *Couldn't Happen*. Display several familiar picture books for students to categorize.

Writing Stories

Objectives
- understand the parts of a story
- choose an animal main character with a problem
- plan, draft, revise, and edit a story

As you discuss the two points to remember, point out that every story has characters, a setting, a problem, and a plot (these are called story elements), and every story has a beginning, a middle, and an ending.

Based on the writing abilities of your students, determine if they are ready to work independently to write a story. If your students would benefit instead from a shared-writing experience, adapt the instruction and the TE notes in this unit for whole-class activities. Individual students who are ready to write on their own will have the added practice and the class writing model.

 Technology Connections

Use this unit's Interactive Whiteboard Lesson to introduce creative writing.

Interactive Whiteboard Lessons

162

Writing Stories

Reading or listening to stories is fun. With some planning, you can write your own made-up stories.

Kaylee writes her story.

Kaylee likes to make up stories of her own. She likes to write about animals.

This chapter will show you how to write a story, too. Remember these points when you write a story.

1. You include characters, a setting, a problem, and a plot.

2. You write a beginning, a middle, and an ending.

Materials

Multiple copies of picture books (TE p. 163)

Colored chalk (TE p. 164)

Drawing materials (TE p. 166)

Highlighters (TE p. 169)

Recording device (TE p. 176)

Copy Masters

Use an Apostrophe (TE p. 164)

Four-Square (TE p. 165)

Editing Checklist (TE p. 168)

Writing Stories   163

Look at the parts of a story.

Characters

The **characters** are the people or animals in the story.

Setting

The **setting** tells when and where the story happens.

Problem

The **problem** is the trouble the main characters face.

Plot

The **plot** is what happens when the characters try to solve the problem.

Look at the parts of a story.

Focus on a familiar fairy tale, such as "Goldilocks and the Three Bears," as you talk about each story element described in the list on the page.
- **Characters** Goldilocks, Papa Bear, Mama Bear, Baby Bear
- **Setting** the bear's house
- **Problem** Goldilocks wanders into the bear's house when they are gone.
- **Plot** Goldilocks eats Baby Bear's porridge, breaks Baby Bear's chair, and falls asleep in Baby Bear's bed before being scared away by the Bears.

Then focus attention on the illustration on the page and ask the following questions:
- What characters is Kaylee thinking about using in her story? (an owl, bees, a squirrel, a snake)
- What story setting is she thinking about for her story? (a forest)

Make sure students understand the relationship between the story problem and the plot by making these points:
- Every story must have a problem that the main character or characters try to solve.
- The plot tells the way the characters solve the problem.

Grammar Connection

Apostrophes
- **Proofreader's Guide** page 274
- **Words** pages 236–237
- *GrammarSnap* Contractions, Contractions Using *Not*
- *SkillsBook* pages 31–32
- **TE copy master** page 372

Read aloud Kaylee's speech balloon at the bottom of the page. Point out that the color coding shows the beginning (green), the middle (orange), and the ending (blue) of Kaylee's story.

Consider introducing apostrophes. Have students locate the two words that use an apostrophe *(Suzi's, couldn't)*. Write them on the board.

Point out the words *could* and *not* in the third sentence. Explain that *couldn't* (in the eighth sentence) is a word made from these two words. It is called a *contraction*, and the apostrophe takes the place of a missing letter *(o)*.

Point out that *Suzi's* is not a contraction. The apostrophe shows that something belongs to Suzi (a hiss).

✱ For information and a worksheet on contractions and apostrophes, see SE pages 236–237 and 274 and TE page 372.

164

Suzi's Missing Hiss

One morning, Suzi the snake woke up. Something was wrong. Suzi could not hiss. She twirled around. She stood on her head. She even tied herself in a knot. Nothing worked. Suzi still couldn't hiss. So she went to see Dr. Owl. He hooted, "You have a cold! Go to bed." Suzi slept and slept. She woke up and hissed a tiny, soft hiss. Then she smiled and hissed a big, loud hiss!

Do you see the **beginning**, the **middle**, and the **ending** of my story?

Struggling Learners

Some students may confuse apostrophes in Kaylee's story with quotation marks placed around dialogue. Tell students that some stories contain words that the story characters speak to each other. This is called *dialogue*. Point out that the exact words of each speaker are set off by a pair of marks called *quotation marks* that look like two apostrophes put together. Ask students to find an example of dialogue in Kaylee's story and have them read it to you as you write on the board. Have a volunteer circle the quotation marks with colored chalk. Then guide students in reading aloud Dr. Owl's words in the way that they think Dr. Owl might say them.

Writing Stories   165

Beginning

The **beginning** names the main character and the setting. It also tells about the problem.

Middle

The **middle** tells how the main character tries to solve the problem.

Ending

The **ending** tells how the problem is solved and how the main character feels.

Talk about it.

1. Who is the main character in this story?
2. What is the problem?
3. How is the problem solved?

As you explore the story elements that Kaylee included in the beginning, middle, and ending of her story, point out how each colored section on the page corresponds to each colored section of Kaylee's story on SE page 164.

■ Who is the main character? (Suzi the snake) When does the story take place? (in the morning) What is the problem? (Suzi can't hiss.) Which part of the story tells you this information? (the beginning)

■ How does Suzi try to solve the **story problem** *(see below)*? (She moves in different ways. Then she visits the doctor.) What advice does Dr. Owl give Suzi? (He tells her to go to bed.) Which part of the story tells you this information? (the middle)

■ How does Suzi feel when her problem is solved? (happy) Which part of the story tells you this information? (the ending)

Answers

1. Suzi the snake
2. She can't hiss.
3. She goes to bed and sleeps.

Prewrite Plan your story.

Explore the steps that Carlo follows to plan his story by asking the following questions:

■ What does Carlo do first? (makes a list of animals)

■ Why does Carlo circle the word *crab*? (to show that he chooses a crab as his main character)

■ How does Carlo make a story plan? (He writes words and draws pictures to show what will be in the beginning, middle, and ending of his story.)

After students write their list and circle their main character, distribute crayons and drawing paper. Show students how to fold their drawing paper into thirds. Have them label each part with the headings *Beginning, Middle,* and *Ending.* Then have them jot down key words and draw pictures under each label to plan their stories.

Technology Connections

Students can use the added features of the Net-text as they explore this stage of the writing process.

☀️*Write Source Online* **Net-text**

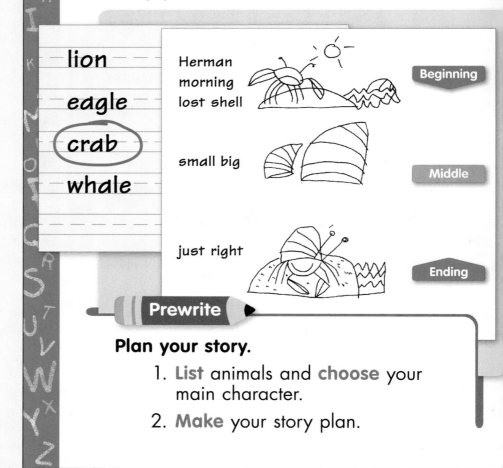

166

Prewrite ▶ Plan your story.

Carlo prewrites to plan his story. First, Carlo lists animals he likes. Then he chooses his main character and makes a story plan.

lion

eagle

crab

whale

Herman
morning
lost shell

Beginning

small big

Middle

just right

Ending

Prewrite

Plan your story.

1. **List** animals and **choose** your main character.

2. **Make** your story plan.

Struggling Learners

Students may benefit from detailed instructions, such as the following.

● List four animals you might write about.

● Choose one animal for your main character. Circle it.

● In the box labeled *Beginning*, write the name of your main character. Now write when or where the story takes place. Write several words telling about the story problem.

Draw a picture showing the character in the setting.

● Think of a few ways the character might solve the problem. In the box labeled *Middle*, write words that remind you of these solutions. Now draw some pictures that show the character trying to solve the problem.

● Decide how the character finally solves the problem. Remember, a

character can do it alone or with the help of another character. In the box labeled *Ending*, write about this solution. Draw a picture showing the solution and how the character feels about it.

Writing Stories   167

Write ▶ **Write your first draft.**

Carlo uses the ideas from his story plan to write sentences. This is his first draft.

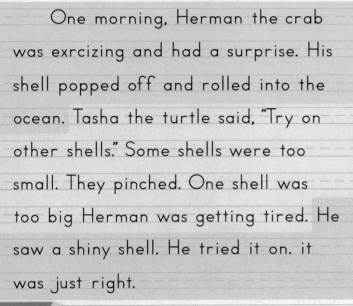

One morning, Herman the crab was exrcizing and had a surprise. His shell popped off and rolled into the ocean. Tasha the turtle said, "Try on other shells." Some shells were too small. They pinched. One shell was too big Herman was getting tired. He saw a shiny shell. He tried it on. it was just right.

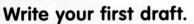

Write

Write your first draft.

1. **Use** the ideas in your story plan.
2. **Write** sentences to make a first draft.

Write **Write your first draft.**

Help students see how Carlo uses his story plan to write his first draft. Point out how the beginning of his draft (green section) relates to his story map by asking these questions:

- Who is the main character? (Herman the crab)
- When and where does the story take place? (morning at the beach)
- What is the story problem? (Herman's shell pops off.)

Ask similar questions to help students compare the middle and the ending of Carlo's first draft and story plan.

Ask students to find action words Carlo uses to describe Herman's problem. Is the story told in the **present tense** or the **past tense** *(see below)*? Past-tense verbs such as *was, popped, rolled,* and *pinched* are clues.

❋ For information about verbs, see SE pages 228–233 and 294–296.

Technology Connections

Students can use the added features of the Net-text as they explore this stage of the writing process.

❋ *Write Source Online **Net-text***

Teaching Tip: Present and Past Tense

Explain that present-tense verbs show that a story is happening now, while past-tense verbs show that a story already happened. Point out that *–ed* is often added to an action verb to form the past tense. Have students look through Carlo's first draft and find examples of past-tense action verbs formed in this way (*popped, rolled, pinched, tried*).

Explain that the past tense of the linking verbs *is* and *are* are completely different words, *was* and *were*. Help students find sentences in Carlo's draft where past-tense linking verbs are used.

❋ For more about linking verbs, see SE page 296.

Struggling Learners

To help students make the comparison between Carlo's first draft and his story plan, be sure they see how the color-coding of the draft corresponds to each part of the story plan. Help visual learners focus their attention by having them slide a piece of paper down the page as you discuss the story.

Revise and Edit Make changes.

Have students identify the revising changes (in blue) Carlo makes. Have them point to places where Carlo uses a caret to make additions to his writing (*Oops!*, *Then*, and a final sentence). Ask students why they think he added this last sentence. (to tell how Herman feels after the problem is solved)

Then discuss the editing changes Carlo makes (in red) to correct capital letters, end marks, and spelling.

Provide photocopies of the reproducible Editing Checklist (TE page 358) for students to use during the editing step. Remind them to check their writing carefully and to make corrections before checking off an item on the checklist.

Technology Connections

Have students use the Writing Network features of the Net-text to comment on each other's drafts.

 Write Source Online **Net-text**

168

Revise and Edit ▸ Make changes.

Carlo reads his story to a partner. He makes changes and checks for conventions.

> One morning, Herman the crab
> was ~~exrcizing~~ exercising and had a surprise. ᴬHis Oops!
> shell popped off and rolled into the
> ocean. Tasha the turtle said, "Try
> on other shells." Some shells were too
> small. They pinched. One shell was too
> big. Herman was getting tired.
> Then hᴬHe saw a shiny shell. He tried it on. It
> was just right.ᴬ Herman liked his new home.

Revise ▸ **and** **Edit** ▸

Make changes and check your story.

1. **Read** your story to a partner.

2. **Change** your story to make it better.

3. **Check** capital letters, end marks, and spelling.

Grammar Connection

Kinds of Sentences

- **Proofreader's Guide** page 290
- *GrammarSnap* Kinds of Sentences

Advanced Learners

Point out that dialogue can make a story more interesting to read. If students haven't included dialogue in their stories, encourage them to add some as they revise.

- Remind students that dialogue is the exact words that the characters say.
- Have students find the dialogue in Carlo's story. ("Try on other shells.") Ask them how they know

these are words that Tasha speaks. (They are enclosed in quotation marks.)

- Explain that the phrase *Tasha the turtle said* tells who is speaking (speaker tag).
- Remind students to choose words that make their characters sound real.

As students write, circulate to help them punctuate the dialogue they include.

Writing Stories   169

Publish ▶ Share your writing.

Carlo adds a title to his story and makes a neat final copy. He shares his story with another class.

"One morning . . ."

Herman's New Home

One morning, Herman the crab was exercising and had a surprise. Oops! His shell popped off and rolled into the ocean. Tasha the turtle said, "Try on other shells." Some shells were too small. They pinched. One shell was too big. Herman was getting tired. Then he saw a shiny shell. He tried it on. It was just right. Herman liked his new home.

Publish

Share your writing.

1. **Add** a title to your story.
2. **Make** a neat final copy of your story.
3. **Read** your story to others.

Publish Share your writing.

Have students identify the three things that Carlo does to publish his story. (He adds a title; he makes a neat copy; he reads it to another class.)

Have students compare the revised and edited first draft on SE page 168 with Carlo's final copy. Point out that when Carlo copies his sentences, he includes the additions (in blue) and corrections (in red) he made. Emphasize that it's important to **double-check corrections** (see below) on the final copy.

Have students come up with two or three possible titles and share them with their revising partners. Then choose the titles that will make others want to read the stories.

⌁ Technology Connections

Remind students that they can use the Writing Network features of the Portfolio to share their work with peers.

☀ *Write Source Online* **Portfolio**
☀ *Write Source Online* **Net-text**

Teaching Tip: Double-Check Corrections

To make sure that all additions and corrections are included in the final copies, have students use highlighters to highlight all revisions and edits on their first draft. After the final copies are made, have students compare these copies to their first drafts to make sure that the highlighted areas were copied correctly.

Struggling Learners

To help students create their final copies, guide them to use Carlo's final copy by asking the following questions:
- Reread Carlo's title. Did you add a title?
- Did you remember to indent the first line of your story like Carlo did?
- Is your story copied neatly like Carlo's so others can read it?

Advanced Learners

Encourage students to practice a fluent and dramatic reading of their story. Point out that as they read aloud, they should make their voices sound as if they are telling the story to interested friends. Remind them to let their voices rise and fall to sound like the story characters. Explain that they can also use their voice to show how characters feel or to show exciting parts of the stories.

Writing Poems

Objectives
- understand the content and form of a list poem
- choose a topic (a favorite thing) to write about
- plan, draft, revise, and edit a list poem

Explore the figurative meaning of *writing poems is like making pictures with words* by pointing out that most writers have pictures in their minds when they write poems. By choosing the right describing words, a writer can "paint this picture" in words for the reader.

Poetry is a kind of writing in which words are chosen for their sounds or the feelings they create. Many poems follow a certain **pattern** *(see below)*. Point out that the pattern of a list poem is a list of sentences that begin the same way, such as Kita's poem on SE page 171.

Read aloud selected poems from a children's anthology to show different kinds of poems and patterns.

170

Writing Poems

Writing poems is like making pictures with words. A list poem is a special type of poem. It follows a pattern.

Kita writes a list poem.

Kita writes a poem about her cat. She thinks of describing words and words that sound fun to use.

You can write poems, too. This chapter will show you how.

1. You think about a special topic.

2. You find just the right describing words to share your ideas.

Materials

Children's poetry anthology (TE pp. 170, 171)

Chart paper (TE p. 177)

Copy Masters

Adjectives 1 (TE p. 171)

Adjectives 2 (TE p. 171)

Cluster (TE p. 173)

Editing Checklist (TE p. 175)

Teaching Tip: Exploring Patterns

Explain that a pattern is any repeated arrangement of sounds or words. To demonstrate visual patterns, arrange several students in an alternating boy-girl pattern. To demonstrate auditory patterns, clap out a pattern and have students repeat the pattern. Point out that in writing, a pattern can be created by repeating words.

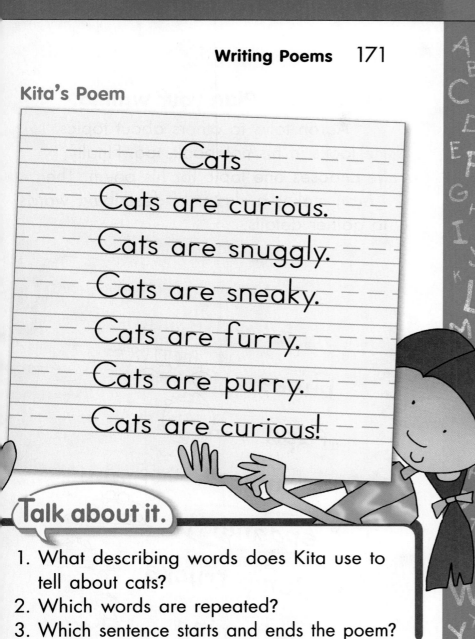

Kita's Poem

Cats

Cats are curious.

Cats are snuggly.

Cats are sneaky.

Cats are furry.

Cats are purry.

Cats are curious!

Talk about it.

1. What describing words does Kita use to tell about cats?
2. Which words are repeated?
3. Which sentence starts and ends the poem?

Kita's Poem

Explain that writers use describing words to make pictures with words. Remind students that describing words, also called **adjectives** *(see below)*, are words that tell details about naming words or *nouns*. Describing words tell which one, what kind, or how many. They also compare.

Call on a volunteer to read aloud the first sentence of Kita's poem. Then ask these questions:
■ What is the naming word in this sentence? (Cats)
■ What is the describing word that tells about cats? (curious)

✱ For information and worksheets on adjectives, see SE pages 238–239 and 297, and TE pages 373–374.

Read aloud Kita's poem several more times and invite students to chime in.

Talk about it.

Answers

1. curious, snuggly, sneaky, furry, purry
2. Cats are
3. Cats are curious.

Teaching Tip: Adjectives

Point out that describing words can be formed by adding *y* to the end of some words; for example, *snuggly* is formed by adding *y* to *snuggle*. Have students identify other adjectives in Kita's poem formed in this way. (sneak/sneaky; fur/furry; purr/purry) Explain that sometimes poets make up words, such as *purry,* to follow a rhyming pattern, or for feeling or sound.

English Language Learners

Define the following words from the poem:
● curious (wanting to learn)
● snuggly (likes to cuddle)
● sneaky (moves quietly)
● furry (lots of fur)
● purry (a made-up word; a cat noise)

Struggling Learners

To help students understand how words can make pictures, have them close their eyes as you read aloud Kita's poem. Ask volunteers to describe the pictures that come to mind. Read aloud other short, descriptive poems such as Carl Sandberg's "Fog" and "Cat Kisses" by Bobbi Katz. Have students describe the pictures they see.

Prewrite Plan your writing.

Explain that Aaron's list of favorite things is in his writer's notebook and that he made this list a while ago. Now, when he needs a topic idea, he looks in his writer's notebook.

Focus attention on the pictures that Aaron draws next to his topics and discuss their purpose. Point out that Aaron made quick sketches rather than drawing detailed pictures because he just wanted to remind himself of his ideas.

If students have a writer's notebook (Teaching Tip, TE page 66) to refer to, ask them to look and see if they have a list of favorite things. If so, they can choose a topic from their list. If not, have them copy the title *My Favorite Things* on their own paper and write a list of at least five topics they might use in a list poem. Encourage students to draw a quick sketch for each topic they list.

Technology Connections

Students can use the added features of the Net-text as they explore this stage of the writing process.

Write Source Online **Net-text**

172

Prewrite ▶ Plan your writing.

Aaron talks to others about topics. He looks in his notebook, too. Finally, he chooses one topic for his poem. Then Aaron makes a cluster of describing words to gather details.

Grammar Connection

Adjectives

- **Proofreader's Guide** page 297
- **Words** pages 238-239 (+)
- *GrammarSnap* Adjectives, Adjectives to Compare
- *SkillsBook* pages 83-84
- **TE copy masters** pages 373, 374

English Language Learners

Develop a word wall of describing words that students can use to complete their clusters. Separate words into sections according to the five senses. As the wall is developed, ask students to draw examples of what the words mean. If students are very limited in their English writing, help them choose appropriate describing words for the topics of their poems.

Struggling Learners

Some students may find it easier to draw a simple picture for each topic and then write a word that names it. To help them find topic ideas for their pictures, suggest that they think of a favorite food, person, animal, place, activity, season, hobby, toy, or game. Remind students to draw quick sketches, not detailed drawings, like Aaron drew in his writer's notebook.

Aaron's Cluster

Writing Poems 173

slurpy

slippry

spaghetti

red

sloppy

meaty

messy

Prewrite

Choose a topic and gather details.

1. **Choose** your topic.
2. **Gather** details about the topic in a cluster.

Aaron's Cluster

Remind students that a cluster is formed by writing the topic in the center and the details around it. Review the information in Aaron's cluster by asking these questions:

- What is Aaron's topic? (spaghetti)
- Which words tell how spaghetti looks? (*red, sloppy, messy*)
- Which words tell how spaghetti tastes, feels, and sounds? (*meaty, slippery, slurpy*)

Point out that Aaron used four of his five senses (see, taste, touch, hear) to choose describing words.

✳ For another example of a cluster, see SE page 249.

Distribute photocopies of the reproducible Cluster (TE page 337) for students to use to **create a cluster** *(see below)* of describing words about their topic.

Teaching Tip: Create a Cluster

Guide students to use their five senses as they create their clusters.

- Ask them to close their eyes and try to picture their topic. Have them list words that tell what they see in their minds (color, size, shape).
- Then have students list words that describe what they would hear (sounds).

- If appropriate, ask them to list words that describe what they would taste or smell.
- Finally, have students list words that describe what they would feel (texture).

Point out that if students cannot think of at least five or six describing words, they should choose a different topic.

English Language Learners

Although most of Aaron's describing words end in *y*, students do not have to use adjectives that end in *y*. Point out examples on the word wall of adjectives that do not end in *y* (English Language Learners, TE page 172). Work with students to think of others to add (*hot, cold, loud, soft, hard*). Encourage them to use describing words for more than just one of the senses.

Write Write your first draft.

Read aloud Aaron's poem several times and invite students to chime in as they become familiar with the words. Then have them identify the pattern Aaron uses in his list poem. (He begins each sentence with the word pattern *Spaghetti is* and ends with a describing word.) Have students compare Aaron's poem and his cluster (SE page 173). Guide them to see that Aaron did not use all the cluster words in his poem.

Have students look at their own cluster and choose the describing words they want to use to write their list of sentences. Emphasize that they don't have to use all of the words on their cluster. Point out that the first and last sentence should be the same.

Remind students that a first draft doesn't have to be perfect. They will have time to make corrections later.

Technology Connections

Students can use the added features of the Net-text as they explore this stage of the writing process.

Write Source Online **Net-text**

174

Write ▶ Write your first draft.

Aaron writes his first draft. He puts his ideas on paper. The pattern of his poem is a list of sentences that begin the same way.

I started each line with "Spaghetti is."

Spaghetti is messy.
Spaghetti is slippry.
spaghetti is sloppy.
Spaghetti is slurpy
Spaghetti is messy.

Write

Write your first draft.

1. **Begin** each sentence the same way.
2. **Add** a new describing word to each sentence.
3. **End** your poem with your first sentence.

Struggling Learners

To help students keep track of the describing words that they use in their poem, suggest that they put a check mark by each word in their cluster as they use it. If their cluster contains more than four words, suggest that they highlight the four describing words they like best and use just these words in their poem.

Writing Poems   175

Revise and Edit ▸ Make changes.

Aaron revises and edits his poem. First, he reads his poem. Then he makes a change and checks his poem for conventions.

> I moved one of my sentences.

Spaghetti is messy.

Spaghetti is ~~slippry~~ *slippery*.

~~s~~S spaghetti is sloppy.

Spaghetti is slurpy.

Spaghetti is messy.

Revise ▸ and Edit ▸

Make changes and check your poem.

1. **Change** the order of your sentences if you wish.

2. **Check** your writing for capital letters, end marks, and spelling.

Revise and Edit Make changes.

Talk with students about the one revision (in blue) that Aaron makes in his poem. (He moves one of his sentences.)

■ Explain that Aaron decided that his poem would sound better if he moved that sentence.

■ Point out that reading aloud a poem is a good way to tell if the order of the sentences sounds right. Read aloud Aaron's poem as he wrote it originally, and then with the revision. Ask students if they think moving the sentence makes the poem sound better.

As students revise their poem, have them read it aloud to a partner and ask if the sentence order sounds right.

Have students identify the editing changes (in red) Aaron made. (He capitalized the first word in one of his sentences. He added a period at the end of a sentence. He corrected his spelling error—*slippery.*)

Provide photocopies of the reproducible Editing checklist (TE page 358) for students to use when editing their list poem.

Technology Connections

Have students use the Writing Network features of the Net-text to comment on each other's drafts.

▸ᐧ= **Write Source Online** *Net-text*

English Language Learners

Teach a minilesson about the correct use of the verb *to be* in the third person. Reread the poem on SE page 171 and point out that the topic *cats* is plural, so it needs the plural verb *are*. Then have students look at Aaron's poem on SE page 175 and explain that the topic *spaghetti* is singular, and so it needs the singular verb *is*.

Ask students to edit their work for the correct form of the *to be* verb in each of their sentences.

✷ For information about subject-verb agreement, see SE pages 234–235.

Grammar Connection

Parts of Speech
■ **Proofreader's Guide** pages 291–297
■ **Words** pages 220–239
■ *GrammarSnap* Parts of Speech
■ *SkillsBook* pages 85–86

Publish **Share your writing.**

Read aloud Aaron's finished poem, using your voice to emphasize the pattern, alliteration, and rhythm. Repeat several times and invite students to chime in. Explain that when students read aloud their own poem, they should read it in a similar way.

Focus attention on the **Publish** steps at the bottom of the page. (See **Write a Title** below.) Call on volunteers to tell in their own words what they will do to publish their poem.

 Technology Connections

Remind students that they can use the Writing Network features of the Portfolio to share their work with peers.

☀ *Write Source Online* **Portfolio**

☀ *Write Source Online* **Net-text**

176

Publish ▶ Share your writing.

Aaron publishes his poem. He makes a neat final copy, adds a title, and shares it with others.

Does my spaghetti sound silly?

Silly Spaghetti

Spaghetti is messy.

Spaghetti is slurpy.

Spaghetti is slippery.

Spaghetti is sloppy.

Spaghetti is messy.

Publish

Share your writing.

1. **Make** a neat final copy of your poem.
2. **Add** a title and a drawing.
3. **Read** your poem to others.

Teaching Tip: Write a Title

Explain that a title should make others want to read the poem. An effective title . . .

- usually gives readers a clue about the topic and
- suggests how the writer feels about the topic. (For example, Aaron could have used the title "I Love Spaghetti.")

Encourage students to think of a couple of titles for their poem and then choose the one they like best. Remind them to capitalize the first word and all the other important words in their title.

English Language Learners

If possible, make a recording of students reading their published poems. Have them practice before recording. Compare this recording to other similar recordings you have them make throughout the school year as a record of development in English language oral skills.

Writing Poems 177

Try other kinds of poems.

ABC Poem

An **ABC poem** uses part of the alphabet to make a list poem.

Jump
Kick
Look at
Me
Now.

Rhyming Poem

My red shoes are really fast.
Ready, set, go! I zoom past!

A **rhyming poem** uses words that rhyme at the ends of the lines.

Try other kinds of poems.

Explain that an ABC poem is similar to a list poem because it follows a pattern; however, the pattern is based on letters of the alphabet instead of repeated words. Point out that each line in the poem begins with a capital letter even though it is not the first word of a sentence.

Write an ABC poem as a class or have students work in small groups to create a poem. Have each group choose a different section of the alphabet (five letters in a row) to create their poem.

Remind students that rhyming words are words that end with the same sound. Have students identify the two words that rhyme in the rhyming poem at the bottom of the page (*fast* and *past*).

If time allows, write a rhyming poem with the class. Begin by brainstorming pairs of rhyming words and write them on the board. Then have students write two-line rhyming poems. Guide students in reciting the poem several times and have them clap on the rhyming words.

English Language Learners

Students may have difficulty hearing all of the sounds in some consonant blends, such as *fast* and *past*. To keep students from becoming frustrated, brainstorm lists of rhyming words that have vowel and single-consonant endings (*red, bed, head*) for students to use when writing rhyming poems.

Struggling Learners

Provide practice identifying words that rhyme by saying word pairs (*coat/boat, ran/tan, cat/cape*). Have students raise their hand each time they hear a pair of rhyming words. Then brainstorm word families for phonograms such as *–et, –amp, –un, –an,* and *–op*. Write them on chart paper and display them as word walls.

Report Writing Overview

Common Core Standards Focus.

Writing 8: With guidance and support from adults, recall information from experiences or gather information from provided sources to answer a question.

Language 2: Demonstrate command of the conventions of standard English capitalization, punctuation, and spelling when writing.

Writing Form
- research report

Focus on the Traits
- **Ideas** Choosing a topic and finding interesting facts about it
- **Organization** Using a gathering grid to take notes
- **Conventions** Checking for errors in capitalization, punctuation, and spelling

 Literature Connections

- ***Amazing Animals*** by Gwendolyn Hooks

 Technology Connections

 Write Source Online
www.hmheducation.com/writesource

- *Net-text*
- *Bookshelf*
- *GrammarSnap*
- *Portfolio*
- *Writing Network features*
- *File Cabinet*

 Interactive Whiteboard Lessons

Suggested Report Writing Unit (Six Weeks)

Day	Writing and Skills Instruction	Student Edition — Report Writing Unit	Student Edition — Resource Units*	Teacher's Edition — Grammar Copy Masters	SkillsBook	Daily Language Workouts	Write Source Online
WEEK 1 1–5	**Finding Information** Literature Connections *Amazing Animals*	179–183				66–67, 95	
WEEK 2 6–10	**Finding Information** (cont.)	184–187				68–69, 96	
	Learning to Interview	206–207					
WEEK 3 11–15	**Writing a Friendly Letter**	102	273	336		70–71, 97	
	Skills Activities: • Capitalization		273		39–40, 91		*GrammarSnap*
	• Punctuation		270–274		33–34		*GrammarSnap*
WEEK 4 16–20	**Writing a Report** (Model, Prewriting)	188–191 (306–307)			89, 98	72–75, 98	*Interactive Whiteboard Lessons, Net-text*
	Skills Activity: • Verbs		294–296				*GrammarSnap*
WEEK 5 21–25	**Report** (cont.) (Writing)	192–195			99	76–77, 99	*Net-text*
	Skills Activities: • Sentence review		288		21–22		*GrammarSnap*
	• Capital-letter review		275–277		41–42		*GrammarSnap*
	Working with a Partner	26–27					
WEEK 6 26–30	**Report** (cont.) (Revising, Editing, Publishing)	196–199				78–79, 100	*Net-text, Portfolio*
	Skills Activities: • Plurals		223 (+), 278, 292	376, 377	47–48		*GrammarSnap*
	• Subject-verb agreement		289	394			*GrammarSnap*
	Working with a Partner	26–27					
	Speaking to Others	202–203					

* These units are also located in the back of the *Teacher's Edition*. Resource Units include "Words," "A Writer's Resource," "Proofreader's Guide," and "Theme Words."
(+) This activity is located in a different section of the *Write Source Student Edition*. If students have already completed this activity, you may wish to review it at this time.

Teacher's Notes for Report Writing

The overview for report writing includes some specific teaching suggestions for the unit.

Finding Information (pages 180–187)

The point of writing a report is doing research and learning something new. Finding the information they need may seem overwhelming to first-grade students. This is a time for them to learn about the library and how to use different kinds of books and reference options (for example, the dictionary, an encyclopedia, computer catalog, and so on). Parts of a book are explained as well.

Writing a Report (pages 188–199)

Children are eager to learn and talk about things that interest them. They often have many interests and often know a lot about particular subjects. "Writing a Report" will help them write about these topics as well. Once students have gathered the information they need, they are ready to begin writing their reports. Again, the steps in the writing process are brought into play. Each step is presented in detail to help the students understand what they are to do.

Academic Vocabulary

Read aloud the academic terms, as well as the descriptions and questions. Model for students how to read one question and answer it. Have partners monitor their understanding and seek clarification of the terms by working through the meanings and questions together.

Minilessons

Map It! — Finding Information

- **HAVE** students **DRAW** a map of the library that shows where fiction, nonfiction, dictionaries, and so on are located.

Fact-Finding Mission — Finding Information

- **CHOOSE** a subject and **GUIDE** the class discussion about it. **LIST** the ideas and facts that are shared on the board. Then **FIND** a book or magazine that contains more information on the topic. **SHOW** students how to find the information. **ADD** some "new" facts to your list. (Do this same lesson on another day with a different topic and a different type of source.)

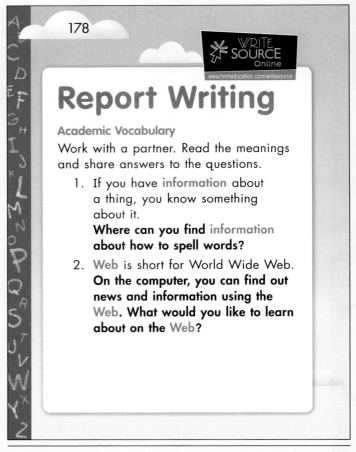

Report Writing

Academic Vocabulary

Work with a partner. Read the meanings and share answers to the questions.

1. If you have information about a thing, you know something about it.
   Where can you find information about how to spell words?

2. Web is short for World Wide Web.
   On the computer, you can find out news and information using the Web. What would you like to learn about on the Web?

Reports — Writing a Report

- **EQUIP** students with notebooks and **TEACH** them how to take notes before they go on a field trip. For example, **ASK** students to **LOOK** out the window and answer these questions: What is the weather like? What is happening outside? Then, on the next field trip, **HAVE** students **TAKE** notes. (These notes can be used to write individual or small-group reports.)

Writing a Report — Writing a Report

- **CHOOSE** a topic (science, health, or social studies related) that your class has recently studied together. **CLUSTER** the important facts about your topic. On another day, **USE** the cluster to **WRITE** sentences (a first draft) about the chosen topic. (Do this on the board so it can be easily revised.)

From Facts to Sentences — Writing a Report

- **WRITE** some short factual phrases on the board. **ASK** students to **MAKE UP** sentences using the facts. **PUT** the sentences next to the phrases. Example:

Fact	Sentence
Rhinoceros—tiny eyes	The rhinoceros has tiny eyes.

179

When you write a report, you share factual information. You share what you have learned about a topic.

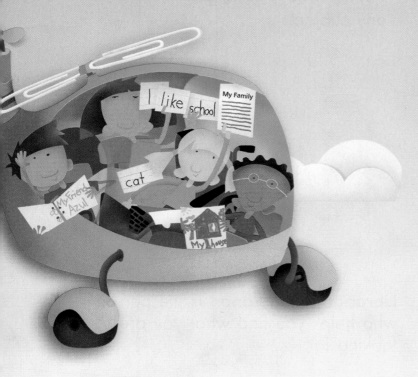

 Literature Connections: Like a report, *Amazing Animals* by Gwendolyn Hooks includes interesting information.

Family Connection Letters

As you begin this unit, send home the Report Writing Family Connection letter, which describes what students will be learning.

○ Letter in English (TE page 403)

○ Letter in Spanish (TE page 412)

Report Writing

Invite students to talk about animals they think are interesting and would like to learn more about. Write a list on the board as students share their responses.

■ Call on volunteers to tell where they could look for information about the animal topics. Encourage students to think of places as well as types of materials (library, Internet, museums, books, magazines). Point out that looking for information about a topic is like being a good detective. Often, students must look in more than one place to find the information they want.

■ Explain that after students find the information, a good way to share what they learn is to write a **report** about it. Have students tell how a report is different from a story they make up. (A report tells information and facts that are true; a made-up story tells something imaginary or not completely true.)

As you introduce report writing, help students understand the specific purpose for writing—to inform or explain. Then discuss the concept of writing to an audience. Point out that whenever students write, they are writing for someone: themselves, teachers, friends, family members, and so on.

 Literature Connections

In the nonfiction text *Amazing Animals*, author Gwendolyn Hooks shares interesting facts about different kinds of animals. Hooks explains how certain animals have special features that help keep them healthy and safe.

Discuss how the author presents intriguing details and asks questions to encourage readers to think about each animal's abilities. For a list of reference books to use when writing a report, see the Reading-Writing Connections beginning on page TE-36.

Finding Information

Invite students to share their experiences using the school or public library by asking the following questions:

- What kinds of books do you like to take out?
- Who helps you find what you are looking for?
- Why is the library a great place to find information?

Review the meanings of the terms *fiction* and *nonfiction*. Remind students that a fiction book is a story that has been made up, and a nonfiction book tells facts about real people, places, and things.

180

Finding Information

A library is a great place to find information. You can read magazines, books, Web pages, and more about any subject.

Books Some books are small, and some books are big. Some are fiction, and some are nonfiction. Some books are all pictures.

Librarian The librarian is the person who helps you find what you are looking for.

Materials

Chart paper (TE pp. 186)

Nonfiction books about animals, including some that have a table of contents and an index (TE pp. 184, 185)

Beginner's dictionary (TE pp. 186, 187)

Alphabet strips (TE p. 186)

Translation dictionary (TE p. 187)

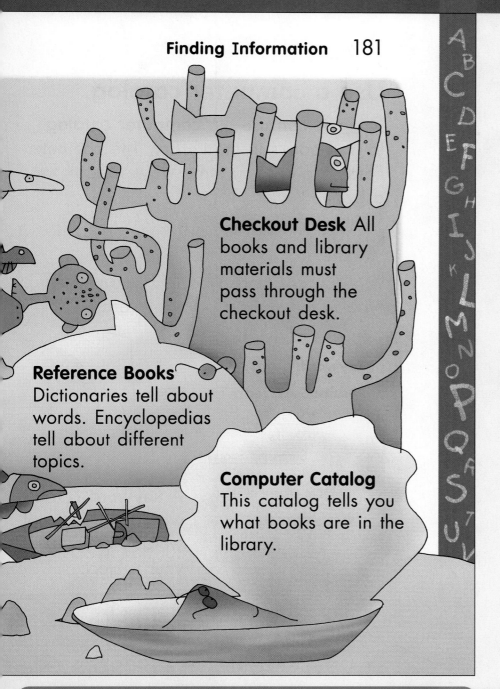

Finding Information 181

Checkout Desk All books and library materials must pass through the checkout desk.

Reference Books Dictionaries tell about words. Encyclopedias tell about different topics.

Computer Catalog This catalog tells you what books are in the library.

Talk about how a library is organized and explain the following:

■ The checkout desk is where students bring the books and other materials they want to borrow so the librarian can check them out. It is also where they can get a library card.

■ Most reference books can be used only in the library and cannot be checked out.

■ A computer catalog lists all the books and materials in a library. Some libraries also have a set of drawers called a *card catalog*. Cards in the drawers tell what materials are in the library and where to find them.

Talk with students about other resources the school and public libraries may offer—books on tape, puzzles, games, magazines, music CD's, and DVD's of movies.

In the next day or two, schedule **a visit to the school or public library** *(see below)* for students to become more familiar with its resources.

Teaching Tip: A Visit to the School or Public Library

Talk to your school librarian or the librarian at your public library to arrange a tour for your class. Before the visit, work with students to prepare questions to ask the librarian:

● What kinds of magazines do you have in the library?

● What kinds of reference books do you have in the library besides dictionaries and encyclopedias?

● How long can I keep a book I have checked out?

● What do I do if I want to keep a book longer?

Encourage students to ask the librarian some of these questions.

English Language Learners

Ask your school librarian to allow you to post large labels in the library that name the different sections and give a brief description of each so that students can learn the words. Use the exact definitions given in the student book for Checkout Desk, Reference Books, and Computer Catalog so that students are familiar with each concept.

Use a computer catalog.

If your school or public library's computer catalog is available online, demonstrate in your classroom how to **find a book using the subject or keyword** *(see below)*. Explain that you use a subject word when you don't know any titles or authors of books on a topic.

If you don't have a computer in your classroom, schedule time in your school library to use the computer catalog with your class. Give students the opportunity to work with partners or in small groups to practice looking up books using subjects or keywords.

A B C D E F G H I J K L M N O P Q R S T U V W X Y Z

182

Use a computer catalog.

You can use the **computer catalog** to find books in the library. The computer catalog gives you three ways to look for a book.

Search for a subject.

You can find a book if you type in the subject or a keyword.

Keyword: Sharks

Results: *Sharks* search found 10 titles.

    Shark Facts
    Sharks
    Surprising Sharks

more titles >>>

A **keyword** is a word or a group of words that tell about your subject.

Teaching Tip: Using the Subject or Keyword to Find a Book

Focus attention on the sample search results. Point out that the keyword *Sharks* is also the subject. Explain that sometimes the keyword is the same word as the subject. Other times, the keyword can be a phrase that contains the subject *(hammerhead sharks)*. The keyword can also be a word or phrase that doesn't use the subject word *(ocean life)*.

English Language Learners

If your school library contains books in students' first language, allow them to practice looking up books using keywords in their first language.

If the library is English only, allow students to think of keywords in their first language, use a Web-based (or online) language translator to look up the keywords in English, and then use the English keywords to look up books.

Finding Information 183

Search for a title.

You can find a book if you type in its title.

Title: Shark Facts

Author: Shaw, Marie.

Publisher: Daniels Press, 2009

Pages: 32

Notes: This book tells about kinds of sharks, where sharks live, and what sharks eat.

Subjects: sharks, ocean life

Search for an author.

You can find a book if you type in the name of the author.

Author: Shaw, Marie

Results: 3

Beautiful Butterflies
Shark Facts
Tigers and Other Big Cats

Demonstrate how to find a book using the title or the author and make the following points:

- Students should use the title when they know the book they want and need to find out where it is located in the library. When they type in the title of a book, they should leave out the word *the* if it is the first word of the title. The computer catalog gives a great deal of information about the title. It tells the name of the author, the publisher, the year the book was published, and the number of pages in the book. It also tells what the book is about and gives related subjects to look up if a student wants to find more information about the topic.

- Students should use the author's name if they know it but can't remember the title, or if they liked a book they read and want to read more books by the same author. When they type in the name of an author, they should type the author's last name first, followed by a comma and the author's first name. The computer catalog tells which books written by that author are in the library's collection, and it lists those titles in alphabetical order.

Struggling Learners

If students are feeling confused by the different ways to search for a book, provide practice with concrete examples.

- Have students look up the subject *honeybee*. Point out how many different books are listed. Explain that when students search by subject, the catalog will list all the library's materials on that subject.

- Then have students look up the title *Are You a Bee?* (by Judy Allen). Read the listing and point out the subjects listed, including *honeybee*. Help students look up *honeybee* again and find *Are You a Bee?*

- Finally, have students look up the author Judy Allen and see all the books she's written. Can they find *Are You a Bee?*

Learn the parts of a book.

Explain that the cover of a book helps you know what the book is about.

Display several nonfiction books about animals. Then have volunteers point to each of the following items and help them track and read each one:
■ the book title
■ the author's name
■ the illustrator's name

If there is a Caldecott medal, explain that it is an award given for excellence in illustration in children's books each year. A gold medal is given to the best book, and silver medals are given to honor (runner-up) books.

If the front cover is illustrated, ask students if the illustration or photograph helps them know what the book is about. Does it make them want to read the book? Why?

Repeat with as many books as necessary until you feel students can easily identify the front cover and its parts. Keep these books on display for demonstrating how to use a **table of contents and index** *(see below)*.

184

Learn the parts of a book.

Books have special parts. The cover identifies the book. Other parts help the reader find information in the book.

Look at the cover.

The **title** names the book.

Shark Facts

by: Marie Shaw   pictures by: Erin Mico

The **author** wrote the book.

The **illustrator** made the pictures.

Teaching Tip: Table of Contents and Index

The following books include a table of contents and an index. All are part of *A True Book* series published by Children's Press.

Alligators and Crocodiles by Trudi Strain Trueit
Ants by Ann O. Squire
Elephants by Melissa Stewart
Snakes by Trudi Strain Trueit
Turtles by Trudi Strain Trueit
Zebras by Melissa Stewart

English Language Learners

If books in a student's first language are read in the opposite direction from how English books are read, ask students to bring from home a book written in their first language.

Compare the way the book is opened and read, and the parts of the cover so that students can adapt to reading a book written in English.

Look inside the book.

Table of Contents

The page numbers and chapters are listed in the front of the book.

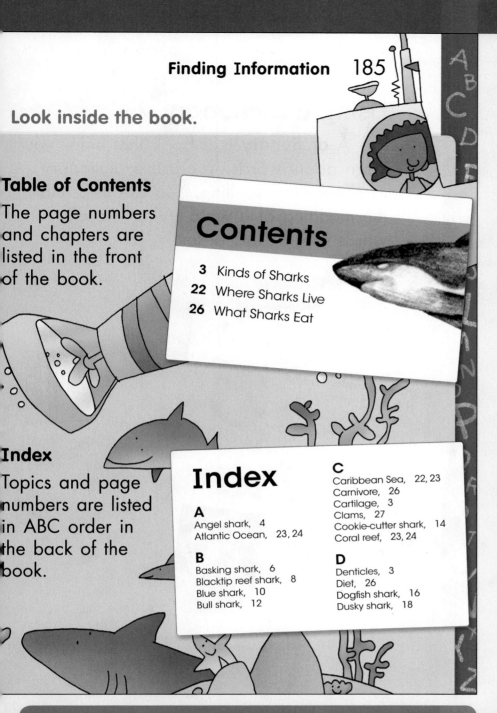

Contents

3 Kinds of Sharks

22 Where Sharks Live

26 What Sharks Eat

Index

Topics and page numbers are listed in ABC order in the back of the book.

Index

A
Angel shark, 4
Atlantic Ocean, 23, 24

B
Basking shark, 6
Blacktip reef shark, 8
Blue shark, 10
Bull shark, 12

C
Caribbean Sea, 22, 23
Carnivore, 26
Cartilage, 3
Clams, 27
Cookie-cutter shark, 14
Coral reef, 23, 24

D
Denticles, 3
Diet, 26
Dogfish shark, 16
Dusky shark, 18

Use one of the nonfiction books you have displayed (TE page 184) and point to the following as you talk about the table of contents:

- The *title of a chapter* tells what that part of the book is about.
- The *page numbers* tell where each chapter begins.

Explain that *contents* means all the information in the book, and that by looking at a table of contents, you can quickly tell if the book has the information you need.

Point to the following as you talk about the *index:*

- The *topics* listed in alphabetical order tell the specific information you can find in the book.
- The *page numbers* tell where each topic can be found.

Focus attention on the sample index at the bottom of the page. Have students tell on what page they could find information about angel sharks. Point out that in the sample table of contents, the first chapter is about kinds of sharks. Explain that you could look there for information about angel sharks, but you'd have to skim the whole chapter. By looking in the index, you can find the exact page number.

Have partners choose a book from your display and explore using the table of contents and the index.

Struggling Learners

To review the parts of a book, have students finish your sentences as you point to each part of a nonfiction book:

- This is the *(cover)*, the book's *(title)*, the name of the *(author)*, and the name of the *(illustrator)*.
- This is the *(table of contents)*, the *(name of a chapter)*, and the *(page where the chapter starts)*.
- This is the *(index)*, a *(topic)*, and the *(page where the topic can be found)*.

Advanced Learners

Point out the title and copyright pages to students and explain the following:

- The title page is usually the first page in the book. It gives the title of the book, the author's and illustrator's names, and the name of the publisher.
- The copyright page tells the year the book was published. This lets you know whether the information is up-to-date.

Using a Dictionary

Make alphabet charts for students to use as a guide when looking up words in a dictionary. On one piece of chart paper, write the heading *Front* and then all of the alphabet letters from *a* to *f*. On another piece of chart paper, write the heading *Middle* and all the letters from *g* to *p*. On a third piece, write the heading *Back* and all the letters from *q* to *z*. Post these on a wall.

Tell students to think of a dictionary as having three parts—a front, a middle, and a back. Point to the alphabet charts as you explain that the front of the dictionary contains words that begin with the letters *a-f*, the middle contains words that begin with *g-p*, and the back contains words that begin with *q-z*.

Point out the guide words at the top of a dictionary page and explain that they help you find the page your word is on. The first guide word shows the word that comes first on the page. The second guide word shows the word that comes last on the page. If the word students are looking for comes alphabetically in between the two guide words, then it is on this page.

Model **how to look up a word in the dictionary** *(see below)*. Have students follow your model to look up other words.

186

Using a Dictionary

A **dictionary** is a book that helps you learn about words. You use a dictionary to check your spelling. You use it to find the meaning of a word. All of the entry words are in ABC order.

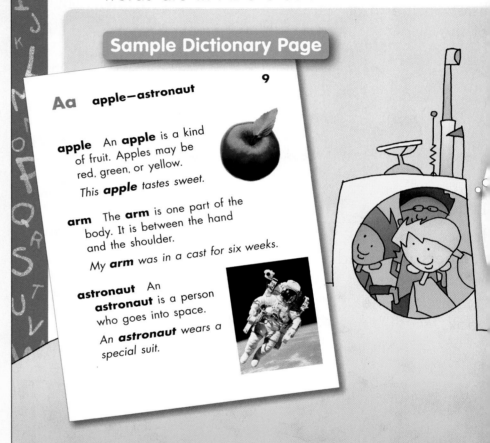

Sample Dictionary Page

9

Aa   apple—astronaut

apple   An **apple** is a kind of fruit. Apples may be red, green, or yellow.
*This **apple** tastes sweet.*

arm   The **arm** is one part of the body. It is between the hand and the shoulder.
*My **arm** was in a cast for six weeks.*

astronaut   An **astronaut** is a person who goes into space.
*An **astronaut** wears a special suit.*

Teaching Tip: How to Look Up a Word in the Dictionary

Model how to look up the word *turtle* in a beginner's dictionary:
- Refer to alphabet wall charts and ask where words that begin with *t* can be found in the dictionary *(back)*.
- Use the guide words to find the page on which the word *turtle* appears.
- Look down the page to find the entry word *turtle*.

English Language Learners

If students are not in command of the English alphabet, teach them the alphabet song (the letters sung to the tune of *Twinkle, Twinkle, Little Star*) so that they can practice on their own. Hang a large alphabet strip with picture support in a visible place in the classroom and provide students with desk-sized alphabet strips as well.

Finding Information   187

> This is an **entry word**.

> The **meaning** of the word follows the entry word.

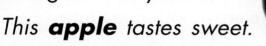

apple   An **apple** is a kind of fruit. Apples may be red, green, or yellow.

*This **apple** tastes sweet.*

> A **sentence** helps you understand the word.

> A **picture** shows you the meaning.

Talk about it.

Name two other entry words shown on the sample dictionary page.

Discuss the different ways a dictionary entry helps students understand a word: It shows the spelling, gives the meaning, uses the word in a sentence, and sometimes provides a picture.

Encourage students to use a dictionary to look up unfamiliar words they read or hear. Explain that the more they **practice using a dictionary** *(see below)*, the better they will become at it.

Whenever students read independently, have them write down any unfamiliar words in their writer's notebook. Then they can look up the words in the dictionary and write down their meanings. At the end of the year, students will see how many new words they have learned.

Talk about it.

Answers
The two other entry words are *arm* and *astronaut*.

Teaching Tip: Practice Using a Dictionary

Keep a beginner's dictionary in the writing center and provide a short list of words for students to look up.
- The list should relate to what students are studying.

- Change the list every few days so that students practice looking up new words.
- Have students write in their writer's notebook the meaning of each word they look up and their own sentence for the word.

English Language Learners

As students learn about English dictionaries, teach them to use a translation dictionary. When they are trying to think of an English word, they can look up the word in their first language. They may find several translations. Tell students to ask for help deciding the correct word for the context.

Writing a Report

Objectives

- understand the content and form of a report
- choose a topic (an animal) to write about
- plan, draft, revise, and edit a report

Begin a discussion of a topic students are studying in science class. Ask volunteers to share facts and details as you list them on the board. Explain that a good way to share facts and details about a topic is to write a **report**.

Focus attention on the illustration at the bottom of the page and ask if anyone knows what kind of animal is pictured (a leafy sea dragon). Point out that Jake chose an unusual animal for his report. Ask students why they think he might have chosen that animal. Guide them to conclude that Jake was probably curious about the animal and wanted to learn more about it. Explain to students that writing a report is a good way to find answers to their questions about an interesting topic.

 Technology Connections

Use this unit's Interactive Whiteboard Lesson to introduce report writing.

Interactive Whiteboard Lessons

188

Writing a Report

In a report, you share facts and information about a topic.

Jake writes a report.

Jake writes a report about an unusual animal that he saw at an aquarium. You can write a report, too. This chapter will show you how.

Materials

Pictures (TE p. 189)

Chart paper (TE p. 190)

Class list of topics, nonfiction books about animals (TE p. 191)

Beginner's dictionary, drawing materials (TE p. 199)

Copy Masters

Gathering Grid (TE p. 191)

Editing Checklist (TE p. 199)

Plurals 1 (TE p. 199)

Plurals 2 (TE p. 199)

Jake's Report

Leafy Sea Dragon

The leafy sea dragon is unusual. It looks like a sea horse with green and yellow leaves.

It lives in the ocean by Australia. It hides in kelp forests. Kelp is giant seaweed.

The sea dragon eats tiny shrimp and small fish. It uses its mouth like a straw.

The father sea dragon takes care of the babies. He keeps them in a pouch on his body.

English Language Learners

Define the following words before reading Jake's report (Use picture and prop support where possible.):

- unusual (strange, not common)
- seaweed (a plant that grows in the ocean)
- shrimp (small animals that live in the ocean)
- straw (a plastic tube used to drink things)
- pouch (a pocket)

Jake's Report

Point out that the report shown here is Jake's final copy. Explain that students will see what Jake did for each step to develop this report.

Then point out the following features in the report:
- It has a title.
- The first sentence of the report introduces the topic (leafy sea dragon).
- It has four paragraphs. Each paragraph tells something about a leafy sea dragon: what it looks like, where it lives, what it eats, and how the babies are cared for.
- Each paragraph is indented, which means a space was left at the beginning of the first line of the paragraph.
- Jake included many interesting facts in his report.

Invite volunteers to tell some of the interesting facts they learned from Jake's report. Emphasize that a report shares facts and details about a topic.

Prewrite Plan your report.

Before reading aloud the page, have students share what they know about the **Prewrite** step in the writing process. Then call attention to the three steps Jake follows to plan his writing:

- **Choose** Explain that Jake's thought balloon shows the class list of topics from which he chooses his topic—the leafy sea dragon.
- **Read** Point out that students can read books, magazines, encyclopedias, and materials from **online sources** *(see below)* to gather facts about their topics.
- **Answer** Guide students to understand that it is helpful to ask questions about a topic and then find the answers.

Invite students to talk about animals they would like to learn more about and make a list on chart paper. As students think about which animals to choose for their topics, suggest that the class choose a variety of animals so that they can learn from one another's reports. Post the list on the wall.

⚙ Technology Connections

Students can use the added features of the Net-text as they explore this stage of the writing process.

➤ *Write Source Online* **Net-text**

Teaching Tip: Online Sources

The following Web sites contain photographs and information about animals. Help students use them to gather details for their reports.

http://animaland.org

http://www.national geographic.com/kids

http://www.nationalzoo.si.edu

http://yahooligans.yahoo.com/ content/ animals/

190

Prewrite ▶ Plan your report.

Before you write a report, you choose a topic and gather details about it. The facts you find are called **details**.

Choose	From the class list, Jake chooses the leafy sea dragon for his topic.
Read	He reads about it.
Answer	He answers the questions on his gathering grid.

electric eel

aardvark

leafy sea dragon

fruit bat

koala

English Language Learners

Students may become frustrated if research materials are too advanced.

- Before having the class talk about animals for the topics list, preview available materials to find topics that have sufficient material at the students' comprehension level.

- Include those topics on the class list and guide students to choose only from those topics.

Writing a Report   191

Jake's Gathering Grid

Gathering Grid

Topic: __leafy sea dragon__

1. What does the animal look like?

sea horse
green and yellow
leaves

2. Where does it live?

kelp forests
ocean
Australia

3. What does it eat?

tiny shrimp
small fish
uses mouth like
a straw

4. What are other interesting facts?

father takes care of
the babys
pouch on his body

Prewrite

Choose your topic and gather details.

1. **Choose** an animal.
2. **Read** about it.
3. **Answer** questions on a gathering grid.

Struggling Learners

Hold individual conferences with students to help them read the information they find about their topics. In some cases, you will have to read aloud sentences and paragraphs to them so they can orally answer each grid question. Help students write the words and phrases that answer the questions on their gathering grids.

Grammar Connection

Verbs

- **Proofreader's Guide** pages 294–296
- *GrammarSnap* Action Verbs, Linking Verbs

Jake's Gathering Grid

Point out the four questions on Jake's gathering grid. Explain to students that these are good questions to ask when writing a report about an animal.

Point out that Jake used words and phrases, not complete sentences, to answer the questions on his gathering grid. The most important thing is to write down the facts and information.

Provide photocopies of the reproducible Gathering Grid (TE page 375).

- Have students choose an animal from the class list of topics (TE page 190) and write their choice on their grids.
- Have students read about the animal, using nonfiction books in the classroom, reference sources in the school library, as well as online sources of information.
- Have students find details for one grid question a day. Remind them to write just words and phrases, not complete sentences.

Write **Write your beginning.**

Point out that when Jake begins to write his report, he concentrates on just the first paragraph.

Explain that when Jake writes his beginning paragraph, he
- **uses** details from his gathering grid;
- **introduces** the topic in the first sentence of the paragraph, which is the first sentence of the report; and
- makes sure the first question is **answered** in the first paragraph.

Literature Connections

Mentor texts: Model strong beginnings by reading to students from age-appropriate expository texts, such as *Air Is All Around You* by Franklyn M. Branley, *Animals in Winter* by Henrietta Bancroft, or *Octopuses* by Lola M. Schaefer. Read the opening paragraph and ask students, "How does the writer get your attention?" Take responses. "How does the writer introduce the topic?" Lead a discussion of beginning strategies and encourage students to use these strategies as they create their reports.

Technology Connections

Students can use the added features of the Net-text as they explore this stage of the writing process.

 Write Source Online **Net-text**

192

Write ▶ **Write your beginning.**

When you write a report, you put facts about your topic into sentences.

> Here is what Jake does to write his beginning paragraph.
>
> **Use**   Jake uses details from his gathering grid.
>
> **Introduce**   He introduces his topic in the first sentence.
>
> **Answer**   Then he answers the first question on his gathering grid.

English Language Learners

Before students begin to write the first paragraph, give a minilesson on how to organize their words into complete sentences, including writing the naming part before the telling part. Then ask students to use what they learn to orally tell you their sentences before writing them.

✱ For information about writing sentences, see SE pages 44–53 and 288.

Writing a Report 193

Gathering Grid

Topic: _**leafy sea dragon**_

1. What does the animal look like?	**2.** Where does it live?
sea horse	**kelp forests**
green and yellow	**ocean**
leaves	**Australia**

The leafy sea dragon is unusual. It looks like green and yellow leaves.

Write ▶

Write your beginning paragraph.

1. **Use** your gathering grid.

2. **Introduce** your topic in the first sentence.

3. **Answer** the first question on your gathering grid.

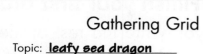

Call attention to Jake's thought balloon at the top of the page. Explain that Jake uses the information in the first box of his gathering grid to write his beginning paragraph. Remind students to use their own gathering grids when they write their beginning paragraphs.

Point out how Jake introduces his topic in the first sentence—by stating that the leafy sea dragon is an unusual animal. Then Jake describes what the animal looks like in the second sentence.

Suggest to students that when they get ready to write their first sentence, they should think about an outstanding feature of their animal. For example, if they are writing about an elephant, their first sentence could be _An elephant is the largest land animal._

Remind students that after they introduce their topics in the first sentence, the next sentences should tell what the animal looks like.

As students **write their beginning paragraph** _(see below)_, circulate and offer help as necessary.

Teaching Tip: Write a Paragraph

Before students begin to write, briefly review the following points:

- A paragraph is a group of sentences about one idea (what the animal looks like).
- The first sentence of the paragraph introduces the topic.
- The other sentences tell more details about the topic.
- Indent the first sentence of a paragraph.

English Language Learners

Students might use the name of their animal to begin each sentence if they have not yet mastered using pronouns in English. Teach a minilesson on how to substitute pronouns for nouns. Point out Jake's use of _it_ and explain that this is a good way to vary sentences.

✱ For information about pronouns, see SE pages 224–227 and 293.

Write Finish your first draft.

Focus attention on Jake's gathering grid and ask the following questions:

■ How many more paragraphs does Jake need to write to complete his first draft? (three, one for each remaining question)

■ What is the next paragraph Jake will write? (the paragraph that answers question 2)

Have students take out their own gathering grids and look at question 2. Explain that the next paragraph they write will answer that question.

Remind students that as they write their first drafts, their paragraphs do not have to be perfect because they will have time to revise and edit later on. For now, they should focus on getting their ideas down on paper.

194

Write ▶ Finish your first draft.

Next, you write the rest of the paragraphs with facts about your topic.

Here is what Jake does to write the rest of his first draft.

Follow Jake follows the order of his gathering grid.

Write He writes a paragraph to answer each question.

Gathering Grid

Topic: **leafy sea dragon**

1. What does the animal look like? **sea horse** **green and yellow** **leaves**	**2.** Where does it live? **kelp forests** **ocean** **Australia**
3. What does it eat? **tiny shrimp** **small fish** **uses mouth like** **a straw**	**4.** What are other interesting facts? **father takes care of** **the babys** **pouch on his body**

It lives in the ocean by Australia it hides in kelp forests.

The sea dragon eats tiny shrimp and small fish. It uses its mouth like a straw.

The father sea dragon takes care of the babys. He keeps them in a pouch.

Write ▶

Finish your first draft.

1. **Follow** the order of your gathering grid.
2. **Write** a paragraph to answer each question.

Show students how each shaded paragraph in Jake's first draft connects to a question on his gathering grid (SE page 194).

Have students match the words and phrases Jake wrote on his grid with the corresponding words and phrases in the sentences of each paragraph in his first draft.

Point out that there are a few mistakes in Jake's sentences, but that it is not important now because this is his first draft. He will make changes and corrections later.

Tell students to have their gathering grids next to them as they finish writing their first drafts. Remind them that the next paragraph they write will answer question 2. Determine if your students are ready to write paragraphs for questions 3 and 4 now, or if it would be better to have them write one paragraph a day.

As students finish their first draft, remind them to focus on putting their facts into sentences and not to worry about whether their sentences are perfect.

English Language Learners

Point out that the sentences in Jake's second paragraph are not in the same order as the details listed on his grid. Tell students to move their sentences around and decide in what order they want them to be. Repeat this process when students are ready to write their third and fourth paragraphs.

Struggling Learners

Work individually with students to help them write sentences from their facts. Before students write each sentence, have them say it aloud to make sure it makes sense. Then help them write the sentence in correct word order.

Grammar Connection

Sentence Review
- **Proofreader's Guide** page 288
- *GrammarSnap* Understanding Sentences
- *SkillsBook* pages 21–22

Capital-Letter Review
- **Proofreader's Guide** pages 275–277
- *GrammarSnap* Capital Letters
- *SkillsBook* pages 41–42

Revise Change your report.

Have students put away their first drafts for a day before revising. This will help them read their draft with "fresh eyes" and see things they want to add or change.

Review the steps in the writing process that students have completed so far. Then focus on what Jake does to revise the first draft of his report:

- **Read** Jake reads his first draft to make sure his writing makes sense. Suggest that students read their first drafts silently and then have partners read them aloud to them. Point out that sometimes they can hear mistakes that they don't see.

- **Add** Jake adds details to make his report clearer and more complete. Suggest that students ask their partners who read their reports aloud if anything is not clear (for example, an unfamiliar word like *kelp* in Jake's report). Encourage students to add details that explain anything that is not clear, such as special vocabulary.

Technology Connections

Have students use the Writing Network features of the Net-text to comment on each other's drafts.

✴ *Write Source Online* **Net-text**

196

Revise ▶ Change your report.

When you revise, you make changes to your report.

Here is what Jake does to revise his first draft.

Read   Jake reads his first draft.

Add   He adds details.

Learning to Listen 205

Sit quietly or **stand** still.

Look at the person who is talking.

Listen for important words.

Ask any questions after the person stops talking.

If needed, **draw** pictures or write notes about what you hear.

As you go over the rules for being a good listener, add comments such as the following:

■ Pay polite attention to what the speaker says.
■ Look at the speaker to show you are interested.
■ Wait until the speaker is finished before asking questions.
■ Try to picture in your mind what the speaker is saying.

Help students remember that when they are good listeners, they learn a lot more.

Explain that **practicing listening** (see below) can help students become good listeners.

In addition to keeping their focus on the speaker when listening to a presentation, students need to ask questions that focus on the speaker's topic. Model questions that follow the topic. Remind students to keep their focus before any oral presentation.

Teaching Tip: Practicing Listening

Provide opportunities for students to practice the rules for good listening.

● Ask volunteers to describe animals without mentioning the names of the animals. Invite students to listen carefully for clues and write down the kind of animals they think they are. Discuss the responses.

● Have students draw pictures about familiar stories that they have read or listened to in class. Have students tell partners what the stories are about and share their pictures, but not mention the titles of the stories. Ask partners to listen carefully and use the information to identify the stories.

Struggling Learners

Provide another mode in which students can practice listening.

Choose a character from a story that students have read or listened to in class. Tell students to listen carefully for clues as you act out and tell what the character did in the story. Have students name the character. Then invite them to take turns role-playing and listening for clues.

Learning to Interview

Objective

- learn what to do before, during, and after an interview

Invite students to talk about various jobs (firefighters, police officers, retail employees, restaurant staff, and so on). What kinds of questions would students like to ask about them in an interview?

Have students use the words *why, how,* and *what* to ask questions about some of these jobs. On the board, write questions students ask, noting that each question begins with a capital letter and ends with a question mark. For example:

- How did you learn to teach?
- What is the hardest part of your job?
- What do you like best about your job?

As you introduce interviewing, help students understand the specific purpose of this type of writing—to gather information.

206

Learning to Interview

In an **interview**, you ask someone questions. Then you write down what you learn.

You can use this plan whenever you do an interview.

First

Before the Interview

Set a time. (Have a grown-up help you.)

Think of questions to ask (*why, how,* and *what*).

Write down your questions.

Take your questions, a pencil, and paper to the interview.

Learning to Interview 207

Next

During the Interview

Ask one question at a time.

Listen carefully to the answer.

Write an answer for each question.

Thank the person.

Last

After the Interview

Write about what you learned.

Students should follow the "Before the Interview" guidelines before the interviewee arrives. If students need ideas for questions, suggest they use the questions they asked you (TE page 206). Students should follow the "During the Interview" rules during the next step. At the conclusion of the interview, have students write about or discuss what they have learned. Repeat the process for each new interview.

Invite several members of the school staff to visit the classroom and be interviewed about their jobs. For example, invite the principal, the librarian, a custodian, and a lunchroom server.

Then arrange for the class to **conduct an interview** *(see below)* with a writer. (See SE page 273 for a model thank-you letter.)

Teaching Tip: Conduct an Interview

Contact your local newspaper and invite a reporter to visit the class and be interviewed. Or ask the public librarian if there is a writer's group that meets at the library, and invite one of the writers to be interviewed. Set a time with the writer for the visit.

Have students think of questions to ask the writer. Write the questions on the board.

- Why do you like to write?
- How do you get ideas?
- What are some revising and editing strategies that you use?

During the interview, call on students to read one question at a time. Remind them to listen carefully so that they can write the answer to each question.

After the interview, have students write a thank-you note to the guest writer.

Ask students to write one thing they learned about being a writer from the interview. Have them share their writing with the class.

Writing in Journals

> **Objectives**
> - understand the purpose of a journal
> - practice writing a journal entry

Point out to students that they can write about anything they wish in a journal. List a few ideas on the board. They can write about . . .

- things that happen
- things they wonder about,
- their thoughts and feelings, and
- things they see and do each day.

Ask students to match what the child in the illustration wrote about in the sample journal entry to one of the ideas listed on the board (something that happened).

✱ For more examples of writing in a daily journal, see SE page 245.

Copy Masters

Daily Journal (TE p. 209)

208

Writing in Journals

A **journal** is a special notebook. You can write about all kinds of things in a journal.

Here are some ideas to write about in your journal.

In your journal, you can write poems, jokes, and stories. You can describe places and list questions you have.

April 6

I had fun yesterday. I rode my bike through some puddles. The tires made tracks on the sidewalk.

English Language Learners

If you have students keep a journal in class that is not used as a dialogue journal and will be read by you only occasionally, allow students to write in their first language if they choose.

Ask students to translate some passages to English when you will be evaluating their writing.

Or have students start by drawing pictures that describe their ideas. Then tell them to write key words in English about the pictures or label parts of the pictures. Hold a writing conference with students to help them use their key words and labels to write complete sentences.

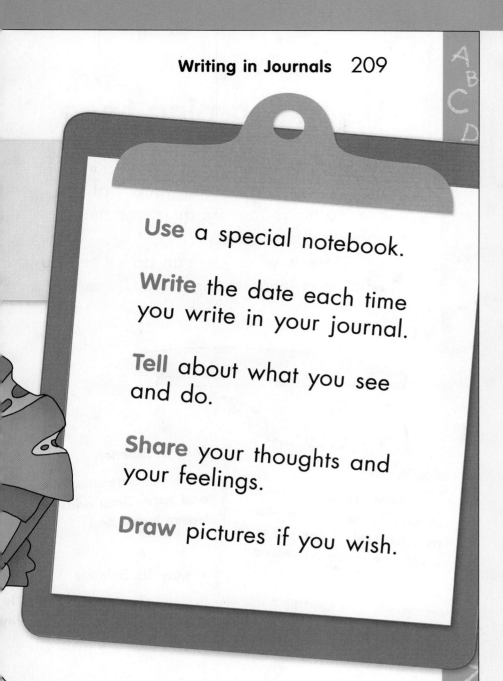

Writing in Journals   209

Use a special notebook.

Write the date each time you write in your journal.

Tell about what you see and do.

Share your thoughts and your feelings.

Draw pictures if you wish.

As you talk about writing in a journal, emphasize the following:

- A journal is for students to write in and read later.
- They shouldn't worry about making mistakes when they write in their journals. They don't need to revise or edit their entries since the purpose is to write ideas and thoughts.
- They can use what they write in their journals to get ideas for writing in school and at home.

On the board, demonstrate how to write in a journal. Conduct a shared writing activity about a class field trip, class contest, or class celebration.

If students do not already keep a journal (Teaching Tip, TE page 17), have them start one now. Distribute photocopies of the reproducible Daily Journal page (TE 333) and have them write a journal entry.

Advanced Learners

Invite students to ask a grandparent or other older family member what life was like when he or she was in first grade.

Have students write about what they learn in their journals. Encourage them to include their feelings about what they learn as well.

Grammar Connection

Writing Dates
- **Proofreader's Guide** pages 272–273, 277
- *GrammarSnap* Commas in Dates and Letters, Capital Letters
- *SkillsBook* pages 27–28

- **TE copy masters** pages 379, 382, 383

Spelling
- **Proofreader's Guide** pages 279–281
- *SkillsBook* pages 49–50, 51–52, 53–54
- **TE copy masters** pages 384, 385, 386

Using Learning Logs

Objectives
- understand the purpose of keeping learning logs
- practice writing learning-log entries

Explain that writing in a learning log is a good way to learn more about a subject.

After reading aloud the page, ask students to identify some facts about caterpillars.

Write their responses in a cluster on the board, with the word *caterpillar* in the center. Point out that a cluster is a good way to organize ideas in a learning log before writing sentences.

✱ For information about making a cluster, see SE page 249.

Point out the underlined word *milkweed* in the sample learning-log entry. Tell students that often they learn new words when they study new topics. Encourage students to include new words in their learning-log entries and to underline the words to show that they are new.

210

Using Learning Logs

A **learning log** is a special kind of journal. You write about facts that you are learning. You ask questions and underline new words.

Here is what you can do when you write in a learning log.

May 4, Science

Sara brought a yellow, white, and black caterpillar to school. Mr. Kane put it in a jar with <u>milkweed</u> leaves.

May 5, Science

The caterpillar eats and eats. Sara adds more leaves every day.

May 18, Science

The fat caterpillar is hanging upside down. Why is it doing that?

Materials

Drawing materials, learning logs— one per student (TE p. 211)

English Language Learners

Students learning English need the reinforcement of having the definitions of new words readily available. Ask students to create a glossary section in their learning logs. In addition to underlining new words in their entries, they should write the words and definitions in their glossaries. Have students use new vocabulary by writing in their learning logs about what they learned.

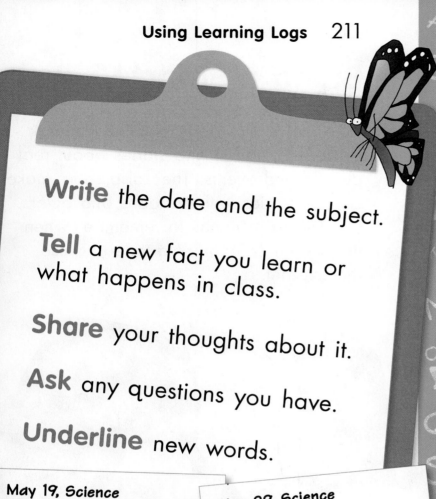

Using Learning Logs 211

Write the date and the subject.

Tell a new fact you learn or what happens in class.

Share your thoughts about it.

Ask any questions you have.

Underline new words.

May 19, Science

Where did the caterpillar go? Mr. Kane says it is inside the green case with gold dots. It is called a chrysalis.

May 29, Science

Surprise! A monarch butterfly came out of the chrysalis. It pumped its orange and black wings. Sara let it fly outside.

Guide students in a discussion about things they have learned in science. Then help them choose topics to write about, making sure they are visual enough for students to draw.

Distribute drawing materials. Invite students to draw pictures that show their chosen topics with labels. Tell students to leave room for writing at the bottom of the paper.

✳ For an example of drawing a picture with labels, see SE page 264.

Have students use the drawings and follow these steps to practice writing learning-log entries underneath their pictures:
- Write the date and subject name.
- Write a description of what they learned.
- Add thoughts and questions.
- Underline new words.

Circulate and offer support as students work. Help them check the accuracy of their facts.

Invite students to share their learning-log entries with the class.

Provide students with learning logs and encourage them to write facts that they are learning in class during a regularly slotted time.

English Language Learners

When beginning a new topic of study with vocabulary that is new to students, help them gain confidence in using a learning log by . . .
- listing on the board new vocabulary students will be encountering,
- defining each word, and
- having students write the definitions in their learning-log glossaries.

This way, students will understand the new words as they come up in the lesson and will also be able to use the words to write their learning-log entries.

Being a Smart Viewer

Take a poll to see how many students view television, videos, or the Internet. Make a chart on the board and tally how many students use each form.

Focus attention on the illustration. Ask students what the children are doing (watching television). Point out that it looks like they are listening and watching carefully and thinking about the show. Remind students what they learned about being good listeners (SE pages 204–205).

Discuss how students view TV, videos, or the Internet. Do they
- listen or read carefully,
- think about what they're viewing or reading, or
- write anything down?

212

Being a Smart Viewer

Television, videos, and the Internet share information and stories about real people and events. They also show make-believe stories with cartoons and actors.

Here are things to remember when you watch TV, look at a video, or use the Internet.

Being a Smart Viewer 213

Ask adults to help you make good choices about what you view.

Remember that commercials and ads are trying to sell you something.

Write down new facts you learn from a show about real people or events.

Share what you have learned.

Talk with students about the following questions:

- How do adults help children make good choices about what they view? (They let children know what programs are suitable for them to see. They limit their viewing time.)
- Why is it important to have an adult approve Web sites? (to make sure they are appropriate for children)
- Why is it important never to give out personal information on the Internet? (to stay safe)
- How do TV **commercials and ads** (see below) get the viewer's attention? (They make the product look good. They are loud.)

Invite students to view an appropriate documentary. Ask them to listen carefully for facts about the topic. As students view, have them write two new vocabulary words. After the program, have students write in their learning log about what they learned. Then have them share and discuss new vocabulary words and facts they learned while viewing the show.

Teaching Tip: Commercials and Ads

Because commercials and ads are trying to sell something, students must be smart viewers as they watch them.

Point out and discuss two ways commercials try to sell products.

- Be just like a famous person. *A rock star uses a certain toothpaste. If viewers use it, they, too, can be a star.*

- Join the crowd. *Buy this product. Everyone has it.*

Have students talk about whether their favorite commercials use either of the two selling methods.

English Language Learners

If students do not have access to the Internet at home, allow them time to search it in class. Show students how to make search engines run in their first language so that they can translate English entries they do not understand.

Taking Tests

Matching Test

Point out that a matching test has two lists of words. Explain that students must match each word in the first list with a word that is in the second list.

Refer to the sample matching test as you offer the following tips:
- Read the directions carefully.
- Look for key words that tell how the two columns go together (*adult* and *baby*).
- Start with the first word in the left list (*dog*).
- Read all the words in the right list to find a word that matches (*puppy*). Continue the process with *cow/calf* and *cat/kitten*.
- Make neat lines to match the words. Ask students what might happen if the lines aren't neat. (They might be marked wrong.)

214

Taking Tests

In school, you learn many new facts and ideas. You study, and then you take tests. A test tells you and your teacher how much you learned.

Matching Test

A **matching test** asks you to choose words that go together.

Read both lists below. Draw a line between the adult animal and the baby animal.

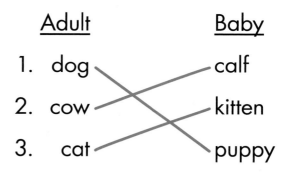

Adult	Baby
1. dog	calf
2. cow	kitten
3. cat	puppy

Multiple-Choice Test

A **multiple-choice test** asks you to choose the best answer.

Fill in the circle next to the correct answer.

1. Kurt had 3 apples. He gave his sister one. How many apples did Kurt have left?

Ⓐ ✖️🍎🍎🍎   4−1 = 3

🅑 ✖️🍎🍎   3−1 = 2

Ⓒ ✖️✖️🍎   3−2 = 1

Multiple-Choice Test

Explain that in a multiple-choice test, students are asked to choose the correct answer from several possible answers. Point out that the correct answer is always given, but students have to decide which one it is.

Ask students to carefully read the sample test directions. Point out the key words *fill in* and *correct answer*.

Ask students what they are being asked to do for this test. (*Fill in* the circle next to the *correct answer*.)

Have students read the sample word problem and then reread it. Ask them to read all the answer choices.

Point out that the circle next to the correct answer B is completely filled in blue. Have a volunteer read that answer and tell why it is correct. (The picture and the number sentence show the math story in the word problem.) Have volunteers explain why A and C are not the correct answers. (Kurt had 3 apples. Answer A shows he had 4 apples. Kurt gave his sister 1 apple. Answer C shows he gave her 2 apples.)

Fill-in-the-Blank Test

Tell students that on a fill-in-the-blank test, there usually is a box that contains words from which to choose for finishing each sentence.

Refer to the sample fill-in-the-blank test as you offer and model the following tips:

- Read the directions carefully before you begin.
- Read each sentence carefully.
- Choose the best word from the box.
- Silently read the sentence with the word in it.
- If the sentence makes sense, write the word on the blank line.
- Silently reread the sentence with the word written in it to be sure your choice makes sense.

As you introduce taking fill-in-the-blank and short-answer tests, help students understand the specific purpose for writing—to clearly express knowledge.

216

Fill-in-the-Blank Test

A **fill-in-the-blank** test usually asks you to finish a sentence.

Choose and write the best word from the box to finish each sentence.

green	blue	yellow
orange	red	purple

1. A stop sign is _____ **red** _____ and white.

2. The school bus is _____ **yellow** _____.

3. On a clear day, the sky is _____ **blue** _____.

4. Mix yellow and blue paint to make **green**.

English Language Learners

Fill-in-the-blank tests can be particularly difficult for students who have not yet mastered English.

- Whenever you give this kind of test, make sure that students understand all of the words in the sentences and are able to understand their overall meaning before writing words in the blanks.

- You may need to read aloud this kind of test to students if you want to get an accurate idea of their comprehension.

- Try to include picture support, like the drawings at the bottom of the page, to help students understand the sentences independently.

Short-Answer Test

A **short-answer** test asks you to answer a question. You may write one word, several words, or a short sentence.

Write a word or words to answer each question.

1. What is something white in your desk?
__paper__

2. What are two green things outside?
__leaves and grass__

3. What are three purple things in the classroom?
__clock__
__block__
__grapes on the color chart__

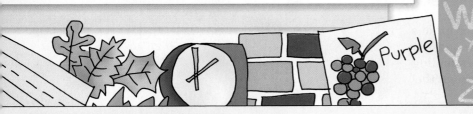

A B C D E F G H I J K L M N O P Q R S T U V W X Y Z

English Language Learners

Point out that the answers to the sample questions are not written in complete sentences, and that students may answer this type of question with a single word or a short phrase. When giving this kind of test, ask students to first paraphrase each question so you can ensure that they understand what they are being asked.

Short-Answer Test

Have students read the first sample question twice. Ask them to identify key words (*something white* and *desk*). Then ask the following questions:

- What is the question asking you to do? (name *something white* that is in your *desk*)
- What information does the question give you? (the thing is white; it's in your desk)
- Why is it important to read the question slowly and carefully? (so you don't name something that doesn't fit the information)

Point out that if the student who took this test hadn't read the end of this question, *in your desk*, she or he might have named something in the school, outside, or at home, and that would have been a wrong answer.

Tell students that after they write their response to a short-answer question, they should read it over and make any additions or corrections.

218

Words

Academic Vocabulary

Work with a partner. Read the meanings and share answers to the questions.

1. A **person** is a man, woman, or child. **What kind of person is your teacher?**

2. Something that is **happening** is going on or taking place. **What is happening in your classroom right now?**

3. If you **compare** two things, you see how they are different and alike. **How would you compare an apple and an orange?**

219

Words are used to share your ideas. You use words when you speak and when you write.

Academic Vocabulary

Read aloud the academic terms, as well as the descriptions and questions. Model for students how to read one question and answer it. Have partners monitor their understanding and seek clarification of the terms by working through the meanings and questions together.

Learning About Nouns

A **noun** is a word that names a person, a place, or a thing.

A lady sits in the park. She feeds a duck.

↑   ↑   ↑
person   **place**   **thing**

More Nouns

Person	Place	Thing
boy	farm	rock
girl	store	cat
doctor	zoo	bus
plumber	school	car

Grammar Practice

Read each sentence. Tell if the underlined **noun** names a person, a place, or a thing.

Example: **Our teacher plays the piano.**

person

1. See the pretty rose.
2. My uncle reads me stories.
3. My dog runs and jumps.
4. Listen to my aunt sing.
5. The library is very quiet.

Grammar Practice
Answers

1. rose—thing
2. uncle—person
3. dog—thing
4. aunt—person
5. library—place

222

Common and Proper Nouns

A **common noun** names any person, place, or thing. A **proper noun** names a special person, place, or thing. It begins with a capital letter.

Common Nouns	Proper Nouns
boy	Frank
river	Ohio River
book	The Zoo Book

Grammar Practice

Read the words below. Tell if the word is a **common noun** or a **proper noun**.

Example: **lake, Frog Lake**

1. family, Watsons
2. sister, Susan
3. Pacific Ocean, ocean

lake—common
Frog Lake—proper

Words 223

Singular and Plural Nouns

A **singular noun** names one person, place, or thing. A **plural noun** names more than one person, place, or thing. Add **-s** to make most nouns plural.

Singular Nouns	Plural Nouns
girl —	girls
garden —	gardens
hammer —	hammers

Grammar Practice

Spell the plural of each **noun** below.

Example: **snack**

1. kite
2. coat
3. orange
4. nest
5. sock
6. car

s-n-a-c-k-s

224

Using Pronouns

A **pronoun** is a word that takes the place of a noun. Some common pronouns are *he*, *she*, and *it*.

> Ellen wiggled the tooth.
> Ellen wiggled it .

> Mike had a loose tooth.
> He had a loose tooth.

Grammar Practice

Choose the right **pronoun** for each underlined noun.

She

Example: **Mom buys a tree.** *(It, She)*

1. Todd helps Mom plant the tree. *(He, She)*
2. Then Todd waters the tree. *(he, it)*
3. Mom thanks Todd for helping. *(It, She)*

Words 225

Using *I* and *Me*

I and **me** are pronouns you use to write about yourself. These pronouns are singular. The word **I** is always capitalized.

> Use I as the **naming part,** or **subject,** of the sentence.
>
> I play in our backyard.
>
> Use me after the **verb** in the **telling part.**
>
> Janey writes me a note.

Grammar Practice

Choose the right **pronoun** for each sentence.

me

Example: **My aunt gave** *(I, me)* **a new book.**

1. My friend and *(I, me)* jump rope.
2. Mom sings to my sister and *(I, me)*.
3. She and *(I, me)* like tomato soup.

Grammar Practice
Answers

1. He
2. it
3. She

Grammar Practice
Answers

1. I
2. me
3. I

226

Using *We* and *Us*

We and **us** are pronouns you use to write about others and yourself. These pronouns are plural.

Use **we** as the **subject** of the sentence.

We have gym every Friday.

Use **us** after the **verb**.

Our teacher shows us new games.

Grammar Practice

Choose the right **pronoun** for each sentence.

We

Example: *(We, Us)* had fun in science today.

1. Mr. King told *(we, us)* about sound waves.
2. *(We, Us)* made waves with string and spoons.
3. He gave *(we, us)* jars full of water.

Using *They* and *Them*

They and **them** are pronouns you use to write about others. These pronouns are plural.

Use **they** as the **subject** of the sentence.

They bake bread every week.

Use **them** after the **verb**.

Nana helps them get ready.

Grammar Practice

Choose the right **pronoun** for each sentence.

They

Example: *(They, Them)* wash their hands.

1. Nana gives *(they, them)* directions.
2. *(They, Them)* each knead the dough.
3. Nana bakes the bread for *(they, them)*.
4. Finally, *(they, them)* eat the warm bread.

Grammar Practice
Answers

1. us
2. We
3. us

Grammar Practice
Answers

1. them
2. They
3. them
4. they

How can I learn new words?

Make your own dictionary.

List new words you want to remember in a notebook. Put words that begin with **A** on the **A** page. Put words that begin with **B** on the **B** page. Do the same for every letter.

Personal Dictionary Page

A

apple   Aunt Ann   alligator

Alex   astronaut   almost

are   all   amazing

Use a classroom dictionary.

A dictionary lists words in ABC order. It shows how a word is spelled and tells what it means.

Sample Dictionary Page

Oo   **oak—ocean**   **25**

oak   An **oak** is a kind of tree. Nuts called acorns grow on oak trees.
*The **oak** tree is big.*

ocean   An **ocean** is a large body of salt water. Many plants and animals live in the ocean.
*Whales and dolphins live in the **ocean**.*

Use a word bank.

A word bank lists many kinds of words. Look at a word bank, or word wall, to find interesting words. Use these words in your writing.

Days	Seasons
Sunday	winter
Monday	spring
Tuesday	summer
Wednesday	fall
Thursday	
Friday	
Saturday	

Colors	Numbers	Months
yellow	one	January
green	two	February
blue	three	March
purple	four	April
brown	five	May
black	six	June
white	seven	July
red	eight	August
orange	nine	September
violet	ten	October
		November
		December

How can I connect sentences?

Use time-order words.

Time-order words tell when things happen in a story or report.

Time-Order Word Chart

first	second	third
yesterday	today	tomorrow
now	then	later
first	next	last

Use place-order words.

Place-order words tell where things are in a description.

on top of
above
in
near
below, under

Place-Order Word Chart

across	between	on
around	by	outside
behind	inside	over
beside	off	up

What can I add to my writing?

Draw a picture.

Add a picture of a detail from your story or report.

Add a speech bubble.

Beside your picture, write words the character might say.

This fruit smoothie is delicious!

Add a photo and a caption.

Use a photo to show a special detail about your story. Under the photo, write a few words or a sentence about it. This is called a **caption**.

Photo

Caption

I love to climb.

Add a drawing with labels.

A drawing with labels can make a report clear and interesting.

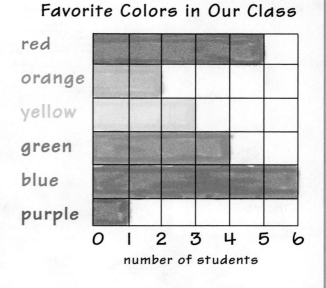

eye

tail

mouth

gill

fins

Fish

A fish has special body parts. Each part does a different job. Eyes let a fish see. A fish eats with its mouth. Gills help a fish breathe. A fish swims with its fins and tail.

Add a bar graph.

A **bar graph** can explain numbers in your writing. The graph below shows how many students chose each color as their favorite.

Favorite Colors in Our Class

red

orange

yellow

green

blue

purple

0   1   2   3   4   5   6

number of students

Write on a computer.

The more you know about a computer, the more you can do with it. Try writing on a computer.

Parts of a Computer

The printer prints your work.

The mouse moves the cursor.

Leafy Sea Dragon

The leafy sea dragon is unusual. It looks like a sea horse with green and yellow leaves.

It lives in the ocean by Australia. It hides in kelp forests. Kelp is giant seaweed.

The sea dragon eats tiny shrimp and small fish. It uses its mouth like a straw.

The monitor shows your work.

The disk saves your work.

Leafy Sea Dragon

The leafy sea dragon is unusual. It looks like a sea horse with green and yellow leaves.

It lives in the ocean by Australia. It hides in kelp forests. Kelp is giant seaweed.

The sea dragon eats tiny shrimp and small fish. It uses its mouth like a straw.

The father sea dragon takes care of the babies. He keeps them in a pouch on his body.

The computer stores information.

The keyboard lets you enter your work.

Proofreader's Guide

Academic Vocabulary

Work with a partner. Read the meanings and share answers to the questions.

1. An **initial** is the first letter of a name.
   What are your initials?

2. A **title** tells the name of something.
   What is the title of your favorite book?

3. If you show **excitement**, you are happy and want to do something very much.
   How do you show excitement when you go out to play?

Follow rules for writing.

All writers follow rules. In this section, you will find rules to help you with your writing.

Academic Vocabulary

Read aloud the academic terms, as well as the descriptions and questions. Model for students how to read one question and answer it. Have partners monitor their understanding and seek clarification of the terms by working through the meanings and questions together.

270

Using Punctuation

Use punctuation marks to make your writing easier to read.

Period

Use a **period** after a telling sentence.

I like to read.

Use a **period** after an initial.

Susan B. Anthony

Use a **period** after an abbreviation.

Mr. Bell
Dr. Wolf

Question Mark

Use a **question mark** after an asking sentence.

Where are my shoes?

Exclamation Point

Use an **exclamation point** after a word that shows excitement.

Wow! Help!

Use an **exclamation point** after a sentence that shows strong feeling.

My dog Coco has my shoe!

Related Skills Activities

- **Sentences and Paragraphs**
  Writing a Sentence, pp. 44–53
  Use end marks, p. 55

- *GrammarSnap*
  Periods

- *SkillsBook*
  Writing Sentences, pp. 5–6
  Telling Sentences, pp. 15–16
  Periods, pp. 23–24

- *Daily Language Workouts*
  Period at the End of a Telling Sentence, pp. 12–13, 28–29
  Period After an Abbreviation, pp. 30–31, 97

Related Skills Activities

- **Sentences and Paragraphs**
  Kinds of Sentences, pp. 54–55

- *GrammarSnap*
  Question Marks
  Exclamation Points

- *SkillsBook*
  Asking Sentences, pp. 17–18
  Exclamatory Sentences, pp. 19–20
  Sentence Review, pp. 21–22
  End Marks, pp. 25–26

- *Daily Language Workouts*
  Question Mark at the End of an Asking Sentence,
      pp. 14–15, 32–33
  Exclamation Point at the End of an Exciting Sentence,
      pp. 16–17, 34–35
  Punctuation Review Sentences, pp. 36–37
  Period, Question Mark, or Exclamation Point; Capital
      Letters for Special Names, p. 93

272

Comma

Commas keep words and numbers from running together.

Use a **comma** between the day and the year.

May 20, 2011

Use a **comma** after the greeting in a letter.

Dear Aunt Janie,

Use a **comma** after the closing in a letter.

Love,
Ryan

Use a **comma** after words in a series.

Today I played catch with Joe, Mike, and Ginny.

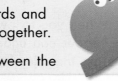

Proofreader's Guide   273

May 20, 2011 Date

Dear Aunt Janie, Greeting

Thanks for the mitt. My dad and my brother throw balls to me. It is fun!

Love, Closing
Ryan

P.S.
Today I played catch with Joe, Mike, and Ginny.

Related Skills Activities

- *GrammarSnap*
  Commas in Dates and Letters
  Commas in a Series

- *SkillsBook*
  Commas 1 and 2, pp. 27–28, 29–30
  Punctuation Review, pp. 33–34
  Writing Friendly Letters, p. 91

- *Daily Language Workouts*
  Comma After the Greeting and the Closing in a Letter,
      pp. 38–41
  Comma Between the Day and the Year, pp. 42–43, 83
  Comma Between Words in a Series, pp. 44–45, 84, 99
  Using the Right Word, Commas in Letters, pp. 72–73,
      74–75
  Using the Right Word, Commas Between Words in a
      Series, pp. 76–77
  Using the Right Word, Comma Between the Day and the
      Year, pp. 78–79, 100

274

Apostrophe

Use an **apostrophe** to make a contraction.

Words	Contractions
I am	I'm
it is	it's
he is	he's
she is	she's
did not	didn't
do not	don't
is not	isn't
let us	let's

Using Capital Letters

When you follow the rules for writing, your reader can understand what you write. Here are the rules for using capital letters.

Capital Letters

Use a **capital letter** for the first word in a sentence.

The walrus has two big tusks.

Use a **capital letter** for the word **I**.

Yesterday I drew a walrus.

Related Skills Activities

- **Words**
  Contractions, p. 236
  Contractions Using *Not,* p. 237

- *GrammarSnap*
  Contractions
  Contractions Using *Not*

- *SkillsBook*
  Apostrophes, pp. 31–32

- *Daily Language Workouts*
  Apostrophe to Make a Contraction,
    pp. 46–47, 85
  Apostrophe to Make a Contraction . . . ,
    pp. 66–67, 95
  Apostrophe to Make a Contraction . . . ,
    pp. 68–69, 96

Related Skills Activities

- **Words**
  Using *I* and *Me,* p. 225

- **Sentences and Paragraphs**
  Writing a Sentence, pp. 44–53

- *GrammarSnap*
  Capital Lettters

- *SkillsBook*
  Writing Sentences, pp. 5–6
  Capital Letters 1, pp. 35–36
  Sentence Review, pp. 21–22

- *Daily Language Workouts*
  Capital Letter for the First Word in a Sentence, pp. 18–19
  Capital Letter for the Word *I,* pp. 22–23
  Capital Letters for First Words . . . , and the
    Word *I,* pp. 24–25
  Capital Letter for the First Word in a Sentence
    . . . , pp. 60–61, 92
  Capital Letter for the Word *I,* Question Mark,
    pp. 64–65, 94

276

Capital Letters

Use a **capital letter** for names of people and places.

| Rosa Parks | Texas |

Use a **capital letter** for name titles.

| Dr. Seuss | Ms. Lim |
| Mrs. Cooper | Mr. Ford |

Use **capital letters** for book titles.

I read the book My Five Senses.

Use a **capital letter** for holidays.

| New Year's Day | Labor Day |
| Thanksgiving | Flag Day |

Proofreader's Guide 277

Use a **capital letter** for the days of the week.

Sunday	Thursday
Monday	Friday
Tuesday	Saturday
Wednesday	

Use a **capital letter** for the months of the year.

January	May	September
February	June	October
March	July	November
April	August	December

Related Skills Activities

- **Words**
  Common and Proper Nouns, p. 222

- *GrammarSnap*
  Capital Letters

- *SkillsBook*
  Capital Letters 2, pp. 37–38
  Capital Letter Review, pp. 41–42
  Common and Proper Nouns, pp. 69–70

- *Daily Language Workouts*
  Writing Sentences (Names), pp. 4–7
  Capital Letters for Special Names, pp. 20–21
  . . . Special Names, and the Word *I*, pp. 24–25
  . . . Capital Letters for Special Names, pp. 62–63, 93

Related Skills Activities

- *GrammarSnap*
  Capital Letters

- *SkillsBook*
  Capital Letters 3, pp. 39–40
  Capital Letter Review, pp. 41–42

278

Making Plurals

Plural means *more than one*. Add an **-s** to most nouns to make the plural.

Singular Nouns	Plural Nouns
book	books
pencil	pencils
teacher	teachers

Some nouns use a new word to make the plural.

Singular Nouns	Plural Nouns
child	children
foot	feet
man	men
woman	women

Checking Spelling

Always check your spelling when you write. Here is an ABC list of words you can use.

Aa
about	and	ask
all	are	at
am	as	away

Bb
be	blue	bus
big	brown	but
black	bug	by

Cc
call	can't	cold
came	car	color
can	circle	come

Dd
day	do	don't
did	does	down
didn't	dog	draw

Related Skills Activities

- **Words**
Singular and Plural Nouns, p. 223

- *GrammarSnap*
Plural Nouns
Irregualr Plurals

- *SkillsBook*
Plurals 1 and 2, pp. 43–46
Plurals Review, pp. 47–48
Singular and Plural Nouns, pp. 71–72

- *Daily Language Workouts*
Plurals That Add -s, pp. 26–27
. . . Plurals That Add -s, pp. 68–69, 96
Plurals That Add -s, . . . , p. 98

Related Skills Activities

- *SkillsBook*
ABC Order 1, 2, 3, 4, 5, and 6, pp. 49–60
Word Dictionary, pp. 101–153

280

Ee
| each | eat | every |
| ear | eight | eye |

Ff
face	first	four
feet	five	Friday
find	for	from

Gg
get	goes	great
give	good	green
go	gray	grow

Hh
had	have	here
hand	he	home
has	help	how

Ii
| I | if | is |
| I'm | in | it |

Jj
| jar | job | jump |
| jelly | joke | just |

Kk
| keep | kitten | knew |
| kind | knee | know |

Ll
last	let	live
left	like	long
leg	little	look

Mm
made	me	most
make	Monday	must
many	more	my

Nn
name	next	nose
need	nine	not
new	no	now

Oo
of	on	orange
off	one	our
old	or	out

Related Skills Activities

- **SkillsBook**
  ABC Order 1, 2, 3, 4, 5, and 6, pp. 49–60
  Word Dictionary, pp. 101–153

282

Pp

paper	please	purple
people	pretty	push
play	pull	put

Qq

quack	quick	quit
question	quiet	quiz

Rr

rain	red	ring
ran	ride	round
read	right	run

Ss

said	say	she
Saturday	see	six
saw	seven	Sunday

Tt

ten	they	Thursday
that	this	Tuesday
the	three	two

Uu

under	up	us
until	upon	use

Vv

van	very	visit
vegetable	vet	voice

Ww

was	Wednesday	what
we	were	white

Xx

x-ray	fi<u>x</u>	si<u>x</u>
fa<u>x</u>	mi<u>x</u>	wa<u>x</u>

Yy

yawn	yellow	you
year	yes	your

Zz

zebra	zigzag	zoo
zero	zip	zoom

Related Skills Activities

- **SkillsBook**
  ABC Order 1, 2, 3, 4, 5, and 6, pp. 49–60
  Word Dictionary, pp. 101–153

Using the Right Word

Some words sound alike, but they are spelled differently and mean different things. These words are called **homophones**.

| ate | Steve ate crackers for a snack. |
| eight | I have eight blocks. |

| blew | The wind blew my kite. |
| blue | My blue pants are too small. |

| buy | The girls buy seeds at the store. |
| by | I live by a park. |

| dear | I wrote "Dear Nana." |
| deer | We saw a deer in the woods. |

| for | This snack is for my brother. |
| four | He is four years old. |

| hear | I can hear music. |
| here | Please come here. |

| its | The bird flaps its wings. |
| it's | It's cold outside. |

| know | Do you know my name? |
| no | "No, I don't," said Theo. |

| one | I lost one sock. |
| won | My team won the game. |

Related Skills Activities

- **SkillsBook**
  Using the Right Word, pp. 61–65

- **Daily Language Workouts**
  Using the Right Word, pp. 48–49, 50–51, 52–53, 54–55, 56–57, 58–59, 60–61, 72–73, 74–75, 76–77, 78–79, 86, 87, 88, 89, 90, 91, 92, 100

286

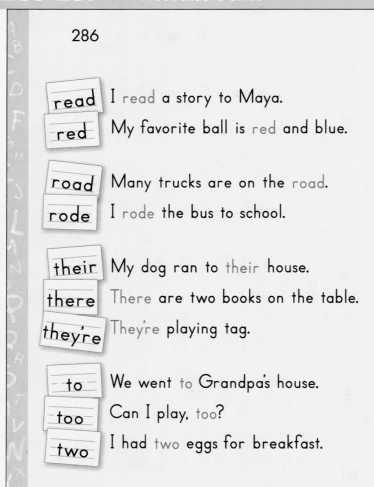

I **read** a story to Maya.

My favorite ball is **red** and blue.

Many trucks are on the **road**.

I **rode** the bus to school.

My dog ran to **their** house.

There are two books on the table.

They're playing tag.

We went **to** Grandpa's house.

Can I play, **too**?

I had **two** eggs for breakfast.

Understanding Opposites

Opposites tell about ideas that are completely different from each other. Opposite words are called **antonyms**.

Related Skills Activities

- **SkillsBook**
  Using the Right Word, pp. 61–65

- **Daily Language Workouts**
  Using the Right Word, pp. 48–49, 50–51, 52–53, 54–55, 56–57, 58–59, 60–61, 72–73, 74–75, 76–77, 78–79, 86, 87, 88, 89, 90, 91, 92, 100

Related Skills Activities

- **SkillsBook**
  Using an Opposite Word, p. 66

288

Understanding Sentences

A sentence tells a complete idea and has two parts.

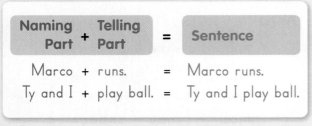

Naming Part	+	Telling Part	=	Sentence
Marco	+	runs.	=	Marco runs.
Ty and I	+	play ball.	=	Ty and I play ball.

A sentence begins with a **capital letter**. It ends with a **period**, a **question mark**, or an **exclamation point**.

Capital Letters — **End Marks**

The boys play basketball.

Does Paulo want to play, too?

He scores the first basket!

Subjects and Verbs That Agree

In every sentence, the subject must agree with the verb.

If the subject names one person, place, or thing, you usually add **-s** to the verb.

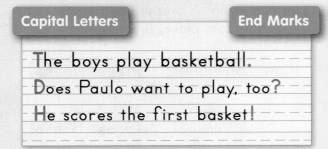

person	Vilay	laughs.
place	The store	opens.
thing	A snake	slithers.

If the subject names more than one person, place, or thing, do not add **-s** to the verb.

people	Vilay and Annie	laugh.
places	The stores	open.
things	Snakes	slither.

Related Skills Activities

- **Sentences and Paragraphs**
  Find the Naming Part, pp. 48–49
  Find the Telling Part, pp. 50–51
  Write Complete Sentences, pp. 52–53
  Kinds of Sentences, pp. 54–55
  Use End Marks, p. 55

- *GrammarSnap*
  Understanding Sentences

- *SkillsBook*
  Writing Sentences, pp. 5–6
  Complete Thoughts, pp. 7–8
  The Naming Part, pp. 9–10
  The Telling Part, pp. 11–12
  Sentence Parts, pp. 13–14
  End Marks, pp. 25–26
  Capital Letters 1, pp. 35–36

- *Daily Language Workouts*
  Period at the End of a Telling Sentence, pp. 12–13, 28–29
  Question Mark at the End of an Asking Sentence, pp. 14–15, 32–33
  Exclamation Point at the End of an Exciting Sentence, pp. 16–17, 34–35

Period, Question Mark, Exclamation Point at the End of a Sentence, pp. 36–37
Period, Question Mark, Exclamation Point . . . , p. 93

Related Skills Activities

- **Words**
  Singular Subjects and Verbs, p. 234
  Plural Subjects and Verbs, p. 235

- **Sentences and Paragraphs**
  Write Complete Sentences, pp. 52–53

- *GrammarSnap*
  Subject-Verb Agreement

- *SkillsBook*
  Sentence Parts, pp. 13–14

290

Different Kinds of Sentences

A **telling sentence** tells about something or someone. It ends with a **period**.

I like to play tag.

An **asking sentence** asks a question. It ends with a **question mark**.

Will you play with me?

An **exclamatory sentence** shows excitement or strong feelings. It ends with an **exclamation point**.

You are it!

Using the Parts of Speech

The words that you use in your writing are called the **parts of speech**.

Nouns

A **noun** is a word that names a person, place, or thing.

person:	boy	nurse
place:	home	school
thing:	book	chair

A **common noun** names any person, place, or thing. A **proper noun** names a specific person, place, or thing.

Common Nouns	Proper Nouns
girl	Julia
school	Grant School

Related Skills Activities

- **Sentences and Paragraphs**
  Kinds of Sentences, p. 54
  Use End Marks, p. 55

- *GrammarSnap*
  Kinds of Sentences

- *SkillsBook*
  Writing Sentences, pp. 5–6
  Telling Sentences, pp. 15–16
  Asking Sentences, pp. 17–18
  Exclamatory Sentences, pp. 19–20
  Sentence Review, pp. 21–22
  End Marks, pp. 25–26

- *Daily Language Workouts*
  Period at the End of a Telling Sentence, pp. 12–13, 28–29
  Question Mark at the End of an Asking Sentence,
      pp. 14–15, 32–33
  Exclamation Point at the End of an Exciting Sentence,
      pp. 16–17, 34–35
  Punctuation Review Sentences, pp. 36–37
  Period, Question Mark, or Exclamation Point, p. 93

Related Skills Activities

- **Words**
  Learning About Nouns, pp. 220–222

- *GrammarSnap*
  Nouns
  Common and Proper Nouns

- *SkillsBook*
  Nouns, pp. 67–68
  Common and Proper Nouns, pp. 69–70

Singular and Plural Nouns

A **singular noun** names one person, place, or thing. A **plural noun** names more than one person, place, or thing.

Singular Nouns	Plural Nouns
cat —— cats	
dog —— dogs	
bug —— bugs	
apple —— apples	
friend —— friends	

Pronouns

A **pronoun** is a word that takes the place of a noun.

Molly likes grapes.

She likes grapes.

(*She* takes the place of the noun **Molly**.)

Robert peeled a banana.

Robert peeled it.

(*It* takes the place of the noun **banana**.)

Common Pronouns

I	we	her	them
it	us	me	they
she	he	his	you

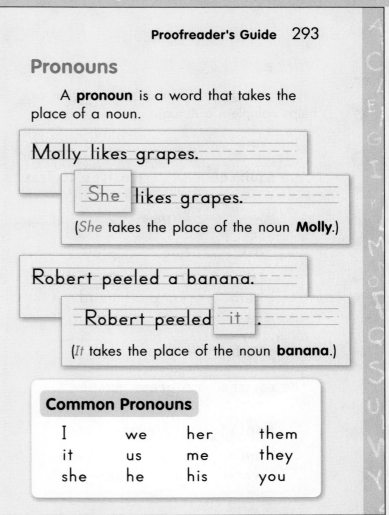

Related Skills Activities

- **Words**
  Singular and Plural Nouns, p. 223

- *GrammarSnap*
  Plural Nouns

- *SkillsBook*
  Plurals 1 and 2, pp. 43–46
  Plurals Review, pp. 47–48
  Singular and Plural Nouns, pp. 71–72

- *Daily Language Workouts*
  Plurals That Add -s, pp. 26–27
  Apostrophe to Make a Contraction, Plurals That Add -s, pp. 68–69, 96
  Plurals That Add -s, Comma After the Greeting and the Closing in a Letter, p. 98

Related Skills Activities

- **Words**
  Using Pronouns, pp. 224–227

- *GrammarSnap*
  Pronouns

- *SkillsBook*
  Pronouns, pp. 73–74
  Parts of Speech Review, pp. 85–86

294

Verbs

A **verb** is a word that shows action or helps complete a thought.

Action **Verb**

The squirrel jumps from tree to tree.

Some Action Verbs

ask	hug	play
fix	go	race
help	jump	read

Linking **Verb**

The squirrel is a great jumper.

Some Linking Verbs

am	is	are	was
were	be	been	

Action-Verb Tenses

Some **action verbs** tell what is happening now, in the **present**.

Sam helps his mother.

Some **action verbs** tell what happened before, in the **past**. Verbs in the past tense usually end in **-ed**.

Sam helped his mother last night.

Present Tense	Past Tense
cook ——	cooked
mix ——	mixed
pull ——	pulled
walk ——	walked

Related Skills Activities

- **Words**
  Learning About Verbs, pp. 228–229

- **Sentences and Paragraphs**
  Writing a Sentence, pp. 44–53

- *GrammarSnap*
  Verbs
  Action Verbs
  Linking Verbs

- *SkillsBook*
  Verbs, pp. 75–76
  Linking Verbs 1 and 2, pp. 79–82

Related Skills Activities

- **Words**
  Present–Tense Action Verbs, p. 230
  Past–Tense Action Verbs, p. 231

- *GrammarSnap*
  Action Verb Tenses

- *SkillsBook*
  Tenses of Action Verbs, pp. 77–78

Linking-Verb Tenses

Linking verbs can complete thoughts in the **present** or in the **past**. Instead of ending in **-ed**, a past-tense linking verb becomes a different word.

I am a first grader.

I was a kindergartner.

The children are happy.

The children were happy.

Present Tense	Past Tense
am	was
is	was
are	were

Adjectives

An **adjective** is a word that tells something about a noun.

Kiki is my silly cat.

(*Silly* tells **what kind** of cat.)

She has three spots.

(*Three* tells **how many** spots.)

An adjective can **compare two** people, places, or things.

Socks is faster than Kiki.

An adjective can **compare more than two** people, places, or things.

Socks is the fastest cat I know.

Related Skills Activities

- **Words**
  Present–Tense Linking Verbs, p. 232
  Past–Tense Linking Verbs, p. 233

- *GrammarSnap*
  Linking Verb Tenses

- *SkillsBook*
  Linking Verbs 1 and 2, pp. 79–82

Related Skills Activities

- **Words**
  Using Adjectives, p. 238
  Using Adjectives to Compare, p. 239

- *GrammarSnap*
  Adjectives
  Adjectives to Compare

- *SkillsBook*
  Adjectives, p. 83
  Adjectives That Compare, p. 84

298

Editing and Proofreading Marks

You can use the marks below to make changes to your writing. Your teacher may also use these marks to help you improve your writing.

Mark	Meaning	Example	Edited
=	Capitalize a letter.	Ezra Jack keats wrote Pet Show.	Ezra Jack Keats wrote Pet Show.
/	Make a capital letter lowercase.	Archie wanted to take the Cat.	Archie wanted to take the cat.
⊙	Add a period.	It was time to go, but the cat was missing⊙	It was time to go, but the cat was missing.
℘	Take something out.	His friends they looked for the cat.	His friends looked for the cat.
∧	Add a letter, a word, or words.	They searched ∧here and there.	They searched here and there.
?∧ ,∧ !∧	Insert punctuation.	Finally∧Archie's friends left for the show.	Finally, Archie's friends left for the show.
sp.	Correct the spelling error.	The endin had some surprises.	The ending had some surprises.

299

Theme Words

In this section, you will find lists about people, places, and things. There are also word lists for animals, foods, and activities.

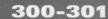

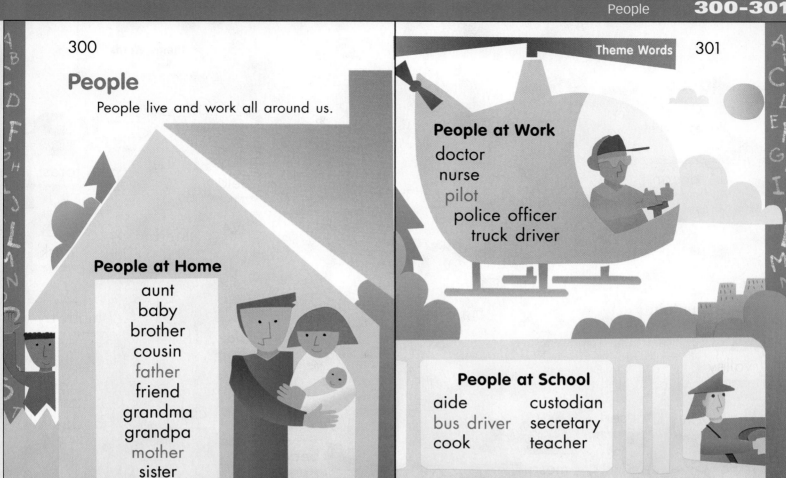

300

People

People live and work all around us.

People at Home

aunt
baby
brother
cousin
father
friend
grandma
grandpa
mother
sister
uncle

People at Work

doctor
nurse
pilot
police officer
truck driver

People at School

aide   custodian
bus driver   secretary
cook   teacher

302

Places

Going
places is fun!

ocean

mountain

valley

canyon   desert

mesa

farm

field

forest

river

island

park

lake

highway

road

city

beach   bridge

street

304

Things

In your classroom centers, you may find interesting things.

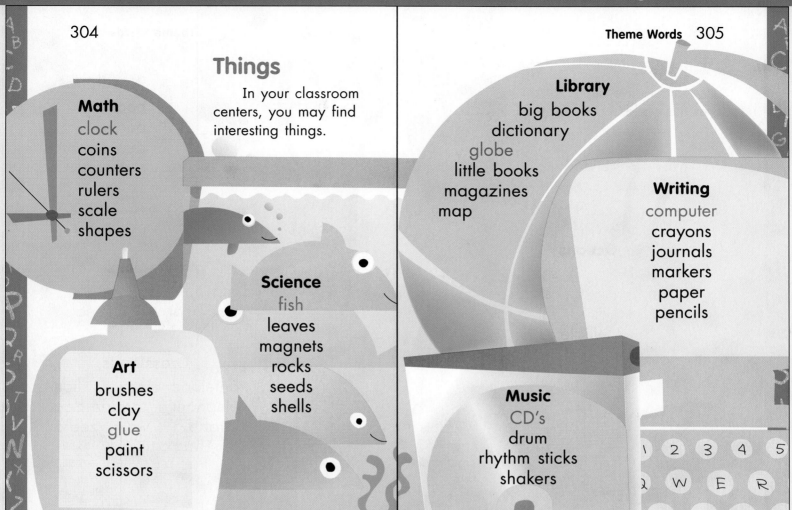

Math
clock
coins
counters
rulers
scale
shapes

Art
brushes
clay
glue
paint
scissors

Science
fish
leaves
magnets
rocks
seeds
shells

Library
big books
dictionary
globe
little books
magazines
map

Writing
computer
crayons
journals
markers
paper
pencils

Music
CD's
drum
rhythm sticks
shakers

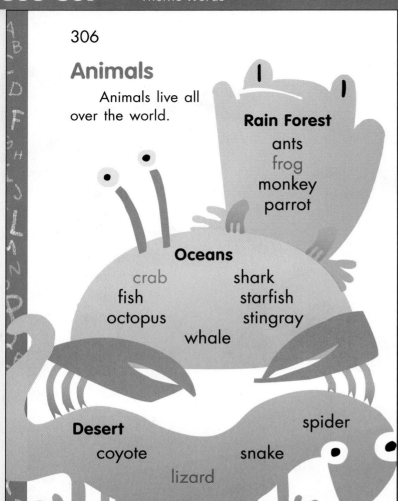

306

Animals

Animals live all over the world.

Rain Forest

ants
frog
monkey
parrot

Oceans

crab
fish
octopus

shark
starfish
stingray
whale

Desert

coyote
lizard

spider
snake

Woodlands

bear
beaver
deer
raccoon
skunk
squirrel

Polar Regions

penguin
polar bear

reindeer
seal

Grasslands

antelope
elephant
giraffe
hippopotamus

lion
prairie dog
zebra

308

Foods

A diet of healthy foods helps you learn and grow.

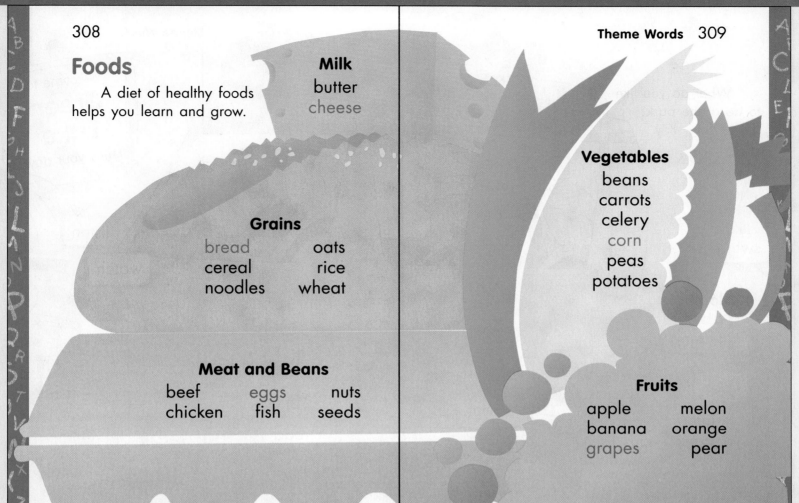

Milk
butter
cheese

Grains
bread   oats
cereal   rice
noodles   wheat

Meat and Beans
beef   eggs   nuts
chicken fish   seeds

Vegetables
beans
carrots
celery
corn
peas
potatoes

Fruits
apple   melon
banana   orange
grapes   pear

310

Activities

What do you like to do at the park?

slide

swing

look

camp

cook

jump

hike

sail

swim

LIFEGUARD

TRAIL

fly

read

Welcome to
Green Lake
Enjoy your day!

listen

watch

play

fish

build

Copy Masters

EDITING AND PROOFREADING MARKS **316**

BENCHMARK PAPERS

Narrative Writing: Pumpkin Farm (strong) Assessment Sheet **317**
Narrative Writing: My Trip (good) **318**
Narrative Writing: Grandma (poor) **320**
Expository Writing: Coins (strong) Assessment Sheet **322**
Expository Writing: Fun with Beads (good) **323**
Expository Writing: Draw (poor) **325**
Responding to Literature: Gutter Ball (strong) Assessment Sheet **327**
Responding to Literature: Bowling (good) **328**
Responding to Literature: Bowl (poor) **330**

CONFERENCE NOTES SHEET **332**

GRAPHIC ORGANIZERS

Daily Journal **333**
Sensory Chart **334**
Story Map/Four-Square **335**
Friendly Letter **336**
Cluster **337**
List **338**
Note **339**

Worksheets

WRITING PROCESS **340**

SENTENCES AND PARAGRAPHS

Sentences 1 . . . . **341**
Sentence Order **342**
The Naming Part **343**
The Telling Part **344**
Writing Sentences **345**
Sentences 2 . . . . **346**
Telling Sentences **347**
Asking Sentences **348**
Exclamatory Sentences **349**
Use a Period 1 . . . . **350**
Use a Question Mark **351**
Use an Exclamation Point **352**

Worksheets

DESCRIPTIVE WRITING

Verbs 1 . . . . **353**
Verbs 2 . . . . **354**
Action Verb Tenses **355**
Linking Verb Tenses **356**
Choose a Topic **357**
Editing Checklist **358**
Thinking About Your Writing **359**

NARRATIVE WRITING

Capital Letters 1 . . . . **360**
Sentence Starters **361**

EXPOSITORY WRITING

Think of Topic Ideas **362**
Order Chart **363**

RESPONDING TO LITERATURE

Nouns 1 . . . . **364**
Nouns 2 . . . . **365**
Nouns 3 . . . . **366**
Capital Letters 2 . . . . **367**
Fiction Details Sheet **368**
Pronouns **369**
Nonfiction Fact Sheet **370**
Poetry Details Sheet **371**

CREATIVE WRITING

Use an Apostrophe **372**
Adjectives 1 . . . . **373**
Adjectives 2 . . . . **374**

REPORT WRITING

Gathering Grid **375**
Plurals 1 . . . . **376**
Plurals 2 . . . . **377**

Worksheets

PROOFREADER'S GUIDE

Use a Period 2 . . . . **378**
Commas in Letters **379**
Capital Letters 3 . . . . **380**
Capital Letters 4 . . . . **381**
Capital Letters 5 . . . . **382**
Capital Letters 6 . . . . **383**
ABC Order 1 . . . . **384**
ABC Order 2 . . . . **385**
ABC Order 3 . . . . **386**
ABC Order 4 . . . . **387**
ABC Order 5 . . . . **388**
Using the Right Word 1 . . . . **389**
Using the Right Word 2 . . . . **390**
Using the Right Word 3 . . . . **391**
Using Opposites **392**
Sentences 3 . . . . **393**
Sentences 4 . . . . **394**

Additional Resources

FAMILY CONNECTION LETTERS

English Letters **395**
Spanish Letters **404**

UNIT-PLANNING WORKSHEET **413**

GETTING STARTED

Scavenger Hunt 1: Find the Threes **415**
Scavenger Hunt 2: What Is It? **416**
Getting to Know *Write Source* **417**
Getting-Started Activity Answer Key **418**

CREDITS **419**

Index **420**

Editing and Proofreading Marks

You can use the marks below to make changes to your writing. Your teacher may also use these marks to help you improve your writing.

Mark	Meaning	Example	Edited
=	Capitalize a letter.	Ezra Jack <u>keats</u> wrote <u>Pet Show</u>.	Ezra Jack <u>Keats</u> wrote <u>Pet Show</u>.
/	Make a capital letter lowercase.	Archie wanted to take the Cat.	Archie wanted to take the cat.
⊙	Add a period.	It was time to go, but the cat was missing⊙	It was time to go, but the cat was missing.
℘	Take something out.	His friends they looked for the cat.	His friends looked for the cat.
∧	Add a letter, a word, or words.	They searched ∧here and there.	They searched here and there.
?∧ ⩘∧ !∧	Insert punctuation.	Finally∧ Archie's friends left for the show.	Finally, Archie's friends left for the show.
sp. ⬭	Correct the spelling error.	The ⟨endin⟩ᵖ had some surprises.	The ending had some surprises.

Conference Notes

Title   *Pumpkin Farm*

Ideas   GREAT!

- Your paragraph tells about one special time.
- Your paragraph tells <u>who</u> you were with when you had fun—with your mother.
- Your paragraph tells <u>where</u> you and your mother went to have fun—a pumpkin farm.
- Your paragraph tells <u>what</u> you did at the farm—picking out a pumpkin, riding on a wagon, and eating apples in the barn.

Organization   GREAT!

- Your first sentence tells readers where you and your mother had fun.
- You use the time-order words <u>first</u> and <u>then</u> in your paragraph. These words connect sentences that describe the different things you did at the farm. This helps readers understand exactly what you did at the farm.

Conventions   GREAT!

- You use the word <u>I</u> to write about yourself and the word <u>We</u> to write about your mom and you.
- You indented the first sentence of your paragraph.
- The first word of every sentence begins with a capital letter.
- Every sentence in your paragraph has an end mark.
- Every word in your paragraph is spelled correctly.

Narrative Writing

My Trip

1   wunce I went to Arcansaw it was very fun. I

2 went swimming. I saw my firend ross. we played

3 games. I wan to go thare agen. the end.

Conference Notes

Title *My Trip*

Ideas   <u>GREAT!</u>

- Your paragraph tells about one special time.
- Your paragraph tells <u>who</u> you were with when you had fun—your friend Ross.
- Your paragraph tells <u>where</u> you went to have fun—Arkansas.
- Your paragraph tells <u>what</u> fun things you did on your trip—swimming and playing games with Ross.

Organization   <u>GOOD!</u>

- Your first sentence names the place that you visited.
- You did not use any time-order words in your paragraph. These words help readers understand how you spent your time. You should revise your writing to include these words.

Conventions   <u>KEEP TRYING!</u>

- You indented the first sentence of your paragraph.
- Be sure the first word of every sentence begins with a capital letter.
- A person's name (<u>Ross</u>) should begin with a capital letter.
- Every sentence in your paragraph needs an end mark.
- You need to check the spelling of several words (<u>wunce, Arcansaw, firend, wan, thare, agen</u>).

Narrative Writing

Grandma

1 i go to flarida i see my grandma Did you rid a
2 plan? i did. it is fun i help in the gardin. we eat
3 out. i like flarida but it is hot

Conference Notes

Title *Grandma*

Ideas   KEEP TRYING!

- Your paragraph tells about three ideas: seeing your grandmother, riding a plane, and Florida. It's not clear how they go together. You should choose one of these topics and write a paragraph that tells only about that one topic.
- You did try to answer the questions <u>who</u>, <u>where</u>, and <u>what</u> in your paragraph. Answer these questions about the one topic you select.

Organization   GOOD!

- Your first sentence names the place that you visited.
- You did not use any time-order words in your paragraph. Be sure to use these words. They help readers understand how you spent your day.

Conventions   KEEP TRYING!

- You need to indent the first sentence of your paragraph.
- The first word of every sentence should begin with a capital letter.
- The name of a state (<u>Florida</u>) should begin with a capital letter.
- Every sentence in your paragraph should have an end mark.
- Several words in your paragraph are not spelled correctly (<u>flarida</u>, <u>rid</u>, <u>plan</u>, <u>gardin</u>).

Conference Notes

Title *Coins*

Ideas
GREAT!

- Your paragraph tells about something that you know how to do well—collect coins.
- Your sentences give details about the coins you collect. This makes your paragraph interesting to readers.

Organization
GREAT!

- Your first sentence names the activity you are going to tell readers about—collecting coins.
- In sentences 2 through 4, you give readers interesting information about this hobby.

Conventions
GREAT!

- You indented the first sentence of your paragraph.
- The first word of every sentence begins with a capital letter.
- Every sentence in your paragraph has an end mark.
- You used commas to separate words in a series (. . . silver, gold, or copper).
- Every word in your paragraph is spelled correctly.

Expository Writing

Fun with Beads

1   do you wear braselets? I do. I make my own.

2   you need beads. and string. you can by them at a

3   store. Tie the string tite. put the beads on the

4   string. Then wear it.

Conference Notes

Title *Fun with Beads*

Ideas <u>GREAT!</u>

- Your paragraph tells about something that you know how to do well—make bracelets.
- Your sentences give details about the things you need to make a bracelet. They also explain the steps to follow when making the jewelry.

Organization <u>GOOD!</u>

- Your first sentence names the activity you are going to tell readers about—making a bracelet.
- You describe most of the steps to follow in order. However, you tell readers to tie the string before they put beads on the string. Is this what you do? Check that the steps are in the correct order.
- You begin the last sentence with the time-order word <u>then</u>. This helps readers understand when they should do this final step.

Conventions <u>GOOD!</u>

- You indented the first sentence of your paragraph.
- Every sentence in your paragraph has an end mark.
- The first word of every sentence should begin with a capital letter.
- Your paragraph contains part of a sentence (and string). Add this to the sentence before it to make a complete sentence (You need beads and string).
- Your writing contains two misspelled words (<u>braselets</u>, <u>tite</u>).

Expository Writing

Draw

1   i like to draw. i do it alot. my pichure is a frog.

2   i saw one wunce. i draw it. i like frogs. i like art.

Conference Notes

Title _Draw_

Ideas   <u>KEEP TRYING!</u>

- Your paragraph tells about drawing and frogs. You need to choose one topic to write about. Name this topic in your opening sentence.
- After you name your topic, write sentences that give information about the topic.

Organization   <u>KEEP TRYING!</u>

- The first sentence tells readers what you know how to do well—draw.
- The other sentences in your paragraph tell about a picture you drew. They also tell why you drew it. These sentences need to explain the steps you follow when drawing a picture.

Conventions   <u>GOOD!</u>

- Every sentence ends with an end mark. Good work!
- You indented the first sentence of your paragraph.
- The first word of every sentence and the word <u>I</u> should start with a capital letter.
- Your paragraph has some misspelled words (<u>alot, pichure, wunce, draw</u>).

© Houghton Mifflin Harcourt Publishing Company

Conference Notes

Title __*Gutter Ball*__

Ideas   GREAT!

- Your opening sentence tells what the poem is about.
- Your paragraph answers the prompt. You name your favorite part. You like this part of the poem because it makes you think of how you feel when you slide on your kitchen floor.

Organization   GREAT!

- The first sentence of your paragraph gives a fact about the poem.
- In sentences 2 and 3, you give interesting details about the poem. These details answer the prompt.

Conventions   GREAT!

- You indented the first sentence of your paragraph.
- Every sentence in your paragraph has an end mark.
- The first word of every sentence begins with a capital letter.
- Every word in your paragraph is spelled correctly.

Bowling

1   The poem tells about bowling. His finger got
2 stuk. My finger got stuk. In a ring. It did not come
3 off. I like the part about getting stuck. It hapened
4 to me.

Conference Notes

Title *Bowling*

Ideas   <u>KEEP TRYING!</u>

- Your opening sentence tells what the poem is about.
- You describe your favorite part of the poem. You also tell why it is your favorite.
- You did not explain how the poem makes you feel. This was part of the prompt. You can revise your paragraph to include this information.

Organization   <u>GOOD!</u>

- The first two sentences of your paragraph give facts about the poem.
- In sentences 3 and 4, you give interesting details about a time when your finger got stuck. This helps the reader understand why you liked this part best.

Conventions   <u>GOOD!</u>

- You indented the first sentence of your paragraph.
- Every sentence in your paragraph has an end mark.
- The first word of every sentence begins with a capital letter.
- Your writing contains part of a sentence (<u>in a ring</u>). Add this part to the sentence before it to form a complete sentence.
- Check the spelling of <u>stuk</u> and <u>hapened</u>.

Responding to Literature

Bowl

1   I bowl. I like it. My feet slide. The ball is hevy. I
2   am stuk. I like to bowl. It is funny.

Conference Notes

Title *Bowl*

Ideas KEEP TRYING!

- Your paragraph should describe the poem. You tell about something that you like to do—bowl, but you do not mention the poem, which tells about bowling, too.
- The prompt asks you to name your favorite part of the poem and tell how it makes you feel. Your writing does not include this information.

Organization KEEP TRYING!

- Your paragraph is about one topic, which is good organization, but it is about the wrong topic.
- The first sentence of your paragraph should give facts about the poem.
- The other sentences should give interesting details about the poem.

Conventions GOOD!

- Every sentence in your paragraph has an end mark.
- The first word of every sentence begins with a capital letter.
- You indented the first sentence of your paragraph.
- Your paragraph contains two spelling errors (hevy, stuk).

Conference Notes

Title _____

Ideas _____

Organization _____

Conventions _____

Name

Daily Journal

Name _____

Sensory Chart

I will describe _____ . (topic)

 see	
 hear	
 smell	
 taste	
 touch	

Name _____

Story Map/Four-Square

1.

2.

3.

4.

336

Narrative Writing 102

Name _____

Friendly Letter

Date _____

Greeting: _____

Message: _____

Closing _____

Name _____

Cluster

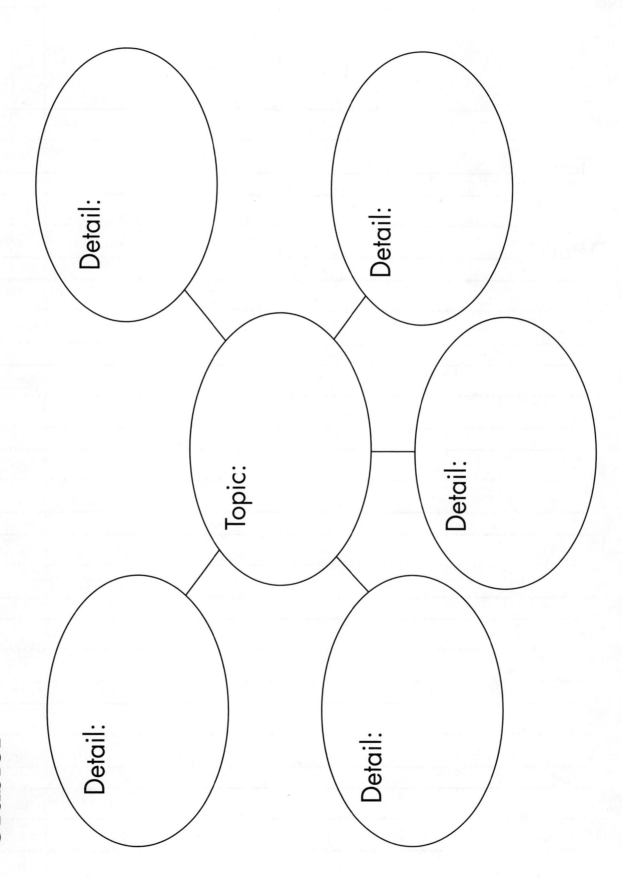

Detail:

Detail:

Topic:

Detail:

Detail:

Detail:

Name _____

List

_____

- -

Topic: _____

_____

- -

Details: _____

_____

- -

_____

_____

- -

_____

_____

- -

_____

_____

- -

_____

_____

- -

_____

_____

- -

_____

Name _____

Note

Greeting: _____

_____

Message: _____

_____

_____

_____

_____

Closing _____

_____

_____

Name _____

The Writing Process

Directions Finish each writing process word. Use page 14 in your book to help you.

> **The Writing Process**

Pr __ __ __ __ __ __

W __ __ __ __

R __ __ __ __ __

E __ __ __

P __ __ __ __ __ __ __

Name _____

Sentences 1

> A sentence tells a complete idea.
>
> **Conall eats his lunch.**

Directions Circle each complete sentence.

1. Conall sits down.

2. Eats cheese.

3. He likes.

4. Conall drinks milk every day.

Next Step: Draw a picture of something you like to eat. Write a complete sentence about it.

Name _____

Sentence Order

Directions Use the words in each box to make a sentence.

| is   brown   My   dog |

1. _____

| run   He   likes   to |

2. _____

Directions Cut out the words at the right.
Put them in the correct order.
Glue one in each box.

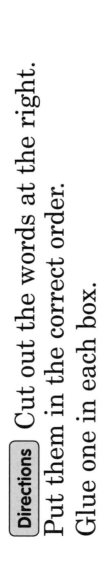

cat		I
love		my

Name _____

The Naming Part

Directions Circle the naming part in each sentence.

1. My cat climbs the tree.

2. I jump up and down.

3. Mom looks up in the tree.

4. Dad gets a ladder.

Directions Choose a naming part from above.
Draw a picture of it.

Name _____

The Telling Part

Directions Circle the telling part in each sentence.

1. I throw a ball to Sadie.

2. She is our new puppy.

3. We play together.

Directions Choose a telling part from above.
Draw a picture of it.

Name _____

Writing Sentences

© Houghton Mifflin Harcourt Publishing Company

Directions Write a **naming part** for each sentence below.

1. _____ jumps.

2. _____ helps me.

Directions Write a **telling part** for each sentence below.

1. The class frog _____

2. The teacher _____

Name _____

Sentences 2

A sentence has a naming part and a telling part.

Naming Part + Telling Part   = Sentence

Mary + jumps rope = Mary jumps rope.

Directions Circle the naming part of each sentence below. (The **naming part** tells who or what the sentence is about.)

1. My brother skates.

2. Nona and Jeff play tag.

3. I run with my dog.

Directions Circle the telling part of each sentence below. (The **telling part** tells more about the naming part.)

1. Devron won the race.

2. The children cheered.

3. They jumped around.

Name _____

Telling Sentences

A telling sentence tells about something or someone. It ends with a period.

The bear lives in the woods.

Directions Circle each telling sentence.

1. Bears eat berries.

2. Do bears eat fish?

3. Bears sleep in winter.

4. Baby bears are cubs.

5. Do you like bears?

Next Step: Write a telling sentence about an animal you know. Use a period.

_____

- -

_____

- -

_____

Name _____

Asking Sentences

An asking sentence asks a question. It ends with a question mark.

Where are you going?

Directions Circle each asking sentence.

1. We will go to the park.

2. Can Ryan come, too?

3. Who will take us to the park?

4. Dad will take us.

5. When are we leaving?

Next Step: Write an asking sentence. Ask your teacher a question. Use a question mark.

_____

- -

_____

- -

_____

Name _____

Exclamatory Sentences

An exclamatory sentence shows strong feeling. It ends with an exclamation point.

Sasha, come quickly!

Directions Circle each exclamatory sentence.

1. Can you swim?

2. Look at that swimmer!

3. She races.

4. Hurray, she wins!

Next Step: Write a sentence about something that excited you. Use an exclamation point.

_____

_____

_____

_____

_____

Name _____

Use a Period 1

Use a period at the end of a telling sentence.
Grandma rides in a cab.

Directions Circle each correct telling sentence below.

1. Mom drives a van.

2. Our neighbor has a black truck

3. I ride a bus to school

4. Grandpa takes a train to work.

5. My sister rides a bike.

Next Step: Write a telling sentence about someone you know. Remember to use a period.

_____

_____

_____

_____

_____

Name _____

Use a Question Mark

Use a question mark at the end of an asking sentence.

What time is it?

Directions Circle the correct questions below.

1. When are we eating

2. Are we having soup?

3. Will you set the table?

4. Where are the cups

5. Are we ready?

Next Step: Write a question to ask your teacher. Remember to use a question mark.

_____

- -

_____

- -

_____

- -

_____

Name _____

Use an Exclamation Point

> Use an exclamation point at the end of an exclamatory sentence.
>
> **My dog Coco has my shoe!**

Directions Circle each exclamatory sentence.

1. The dog is chewing my shoe!

The dog is chewing my shoe.

2. Come here, Coco.

Come here, Coco!

3. Good girl, Coco!

Good girl, Coco.

Next Step: Write a sentence that shows strong feeling. Remember to use an exclamation point.

_____

_____

_____

Name _____

Verbs 1

An action verb tells what the naming part does.

jump   make   run

Mom makes a snack.

Directions Circle the verb in each sentence.

1. Mom cooks popcorn.

2. I smell butter.

3. Mom adds some salt.

4. Mom and I eat the popcorn.

Next Step: Write a sentence using the action verb *jump*.

_____

- - - - - - - - - - - - - - - - - - -

_____

- - - - - - - - - - - - - - - - - - -

_____

- - - - - - - - - - - - - - - - - - -

_____

Name _____

Verbs 2

A linking verb tells what the naming part is.

am   are   was   were   is   been

The lizards <u>are</u> fast.

Directions Circle the linking verb in each sentence.

1. Where are the lizards?

2. They were in the desert.

3. I am in the desert now.

4. Tom was there last summer.

Next Step: Write a sentence using the verb *am*.

_____

- -

_____

_____

- -

_____

_____

- -

_____

Name _____

Action Verb Tenses

Some verbs tell what is happening now, in the present.

Fern <u>walks</u> in the woods.

Some verbs tell what already happened in the past. Action verbs in the past tense usually end in *–ed*.

Fern <u>walked</u> in the woods yesterday.

Directions Draw a line from the present-tense verb to the correct past-tense verb.

1. pack   cooked

2. play   jumped

3. jump   mixed

4. cook   played

5. mix   packed

Name _____

Linking Verb Tenses

Some past-tense verbs do not end in *–ed*. They use a different word to show what already happened.

Present Tense	Past Tense
am	was
is	was
are	were
I am hungry.	**I was hungry.**

Directions Replace each underlined verb with the correct past-tense verb.

_____
- -

1. I <u>am</u> thirsty. I _____ thirsty.

_____
- -

2. Tomás <u>is</u> cold. Tomás _____ cold.

3. The children <u>are</u> happy.

_____
- -

The children _____ happy.

Name _____

Choose a Topic

Directions Think of some things to describe. List the words below.

_____

- -

_____

- -

_____

- -

_____

- -

_____

Directions Choose one thing you would like to describe. Draw a picture of it, and color it.

Name _____

Editing Checklist

☐ Capital letters

☐ End marks

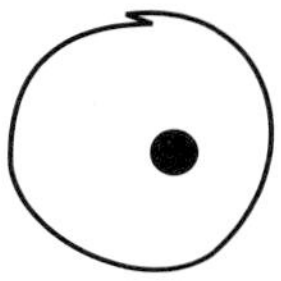

☐ Spelling

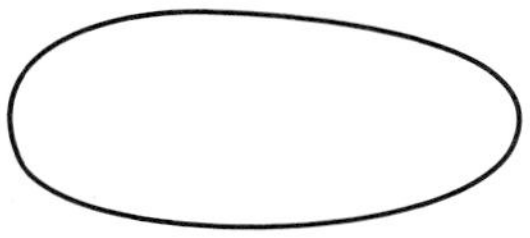

Name _____

Thinking About Your Writing

Title: _____

1. I picked this topic because

_____

_____

_____

_____

2. The best thing about my writing is

_____

_____

_____

_____

_____

*Name*_____

Capital Letters 1

Use a capital letter for the first word in a sentence.

My aunt took me to the zoo.

Use a capital letter for the word "I."

I had fun with my aunt.

Directions Read each sentence. Put three lines (≡) under the letter that should be a capital letter. Then write the word correctly on the line.

1. we saw many birds.

_____

2. the penguin was funny.

_____

3. Look, i can walk like a penguin.

_____

4. My aunt and i laughed.

_____

Name _____

Sentence Starters

_____

1. One summer, _____

_____

_____

_____

_____

2. One day, _____

_____

_____

_____

_____

3. One night, _____

_____

_____

_____

Name

Think of Topic Ideas

I can explain how to

I can explain how to

I can explain how to

I can explain how to

Name _____

Order Chart

Directions Draw a picture about each step you will explain. Label each step.

Topic: _____

Step 1	
Step 2	
Step 3	

Name_____

Nouns 1

A noun is a word that names a person, place, or thing.

person:	girl	teacher
place:	home	park
thing:	pencil	flower

Directions Circle the noun in each sentence.

1. The green parrot yells.

2. A man feeds the elephant.

3. One lion roars.

4. The zoo is noisy.

Next Step: Write a sentence. Circle the noun in the sentence.

_____

- - - - - - - - - - - - - - - - - - -

_____

- - - - - - - - - - - - - - - - - - -

_____

- - - - - - - - - - - - - - - - - - -

_____

Name _____

Nouns 2

Nouns can be common or proper.

A common noun names any person, place, or thing.

A proper noun names a special person, place, or thing. Proper nouns begin with capital letters.

Common Nouns	Proper Nouns
school	Salem School
cat	Smokey

Directions Draw a line from the common noun to the correct proper noun.

1. boy   Star Park

2. woman   Will

3. park   Mr. Wren

4. man   Mrs. Green

Next Step: Use the name of a friend in a sentence.

_____

_____

_____

Name _____

Nouns 3

A singular noun names one person, place, or thing.

A plural noun names more than one person, place, or thing. Many plural nouns end in –s.

Singular Nouns	**Plural Nouns**
bag	bags
pear	pears

Directions Add an -s to make each word plural. Write the new word on the line.

1. bike _____

2. book _____

3. car _____

4. house _____

Name _____

Capital Letters 2

Use a capital letter to write special names.

People	**Places**
<u>M</u>arc <u>B</u>rown	<u>A</u>frica
<u>M</u>ona <u>L</u>isa	<u>N</u>evada

Directions Write the underlined words correctly.

1. This is <u>zoe smith</u>. _____

2. She lived in <u>montana</u>. _____

3. Her family moved to <u>chicago</u>. _____

4. She plays with <u>ruth hall</u>. _____

Next Step: Write two special names.

_____

_____

_____

_____

Name _____

Fiction Details Sheet

Directions To gather details, you can complete these sentence starters.

1. I read _____

by _____

2. The story is about _____

_____

_____

_____

3. The problem is that _____

_____

_____

_____

4. I like this book because _____

_____

_____

_____

Name _____

Pronouns

A pronoun takes the place of a noun. Here are some common pronouns.

he	**she**	**it**	**they**

Directions Write the pronoun from the box above that takes the place of the underlined word or words.

1. <u>Frank</u> makes a sign.

_____

_____ makes a sign.

2. Ruby colors <u>the sign</u>.

_____

Ruby colors _____ .

3. <u>Frank and Ruby</u> work together.

_____

_____ work together.

4. <u>Mrs. Miller</u> looks at the sign.

_____

_____ looks at the sign.

Name _____

Nonfiction Fact Sheet

Directions Complete these sentence starters to gather details.

1. I read _____

by _____

2. The book is about _____

_____

_____

_____

3. I learned that _____

_____

_____

_____

4. I like this book because _____

_____

_____

_____

Name _____

Poetry Details Sheet

1. What is the poem about?

_____

_____

_____

_____

2. What is your favorite line?

_____

_____

_____

_____

3. Why do you like this line or part?

_____

_____

_____

_____

Name _____

Use an Apostrophe

An apostrophe (') shows where a letter or letters have been left out when two words are combined. The new word is called a contraction.

is not   **isn't**

Directions Choose the correct contraction from the word box for the underlined words in each sentence. Write the contraction on the line.

isn't	don't	wasn't	didn't	hasn't

The dog <u>is not</u> old. _____ isn't _____

1. The dog <u>did not</u> jump. _____

2. <u>Do not</u> wake the dog. _____

3. Mrs. Fin <u>was not</u> home. _____

4. She <u>has not</u> seen the dog. _____

Name _____

Adjectives 1

An adjective is a word that tells more about a noun.

Socks is a friendly cat.

She has striped fur.

Directions Write an adjective that makes sense in each sentence. Use the words from the box below.

four	sharp	long

1. Socks has a _____ tail.

2. She has _____ feet.

3. My cat has _____ claws.

Name _____

Adjectives 2

An adjective can compare two nouns.

Grandpa is <u>older</u> than I am.

An adjective can compare more than two nouns.

He has the <u>longest</u> beard of anyone I know.

Directions Circle the correct adjective to finish each sentence.

1. Grandpa has *(shorter, shortest)* hair than I do.

2. His hair is the *(shorter, shortest)* in the family.

3. Dad is *(taller, tallest)* than Grandpa.

4. Grandpa tells the *(funnier, funniest)* jokes.

Name _____

Gathering Grid

To gather details, you can complete these sentence starters.

Topic: _____

1. What does the animal look like?	**2.** Where does it live?
3. What does it eat?	**4.** What are other interesting facts?

Name _____

Plurals 1

Add an *-s* to make the plurals for most nouns.

Singular Nouns	Plural Nouns
book	books
teacher	teachers

Directions Add an *-s* to make each word plural.
Write the new word on the line.

1. bug _____

2. cap _____

3. toy _____

Name _____

Plurals 2

Some nouns use new words to show more than one.

Singular Nouns	Plural Nouns
child	children
foot	feet
goose	geese
mouse	mice

Directions Circle the correct word to finish each sentence.

1. Two *(child, children)* play at the park.

2. Each child hops on one *(feet, foot)*.

3. The children saw a *(mice, mouse)*.

4. The children saw two *(geese, goose)*.

Next Step: Write a sentence using the word *children*.

_____

- -

_____

_____

- -

_____

Name _____

Use a Period 2

Use a period after the abbreviations *Mr.*, *Mrs.*, *Ms.*, and *Dr.*

Mr. Brown lives on a farm.

Directions Add a period after each abbreviation below.

1. Mrs Fine lives in a town.

2. Does Ms Hall live by a lake?

3. They go to Dr Sing.

4. Mr Peet lives in a big city.

Next Step: Write a sentence about a person you know. Use one of these abbreviations: *Mr.*, *Mrs.*, *Ms.*, or *Dr.*

_____

_____

_____

_____

_____

Name _____

Commas in Letters

Use a comma

- between the day and the year: **May 21, 2012**
- after the greeting in a letter: **Dear Tess,**
- after the closing in a letter: **Your friend,**
  Cole

Directions Add three commas to this letter.

April 5 2012

Dear Pam

The tree in our yard is pretty. Here is a picture for you.

Your friend
Ellie

Next Step: Write today's date. Write the month, the day, and the year. Remember to use a comma.

_____

_____

Name_____

Capital Letters 3

Use a capital letter for titles in names.

<u>D</u>r. Mike   **<u>M</u>rs. Lions**   **<u>M</u>r. Fell**

Directions   Write each name correctly.

_____

1. mr. Mills _____

_____

2. mrs. May _____

_____

3. dr. Lee _____

Next Step: Write a sentence about a doctor. Use the abbreviation *Dr.*

_____

_____

_____

Name _____

Capital Letters 4

Use a capital letter for holidays.

_President's _Day   **_New _Year's _Day**

Directions The underlined word names a holiday.
Write it correctly on the line.

1. On <u>thanksgiving</u>, Joe ate turkey.

_____

- -

_____

2. One <u>labor day</u>, Carol went to a picnic.

_____

- -

_____

3. I saw a parade on <u>memorial day</u>.

_____

- -

_____

Name _____

Capital Letters 5

Use a capital letter for days of the week.

<u>W</u>ednesday   **<u>T</u>hursday**   **<u>S</u>aturday**

Directions Write each day of the week correctly.

_____

1. tuesday _____

2. sunday _____

3. monday _____

4. friday _____

Next Step: Write the name of your favorite day of the week.

_____

_____

Name _____

Capital Letters 6

> Use a capital letter for months of the year.
>
> **F**ebruary   **A**ugust   **N**ovember

Directions Write each month of the year correctly.

_____

1. march _____

_____

2. may _____

_____

3. july _____

Next Step: Write a sentence using the name of a month.

_____

_____

_____

Name _____

ABC Order 1

Directions Write the words below in ABC order.

dog	can	all	bug

1. _____

2. _____

3. _____

4. _____

Name _____

ABC Order 2

Directions Write the words below in ABC order.

| feet | hand | in | eat | go | job |

1. _____

2. _____

3. _____

4. _____

5. _____

6. _____

Name _____

ABC Order 3

Directions Write the words below in ABC order.

one	me	kitten	nose	leg

1. _____

2. _____

3. _____

4. _____

5. _____

Name _____

ABC Order 4

Directions Write the words below in ABC order.

ring	quack	ten	saw	pull

1. _____

2. _____

3. _____

4. _____

5. _____

*Name*_____

ABC Order 5

Directions Write the words below in ABC order.

year	van	zero	x-ray	up	we

1. _____

2. _____

3. _____

4. _____

5. _____

6. _____

Name _____

Using the Right Word 1

Some words sound alike but are spelled differently and mean different things. These words are called homophones.

A spider has <u>eight</u> legs.

Tim <u>ate</u> green beans.

Directions Choose the correct word to finish each sentence. Write the word on the line.

1. Mike rides his _____ bike.

　　　　　　　　　　blew　　　blue

2. Did Nan _____ milk at the store?

　　　　　　　　buy　　　by

3. A _____ jumped into the yard!

　　　dear　　　deer

Name _____

Using the Right Word 2

Some words sound alike but are spelled differently and mean different things. These words are called homophones.

Four puppies played.

The letter is for Jim.

[Directions] Choose the correct word to finish each sentence. Write the word on the line.

1. Can you _____ the bird sing?

hear   here

2. My brother is _____ year old.

one   won

Next Step: Write a sentence using the word *it's.*

_____

- -

_____

_____

- -

_____

Name _____

Using the Right Word 3

Some words sound alike but are spelled differently and mean different things. These words are called homophones.

Their brother is tall.

There is one box.

They're going to town.

Directions Choose the correct word to finish each sentence. Write the word on the line.

1. Julie _____ in a bus.

        road   rode

2. Green says "Go." _____ says "Stop."

        Read   Red

3. The bike has _____ tires.

        to   two

Name _____

Using Opposites

Opposites tell about ideas that are completely different from each other.

happy    sad

Directions Draw a line from each word to its opposite.

1. left   hot

2. cold   up

3. down   night

4. day   right

Next Step: Write sentences using the words *on* and *off*.

_____

_____

_____

_____

_____

_____

Name _____

Sentences 3

Every sentence begins with a capital letter and ends with an end mark. The end mark can be

- a period **(.),**
- a question mark **(?),** or
- an exclamation point **(!)**.

Directions Circle each sentence that is written correctly.

1. What does the plant need?

2. it needs the sun.

3. Water the plant

4. Wow, the plant grows and grows!

Next Step: Write a sentence about something that grows. Use a capital letter and an end mark.

_____

- -

_____

- -

_____

Name _____

Sentences 4

> In every sentence the subject and verb must agree.
>
> • If the subject names one person, place, or thing, the verb usually ends with –s.
>
> **Sally <u>likes</u> soup.**
>
> • If the subject names more than one person, place, or thing, the verb does not end with –s.
>
> **Jo and Hal <u>like</u> potatoes.**

Directions Circle the correct verb to finish each sentence.

1. Sophie *(make, makes)* soup every week.

2. She *(share, shares)* it with Ted.

3. Ted and Sophie *(like, likes)* the soup.

Next Step: Write a sentence using the subject *they*. Make sure the subject and the verb agree.

_____

_____

_____

Dear Families,

Ty can write a few letters. Jessica can write her name. Asa can write *cat, dog,* and *I love you.* Mia can write a paragraph. No matter where your first grader is on the writing continuum, you'll be pleased to know he or she is learning the same **writing process** used by professional authors. What is the writing process? Let's follow Kyle as he writes a three-sentence "story."

First, Kyle **prewrites**. He thinks about a topic, makes a list, and draws a picture about the idea he chooses. Next, Kyle **writes**. He gets ideas from his picture and puts them down on paper. Now Kyle is ready to **revise**. He reads his story to a partner, listens to his partner's questions, and makes needed changes. No story is complete without an **edit**. Kyle reads the story and makes corrections in capital letters, end marks, and spelling. Finally, Kyle **publishes** his work. He thinks of a title, writes a neat final copy, and shares his writing and picture with the class. Success!

Besides the writing process, your child will learn to use the six **traits** of writing—**ideas, organization, voice, word choice, sentence fluency,** and **conventions.**

To help your child with the writing process:
- Read together daily. Talk about how authors might get ideas.
- Provide opportunities to make lists at home.
- Follow step-by-step directions to create a craft together.
- Tell your child how you use writing each day.

Thank you!

Dear Families,

Did you e-mail a friend, jot a message on a greeting card, or take notes about a project at work today? Think of all you had to learn before you could complete such a task!

First, you learned to write a few words. Then you learned to put these words together into a sentence. You learned that a sentence doesn't sound right unless the words are in a certain order and state a complete thought. You also learned that a sentence doesn't look right unless you begin with a capital letter and finish with an end mark. Next, you learned to put sentences about the same topic together into paragraphs. You stated the main idea and added details and thoughts. You wanted your paragraph to look right, too, so you indented the first line.

Your first grader is learning about sentences and paragraphs right now. To foster this important foundation for writing:

- Cut out a brief article from a newspaper. Give your child a crayon and take a different color for yourself. Take turns highlighting sentences in the article. Then count the number of sentences in each paragraph.
- Play "Fill in the Blank." Say a sentence, leaving out one word, and challenge your child to guess the word. Then switch roles.
- Write several topics on slips of paper. Take turns selecting one and making up a sentence, a question, and an exclamation about the topic.

Thank you!

Dear Families,

*I'm thinking of a room. I **see** shiny appliances. I **touch** cool, smooth countertops. I **smell** baking bread and **taste** the grape jam that will go on it. I **hear** children playing outside. Where am I?* Did an image of a kitchen form in your mind? As we move into the study of descriptive writing, your child will learn to paint "word pictures" like this, using the five senses.

First, we decide on a topic. Next, we focus on the **word choice** writing trait by making a list of sensory words and pictures about the topic. Then we write an introductory sentence, use ideas from the list to write more sentences, and end with a final thought.

Your child is also learning to reflect on her or his work by completing two sentences: *I picked this topic because . . .* and *The best thing about my writing is . . .* This helps us get the most out of our writing and apply our skills to future projects.

To help your child think descriptively:

- State three clues about a person, a place, or an object, and invite your child to guess who or what it is. Then switch roles.
- Write "favorites" on slips of paper, such as *favorite food, favorite game,* and *favorite animal.* Take turns choosing one and describing it to the family.
- Before bedtime each evening, invite your child to draw and tell you about something interesting seen that day.

Thank you!

Dear Families,

What does your family talk about at the dinner table? Possibly, each person tells about the day's events. As we study personal narratives, students will learn to write about their memorable experiences.

First, we decide on a topic by completing sentence starters such as *One day . . .* or *One summer . . .* Next, we create a "story map" by drawing a series of pictures showing who was there, what happened, and where it happened. Then we write an introductory sentence and a sentence about each picture. We use the word *I* because we're writing about ourselves. A trait important to narration is **organization**. To make sense, details must be arranged in time order using words such as *first, next, then,* and *later.* After revising, editing, and publishing comes the best part— sharing our stories with one another. Finally, we reflect on our writing by answering *I picked this topic because . . .* and *The best thing about my writing is . . .*

To help your child start thinking about narration:

- When guests visit, encourage your child to ask about their childhoods—games, friends, school, and so on.
- Write a letter to a friend together telling about a fun experience. Ask your child to add a drawing.
- Write about a shared experience in short, simple sentences. Read it together. Then cut the sentences apart, scramble them, and help your child put the events back in order.

Thank you!

Dear Families,

Your child can answer the phone, set the table, and play some games. How? You've given him or her step-by-step instructions. As we move into the study of expository writing, your child will have the chance to tell someone else how to do something. An important trait for this genre is **ideas**. We want to choose something we know how to do well and something we can explain.

First, we decide on a topic. Next, we draw the steps in order and label any details on our pictures. Then we write an introductory sentence beginning with *You can . . .* and a sentence about each picture. We use time-order words in our sentences to emphasize the steps, such as *first, then,* and *finally*. After revising, editing, and publishing, we share our how-to paragraphs with one another. We hope someone will try our idea! Then, as always, we reflect on our topic and what we like best about our writing.

To help your child with expository text:

- Together, explore some "how-to" materials, such as books and articles on cooking, crafts, and home repair.

- Have a family talent show in which everyone demonstrates and explains something she or he knows how to do.

- Draw a picture of something you have made. Share it with your child, explaining the process step-by-step. Then invite your child to do the same.

Thank you!

Dear Families,

First graders have opinions! They share their feelings about what to wear, what to eat, TV and computer privileges, and rules they consider unfair. As students move into the study of persuasive writing, they'll learn that stating an opinion is not enough. We must be able to give reasons why others should agree. Convincing someone to agree requires skill in the writing trait called **voice**. Since the opinions expressed are our own, our writing must sound as if we are talking.

First, we decide on an opinion. Next, we make a list of three reasons why others should agree with us. Then we write an introductory sentence using the word *should,* write a sentence for each reason on our list, and state our opinion one more time. With input from a partner, we revise and edit our persuasive paragraph. Finally, we publish it, share it with the class, and reflect on our writing.

To help your child with persuasion:

- Read some fairy tales together. How did the dwarves persuade Snow White to stay? How did the wolf persuade Red Riding Hood to tell him about her grandmother?
- Invite each family member to write down the name of a movie they want to see. Then take turns giving at least three reasons why the family should agree.
- Discuss TV commercials you view together and how they try to persuade people to do or buy certain things.

Thank you!

Dear Families,

Do you like to read fiction? Nonfiction? Poetry? In first grade, we read all three. We learn to tell others about the books and poems so they'll want to read them, too.

To respond to a fiction book, we write the title and author and tell what the book is about, including the main problem. Then we tell why we like the book. We're careful not to give away the ending!

To respond to nonfiction, we write the title and author and tell what the book is about. Then we share some interesting facts we learned and tell why we like the book.

To respond to poetry, we write the title and author and tell what the poem is about. Then we tell about our favorite part and how it makes us feel.

While responding to literature, we continue to follow the writing process and work with the six traits of writing we've mentioned—**ideas, organization, voice, word choice, sentence fluency,** and **conventions.**

To help your child with literature response:

- Look through some children's books together. Talk about what makes readers choose certain books. The title? The art? A favorite author?
- Watch an informational children's show on TV. Ask one another, *What interesting facts did you learn?*
- Invite family members to tell about books they've read. Remind them not to give away the endings!

Thank you!

Dear Families,

Have you ever seen a list poem? It names a topic and uses interesting words to describe it. The first and last sentence is repeated, like this:

> ### *Clowns*
> *Clowns are friendly.*
> *Clowns are colorful.*
> *Clowns are creative.*
> *Clowns are clever.*
> *Clowns are comical.*
> *Clowns are friendly.*

As we move into the study of creative writing, we'll also study ABC and rhyming poems. Besides poems, we'll write stories that focus on **characters** (who), **setting** (where and when), a **problem** (the trouble the characters face), and a **plot** (what happens when the characters try to solve the problem). An important writing trait for the creative genre is **sentence fluency**, where we make our writing easy to read and use both short and long sentences. Above all, we use our imaginations!

To help your child think creatively:

- Read a story together and then retell it in three sentences: beginning, middle, and end.
- Make up sequels to stories you read together.
- Read some poems together. Take turns choosing your favorite words or phrases and telling why you like them.

Thank you!

Dear Families,

How many questions has your first grader asked you today? Children this age seek information morning, noon, and night. However, they are also learning to find answers on their own and share interesting facts with others.

As we move into our report writing unit, we'll first visit the library. We'll look for information in magazines, in books, and on the Internet. We'll use a table of contents and an index to help us find the pages we need. We'll look up words in a dictionary. We'll also learn to use a computer catalog and all the ways the librarian can help us.

When we write our reports, we'll choose a topic, read about it, and gather details. We'll write an opening paragraph to introduce the topic and give the first detail. Then we'll add new paragraphs for additional details. An important trait in report writing is **conventions**. We need to make sure our published work has correct capital letters, end marks, and spelling. Look forward to learning some new fun facts from your first grader soon!

To help your child with reports:

- Explore interesting topics together on the Internet. For quality and safety, look for sites that end with *.edu* (education), *.org* (organizations), or *.gov* (government).
- Call your local library and arrange for a guided tour for you and your child. Take advantage of the many resources available to your family.

Thank you!

Queridas familias,

Ty puede escribir algunas cartas. Jessica puede escribir su nombre. Asa puede escribir *gato, perro* y *te quiero*. Mia puede escribir un párrafo. No importa dónde se encuentre su hijo de primer grado en el proceso de escritura, usted puede sentirse satisfecho de que él o ella está aprendiendo el mismo **proceso de escritura** que usan los autores profesionales. ¿De qué se trata este proceso de escritura? Veamos qué hace Kyle a medida que escribe un "cuento" de tres oraciones.

Lo primero que hace Kyle es **preescribir**. Piensa en un tema, hace una lista y luego hace un dibujo sobre el tema que escogió. Después **escribe**. Toma ideas de su dibujo y las anota en una hoja de papel. Ahora, Kyle está listo para **revisar**. Lee su cuento a un compañero, escucha las preguntas de su compañero y hace los cambios necesarios. Para que el cuento quede completo, tiene que **editarlo**. Kyle lo lee y corrige las letras mayúsculas, los signos al final y la ortografía. Finalmente **publica su trabajo**. Piensa en un título, escribe la versión final y comparte su escrito y su dibujo con la clase. ¡Un éxito!

Además del proceso de escritura, su hijo aprenderá a usar los seis rasgos de la escritura: **ideas, organización, voz, escogencia de palabras, fluidez de las oraciones** y **convenciones**.

Ayúdele a su hijo con el proceso de escritura:

- Lean juntos todos los días. Hablen acerca de cómo obtienen los autores sus ideas.
- Piense en maneras de hacer listas en el hogar.
- Hagan juntos un trabajo manual siguiendo instrucciones paso a paso.
- Explíquele a su hijo cómo usa usted la escritura todos los días.

¡Gracias!

Queridas familias,

¿Hoy le han escrito un correo electrónico a un amigo, una tarjeta de saludo o tomaron notas sobre un proyecto en el trabajo? ¡Piensen en todo lo que tuvieron que aprender para poder completar esas tareas!

Primero aprendieron a escribir algunas palabras. Luego aprendieron a poner esas palabras juntas en una oración. Aprendieron que una oración no suena bien a menos que las palabras estén en cierto orden y expresen una idea completa. También saben que una oración no está bien si la primera letra no está en mayúscula y no tiene signo de puntuación al final. Después aprendieron a poner las oraciones que tratan del mismo tema en párrafos. Expresaron la idea principal y agregaron datos y pensamientos. También querían que el párrafo se viera bien y por eso dejaron sangría en la primera línea.

Su hijo de primer grado está aprendiendo sobre oraciones y párrafos. Para fomentar esta importante base de la escritura:

- Recorte un artículo corto del periódico. Déle a su hijo un creyón y tome uno de diferente color para usted. Túrnense para resaltar oraciones en el artículo. Luego cuenten el número de oraciones en cada párrafo.

- Jueguen a "llenar el espacio en blanco." Diga una oración, pero deje una palabra por fuera. Pídale a su hijo que adivine la palabra. Después cambien de papeles.

- Escriba varios temas en trozos de papel. Túrnense para seleccionar un tema y formar una oración, una pregunta o una exclamación sobre el tema.

¡Gracias!

Queridas familias,

Pienso en un cuarto. **Veo** *electrodomésticos que brillan.* **Toco** *unos mesones lisos y frescos.* **Huelo** *el pan horneado y* **pruebo** *la jalea de uvas que le unto al pan.* **Oigo** *niños que juegan afuera. ¿Dónde estoy?* ¿Formaron mentalmente la imagen de una cocina? A medida que avancemos en el estudio de la escritura descriptiva, su hijo aprenderá a crear "imágenes de palabras" como las anteriores, usando los cinco sentidos.

Primero elegimos un tema. Luego nos concentraremos en el rasgo de la **escogencia de palabras,** haciendo una lista de palabras sensoriales y dibujos sobre el tema. Después escribiremos una oración introductoria, tomaremos ideas de la lista para escribir más oraciones y terminaremos con una idea final.

Su hijo(a) también está aprendiendo a reflexionar sobre su propio trabajo, completando dos oraciones: *Escogí este tema porque. . .* y *Lo mejor de mi ensayo es . . .* Esto nos ayuda a aprovechar al máximo lo que escribimos. Así podremos aplicar nuestras destrezas en proyectos futuros.

Ayúdele a su hijo a pensar descriptivamente:

- Diga tres pistas sobre una persona, un lugar o un objeto. Pídale a su hijo que adivine de quién o de qué se trata. Luego cambien de papeles.
- Escriba algunos "favoritos" en hojas de papel. Por ejemplo *comida favorita, juego favorito* y *animal favorito.* Túrnense para escoger un favorito y describirlo para la familia.
- Todas las noches, antes de irse a la cama, invite a su hijo a dibujar y a contar algo interesante que haya visto durante el día.

¡Gracias!

Queridas familias,

¿Sobre qué tema habla la familia a la hora de cenar? Tal vez cada persona cuenta los sucesos del día. A medida que estudiemos las narrativas personales, los estudiantes aprenderán a escribir sobre sus experiencias más memorables.

Primero escogeremos un tema, completando oraciones de inicio como *Un día . . . o Un verano . . .* Luego crearemos un "mapa del cuento" con dibujos que muestren quién estuvo allí, qué sucedió y dónde sucedió. Después escribiremos una oración introductoria y una oración sobre el dibujo. Usaremos la palabra *yo* porque vamos a hablar sobre nosotros mismos. Un rasgo importante de la narración es la **organización**. Para que los detalles tengan sentido, se deben poner en orden cronológico usando palabras como *primero, luego, después* y *más tarde.* Después de revisar, editar y publicar viene lo mejor: compartir nuestros cuentos con los demás. Finalmente, reflexionaremos sobre nuestro escrito respondiendo a: *Escogí este tema porque . . .* y *Lo mejor de mi escrito es . . .*

Ayúdele a su hijo a pensar en la narración:

- Cuando tenga invitados en casa, motive a su hijo para que les pregunte sobre su infancia—juegos, amigos, la escuela, etc.

- Escríbanle juntos una carta a un amigo o amiga contándole una experiencia divertida. Pídale a su hijo que haga un dibujo.

- Escriban acerca de una experiencia que hayan compartido. Háganlo en oraciones cortas y sencillas. Léanla juntos. Luego, corten las oraciones, mezclen las partes y pídale a su hijo que ponga los sucesos en orden.

¡Gracias!

Queridas familias,

Su hijo puede responder el teléfono, poner la mesa y jugar. ¿Cómo? Usted le da instrucciones paso a paso. A medida que avancemos en la escritura explicativa, su hijo podrá explicarle a otra persona cómo se hace una cosa. Un rasgo importante de este género son las **ideas**. Vamos a escoger algo que sepamos hacer bien y que podamos explicar.

Primero, escogemos un tema. Luego dibujaremos los pasos en orden y anotaremos los detalles en nuestros dibujos. Después escribiremos una oración introductoria que empezará con *Tu puedes . . .* y una oración sobre cada dibujo. Usaremos palabras que indican orden para enfatizar los pasos. Por ejemplo, *primero, luego* y *finalmente*. Después de revisar, editar y publicar, vamos a compartir nuestros párrafos explicativos con los demás. ¡Ojalá que alguien ensaye nuestra idea! Luego, como de costumbre, reflexionaremos sobre nuestro tema y sobre lo que más nos gusta de nuestra escritura.

Ayúdele a su hijo con textos explicativos:

- Busquen juntos información sobre "cómo hacer cosas", por ejemplo en libros y artículos de cocina, de manualidades o de arreglos en el hogar.
- Organicen una función familiar de aptitudes para que cada uno demuestre o explique algo que sepa hacer.
- Haga un dibujo de alguna cosa que usted haya hecho. Muéstreselo a su hijo y explíquele el proceso paso a paso. Luego invítelo a que haga lo mismo.

¡Gracias!

Queridas familias,

¡Los niños de primer grado también opinan! Ellos expresan lo que sienten sobre la ropa, la comida y la televisión. También lo hacen sobre el uso de la computadora y sobre las reglas que consideran injustas. A medida que los estudiantes avancen en el estudio de la escritura persuasiva, aprenderán que a veces no sólo es suficiente expresar una opinión. Tenemos que ofrecer razones para que los demás estén de acuerdo. Convencer a una persona requiere la destreza de la escritura que se llama **voz.** Dado que las opiniones que expresamos son las nuestras, lo que escribimos debe sonar como si estuviéramos hablando.

Primero escogemos nuestra opinión. Luego escribiremos tres razones por las cuales los demás deberían estar de acuerdo con nosotros. Después escribiremos una oración introductoria usando la palabra *deberían,* una oración por cada palabra de la lista, y expresaremos de nuevo nuestra opinión. Luego revisaremos y editaremos nuestro párrafo persuasivo después de escuchar los comentarios de algún compañero. Finalmente lo publicaremos, lo compartiremos con la clase y reflexionaremos sobre lo que escribimos.

Ayúdele a su hijo a ser persuasivo:

- Lean juntos algunos cuentos de hadas. ¿Cómo persuadieron los enanitos a Blanca Nieves para que se quedara? ¿Cómo persuadió el lobo a Caperucita Roja para que le contara sobre su abuelita?

- Invite a cada miembro de la familia a escribir el título de una película que quiere ver. Luego túrnense ofreciendo tres razones por las cuales la familia debería estar de acuerdo.

- Hablen acerca de los comerciales de la televisión que ven juntos y cómo tratan de persuadir a las personas para que compren o usen ciertas cosas.

¡Gracias!

Queridas familias,

¿Les gusta la lectura de ficción? ¿De no ficción? ¡La poesía? En primer grado leemos los tres tipos de literatura. Aprendemos a contar a los demás los libros y poemas para que se interesen en leerlos.

Para reaccionar frente a un libro de ficción, escribiremos el título y nombre del autor y contaremos de qué trata el libro, incluso el problema principal. Luego diremos por qué nos gusta el libro, ¡pero tendremos cuidado de no revelar el final!

Para reaccionar frente a la literatura que no es de ficción, escribiremos el título y nombre del autor y contaremos de qué trata el libro. Luego comentaremos algunos hechos interesantes que hayamos aprendido y diremos por qué nos gustó el libro.

Para reaccionar frente a la poesía, escribiremos el título y nombre del autor y diremos de qué trata el poema. Luego hablaremos sobre la parte que más nos gustó y cómo nos hace sentir.

A medida que reaccionamos frente a la literatura, seguiremos el proceso de escritura y trabajaremos con los seis rasgos de la escritura que ya hemos mencionado: **ideas, organización, voz, escogencia de palabras, fluidez de oraciones** y **convenciones.**

Ayúdele a su hijo a reaccionar frente a la literatura:

- Miren juntos algunos libros infantiles. Hablen acerca de qué hace que las personas escojan ciertos libros para leer: ¿el título? ¿las ilustraciones? ¿un autor o autora preferidos?
- Miren un programa de televisión infantil educativo. Pregúntense: *¿qué hechos interesantes aprendimos?*
- Invite a los miembros de la familia a que hablen de los libros que han leído. ¡Recuérdeles que no deben contar el final!

¡Gracias!

Queridas familias,

¿Alguna vez han leído un poema de frases? Estos poemas tienen un tema y usan palabras interesantes para describirlo. La primera oración y la última se repiten así:

Payasos
Los payasos son amigables.
Los payasos son de colores.
Los payasos son creativos.
Los payasos son listos.
Los payasos son cómicos.
Los payasos son amigables.

A medida que avancemos en el estudio de la escritura creativa, estudiaremos poemas con el abecedario y poemas que riman. Además de poemas, escribiremos cuentos cortos que se concentran en los **personajes** (quién), la **escena** (dónde y cuándo), un **problema** (las dificultades que afrontan los personajes) y la **trama** (qué sucede cuando los personajes tratan de resolver el problema). Un rasgo importante del género creativo es la **fluidez de las oraciones.** Con ella hacemos que nuestro escrito sea fácil de leer y usamos oraciones cortas y largas. ¡Pero sobre todo usamos la imaginación!

Ayúdele a su hijo a ser creativo:

- Lean juntos un cuento y luego cuéntenlo en tres oraciones: principio, desarrollo y final.
- Inventen secuencias de los cuentos que leyeron juntos.
- Lean juntos algunos poemas. Túrnense para escoger sus palabras o frases preferidas. Expliquen por qué les gustan.

¡Gracias!

Queridas familias,

¿Cuántas preguntas le ha hecho su hijo de primer grado hoy? A esta edad, los niños buscan información mañana, tarde y noche. Pero además están aprendiendo a buscar respuestas por sí mismos y a compartir datos interesantes con sus compañeros.

A medida que avanzamos en la unidad que trata sobre escribir informes, visitaremos primero la biblioteca. Buscaremos información en revistas, libros e Internet. Usaremos la tabla de contenido y el índice para buscar las páginas que necesitamos. Buscaremos palabras en el diccionario. También aprenderemos a usar los archivos de una computadora y lo que un bibliotecario puede hacer por nosotros.

Al escribir nuestros informes, escogeremos un tema, leeremos sobre el tema y reuniremos datos. Escribiremos un párrafo inicial para presentar el tema y suministraremos el primer dato. Luego añadiremos nuevos párrafos con datos adicionales. Un rasgo importante de la escritura investigativa es el uso de **convenciones.** Debemos asegurarnos de que nuestras publicaciones salgan sin errores de puntuacón, de mayúsculas y de ortografía.

¡Dentro de poco aprenderá datos nuevos y divertidos de su hijo de primer grado!

Ayúdele a su hijo(a) a escribir informes:

- Exploren juntos algunos temas de interés en Internet. Para obtener buena calidad y seguridad, ingresen a sitios con las terminaciones *.edu* (educación), *.org* (organizaciones), o *.gov* (gobierno).
- Llame a su biblioteca local y solicite una visita guiada para ustedes. Aproveche las ventajas que hay disponibles para usted y su familia.

¡Gracias!

Unit Planning   Writing Form

START-UP
_____ days

- **Focus**

- **Skills**

PARAGRAPH
_____ days

Prewriting

- **Focus**

- **Skills**

Writing
_____ days

- **Focus**

- **Skill**

Revising
_____ days

- **Ideas**

- **Organization**

- **Word Choice**

See Lesson Planning Guidelines on pages TE 32–35.

Unit Planning (continued)

Editing ____ days

- **CAPITALIZATION**

- **PUNCTUATION**

- **SPELLING**

Publishing ____ days

- **OPTIONS**

Assessment ____ days

- **BENCHMARK PAPERS**

Across the Curriculum ____ days

- **MATH**

- **SCIENCE**

- **SOCIAL STUDIES**

- **OTHER**

Scavenger Hunt 1: Find the Threes

© Houghton Mifflin Harcourt Publishing Company

◀ Directions ▶ Find the following "threes" in your book by turning to the pages listed in parentheses.

1. Three writing traits (page 36)

_____

_____

_____

2. Three things you can do to choose a topic (page 66)

_____

_____

_____

3. Three ways to find a book in a computer catalog (page 182)

_____

_____

_____

4. Three kinds of sentences (page 290)

_____

_____

_____

Scavenger Hunt 2: What Is It?

© Houghton Mifflin Harcourt Publishing Company

◄ Directions ► Find the answers to the following questions using the index in the back of the book. The underlined words below tell you where to look in the index.

1. What are <u>antonyms</u>?

_____

_____

_____

2. What is a <u>daily journal</u>?

_____

_____

_____

3. What are the <u>parts of a book</u>?

_____

_____

_____

4. What is a <u>story plot</u>?

_____

_____

_____

Getting to Know *Write Source*

 **Directions** Locate the pages in *Write Source* where answers to the following learning tasks can be found. Both the index and the table of contents can help you.

1. You need to learn about working with a partner.

page _____

2. You need ideas for ways of publishing your writing.

page _____

3. You need to know how to find information about an animal for a report.

pages _____

4. You need ideas for a good writing topic.

pages _____

5. You need help with checking your spelling.

pages _____

Getting Started Activity Answers

Scavenger Hunt 1: Find the Threes
1. ideas, organization, conventions
2. think, list, choose
3. search for a subject, a title, or an author
4. telling sentence, asking sentence, exclamatory sentence

Scavenger Hunt 2: What Is It?
1. words that are opposites (page 287)
2. a special notebook in which you can write all kinds of things (pages 208–209, 245)
3. cover, table of contents, index (pages 184–185)
4. what happens when the characters try to solve the problem (page 163)

Getting to Know *Write Source*
1. 26
2. 38
3. 180–187
4. 242–247
5. 279–283

Credits

Student Edition

Photos:

127 ©Corbis; 186 top, 186 bottom 187 ©Photodisc/Getty Images; 247 ©Ar iel Skelley/Getty Images; 263 ©George Doyle/Getty Images

Teacher's Edition

Photos:

TE-8 ©Tim Pannell/Corbis; TE-10–TE-11 ©Andrzej Tokarski/Alamy; TE-12 ©Image Source/ Getty Images; TE-16–TE-17 Harcourt.

Text:

Index

A

Abbreviations, punctuation of, 270
ABC poem, 177
ABC order, 384–388
Academic Vocabulary, 12, 42, 60, 82, 106, 130, 140, 160, 178, 200, 218, 240, 298

Across the curriculum, writing
    Health, 139
    Math, 80, 126
    Music, 103
    Reading, 102
    Science, 81
    Social studies, 127

Action verbs, 228–231, 294–295, 353, 355
Adjectives, 238–239, 297, 373–374
Advanced learners, 19, 21, 22, 24, 27, 35, 37, 47, 49, 52, 57, 59, 70, 93, 101, 110, 111, 119, 121, 123, 124, 126, 127, 149, 165, 168, 169, 185, 209
Agreement, subject-verb, 234–235, 289
Antonyms, 287
Apostrophes, 236, 274, 372
Asking sentences, 54–55, 271, 290, 348

Assessment,
    Rubrics, 36–37
    Expository prompts, 128–129
    Narrative prompts, 104–105
    Response to literature prompts, 158–159

Ate/eight, 284
Author card/entry, 183

B

Bar graphs, 265
Benchmark papers, 317–331
Beginnings, 56, 143, 151, 165–167, 192–193
    MODELS 57, 143, 151, 164, 193
Blew/blue, 284

Book reviews, 140–157
    Fiction, 142–149
    Nonfiction, 150–157
Books, parts of, 184–185
By/buy, 284

C

Capital letters, 275–277, 288
    Book titles, 276
    Days of the week, 277, 406
    First words, 53, 275, 288, 360
    Holidays, 276, 381
    Months of the year, 277, 383
    Name titles, 276, 380
    Places, 276, 367
    Proper nouns, 276–277, 365, 367
    Word "I," 275, 360
Captions, 263
Caret, 72, 94, 118
Catalog, computer, 181–183
Characters, 163, 165–167
Charts,
    Five W's, 252
    Order, 114–115, 253, 363
    Sensory, 68–71, 250, 334
Checklists for conventions, 22, 35, 75, 97, 121, 137, 148, 156, 198
Classroom portfolios, 40–41
Closing, 272–273
Cluster diagrams, 128, 173, 249, 337
Commas, 272–273, 379
Commercials, viewing, 212–213
Common nouns, 220–222, 291–292, 365
Compare, adjectives that, 239, 297, 374
Complete sentences, 44, 53, 288
Computer,
    Catalog, 181–183
    Parts of, 266–267
    Web sites, viewing, 212–213
    Writing with a, 38, 198–199
Conference notes sheet, 332
Contractions, 236–237, 274

Conventions (writing trait), 28, 35–37
    Descriptive writing, 65, 74–75
    Expository writing, 111, 120–121
    Narrative writing, 87, 96–97
    Persuasive writing, 137
    Poems, 175
    Report writing, 197
    Response to literature, 148, 156
    Stories, 168

Covers, book 184
Creative writing, 160–177
    Poems, 170–177
    Stories, 162–169

D

Daily journals, 208–209, 245, 333
Dates, punctuation of, 273
Days of the week, capitalization of, 277, 382
Dear/deer, 284
Describing words, 62–63, 65, 68–69, 170–174

Descriptive writing, 60–81
    Across the curriculum,
        Math, 80
        Science, 81
    MODELS 64, 78, 80, 81
    Paragraph, 64–81
    Poems, 170–177
    Process of,
        Editing, 74–75
        Prewriting, 66–69
        Publishing, 76–78
        Revising, 72–73
        Writing, 70–71
    Reflecting on, 79
    Sensory details, 68–73, 250, 334
    Topics, 66–67, 244
    Voice, 254

Details, 72–73, 90–91, 144–147, 190–191
    Chart, 159, 368, 371

Details, (continued)
Clustering (web), 128, 173, 249, 337
Five W's, 252
Gathering, 68–69, 90–91, 114–115, 144–145, 375
Order, 253, 363
Sensory, 68–73, 250, 334
Sheet, 145, 159, 368, 371
Story map, 251, 335

Diagrams, 128, 173, 249

Dictionary, using a, 186–187, 256–257

Differentiated instruction, *see* Advanced Learners, English Language Learners, Struggling Learners

Editing, 14, 35, 59,
Conventions, *see* Conventions
Descriptive writing, 74–75
Expository writing, 120–121
Narrative writing, 96–97
One writer's process, 22–23
Persuasive writing, 137
Poems, 175
Report writing, 198–199
Response to literature, 148, 156
Stories, 168

Editing and proofreading marks, 298, 316 and inside back cover

Editing checklist, 358

Eight/ate, 284

End marks, 22, 55, 270–271, 288

Endings, 56, 142–143, 150–151, 165–167
MODELS 57, 143, 151, 164, 167

English language learners, 18, 19, 20, 22, 24, 25, 29, 30, 31, 32, 33, 34, 35, 37, 45, 46, 48, 49, 50, 52, 57, 59, 64, 65, 67, 68, 69, 70, 72, 74, 75, 76, 77, 78, 80, 81, 85, 86, 88, 89, 91, 92, 93, 94, 95, 96, 97, 99, 101, 102, 103, 104, 105, 111, 112, 113, 114, 115, 116, 117, 118, 120, 122, 123, 125, 126, 129, 133, 134, 136, 137, 138, 139, 143, 144, 145, 151, 152, 153, 155, 156, 158, 159, 163, 164, 171, 172, 173, 175, 176, 181, 182, 184, 186, 187, 189, 190, 191, 192, 193, 195, 197, 198, 199, 202, 204, 208, 209, 210, 211, 212, 213, 216

Entry words, dictionary, 186–187

Exclamation points, 55, 271, 288, 290, 352

Exclamatory sentences, 54–55, 271, 290, 349

Expository writing, 106–129
Across the curriculum,
Math, 126
Social Studies, 127
Assessment, writing for, 128–129
How-to writing, 108–125, 253
Learning logs, 210–211
Paragraphs, 110–129
Process of,
Editing, 120–121
Prewriting, 112–115
Publishing, 122–124
Revising, 118–119
Writing, 116–117
Prompts, 128–129
Reflecting on, 125
Reports, 188–199
Response to literature, 140–159
Topics, 112, 113, 244
Traits of, 111
Voice, 255

Fact sheets, 153, 370

Facts, 152–153

Family Connection letters, 395–412

Fiction books, review of, 142–149

Fill-in-the-blank tests, 216

Final copy, 25, 76–77, 98, 122–124, 138, 149, 169, 176, 262–267

Finding information, 180–187

First drafts, 18–19, 70–71, 92–93, 116, 135, 167, 192–195

First words, capitalizing, 53, 275, 288, 360

Five W's chart, 252

For/four, 285

Forms of writing, 42–199

Four-Square, 335

Friendly letters, 272–273

Gathering grid, 191–195, 375

Getting-started activities, 415–417,

Goals, understanding your, 65, 87, 111

Grammar,
Parts of speech, 291–297
Sentences, 42–55, 234–235, 288–290, 343–352, 393–394

Graphic organizers,
Bar graph, 265
Cluster diagram, 128, 173, 249, 337
Daily journal, 333
Details sheet, 145, 159
Fact sheet, 153
Five W's, 252
Four-Square, 335
Friendly letter, 336
Gathering grid, 190–195, 375
Graphs, 265
Lists, 16–17, 66–67, 112–113, 243, 248, 338
Note, 347
Order chart, 115, 253, 363
Sensory chart, 68–71, 250, 344
Story map, 90–91, 104, 251, 335
Story plan, 166
Web, *see* Cluster diagrams

Graphs, 265

Greetings, letter, 272–273, 336

Grids, gathering, 190–195, 375

Health, 139

Hear/here, 285

Holidays, capitalization of, 276, 381

Homophones, 284–286

How-to writing, 108–125, 253

Ideas, finding topics, 242–247

Ideas (writing trait), 28, 30, 36–37, 242–247
Descriptive writing, 65, 67
Expository writing, 111, 113
Narrative writing, 87, 89
Persuasive writing, 130

Ideas list, 16–17, 66–67, 112–113, 243, 248
Indenting, 57, 76–77, 98–99, 122–123
Index, teacher resources, 185
Information, finding, 180–187
Initials, punctuation of, 270
Instructional approaches,
Internet, using the, 212–213
Interviews, 206–207
Irregular nouns, 278
Its/it's, 285

Journals,
Daily, 208–209, 245, 333
Learning log, 210–211
Reading, 242

Keywords, computer catalog, 182
Kinds of sentences, 54–55, 270–271, 290, 347–349
Know/no, 285

Labels, 80, 264
Learning logs, 210–211
Lesson planning, TE-32–TE-61
Letters, 102, 336
Parts of, 272–273
Library, using the, 180–183
Linking verbs, 232–233, 294, 296, 354, 356
Listening rules, 204

Listening skills, 200–207
List poem, 170–171, 176–177
Listing, 16–17, 66–67, 112–113, 243, 248, 338
Literature, response to, 140–159
Literature Connections, 61, 83, 107, 131, 161, 179

Map, story, 90–93, 104, 251, 335
Matching tests, 214
Math,
Addition, 126
Shape description, 80
Meanings, word, 186–187
Middle of paragraphs, 56, 143, 151, 165–167
MODELS 57, 143, 151, 164
Months, capitalization of, 277, 383
Multiple-choice test, 215
Music, personal story, 103

Names, capitalization of, 276, 367
Naming parts, sentence, 48–49, 52–53, 229, 288, 343, 345, 346

Narrative writing, 82–105
Across the curriculum,
Music, 103
Reading, 102
Assessment, writing for, 104–105
Paragraphs, 86–105
Process of, 88–100
Editing, 96–97
Prewriting, 88–91
Publishing, 98–100
Revising, 94–95
Writing, 92–93
Prompts, 104–105
Reflecting on, 101
Voice, 254

New words, learning, 256–259
No/know, 285
Nonfiction books, review of, 150–157

Note,
Notebook, writer's, 66, 67, 172, 243
Nouns, 220–223, 364–366
Agreement with verbs, 234–235, 394
Common, 222, 291–292, 365
Irregular, 278
Plurals of, 223, 278, 292, 366, 376–377
Proper, 222, 291, 365
Singular, 223, 278, 292, 366

One/won, 285
One writer's process, 16–27
Opinions, 130–135
Opposites (antonyms), 287, 392
Order,
Chart, 114–115, 253, 363
Place, 261
Time, 95, 111, 116, 260
Word, 46–47, 342

Organization (writing trait), 28, 31, 36–37, 248–253
Expository writing, 111, 115
Narrative writing, 87, 95

Paragraphs, 56–59
Beginning, 56, 142, 150, 165–166, 192–193
MODELS 57, 143, 151, 164, 193
Descriptive, 64–81
Ending, 56, 143, 151, 165–167
Expository, 110–129
Middle, 56, 143, 151, 165–167
Narrative, 86–105
Parts of, 56–57
Persuasive, 134–139
Response to literature, 143–159
Writing guidelines, 56–57
Partners, working with, 26–27
Parts of a book, nonfiction, 184–185
Parts of a letter, 272–273, 336
Parts of a sentence, 48–53, 288

Parts of speech,
Adjectives, 238–239, 297, 373–374
Nouns, 220–223, 234–235, 291–292, 364–366
Pronouns, 224–227, 293, 369
Verbs, 228–235, 294–296, 353–356

Past tense, 231, 233, 295–296, 355, 356

Periods, 55, 270, 288, 290, 350, 378

Persuasive writing, 130–139
Across the curriculum,
Health, 139
Opinion, 130–135
Paragraphs, 134–139
Posters, 133
Process of,
Editing, 137
Prewriting, 134
Publishing, 138
Revising, 136
Writing, 135
Supporting an opinion, 134
Voice, 255

Place order, 261
Places, capitalization of, 276, 367
Plot, 163
Plural nouns, 223, 278, 292, 366, 376–377
Plural pronouns, 226–227
Plural subjects, 235
Poems,
ABC, 177
Kinds of, 177
List poem, 170–171, 176–177
Publishing, 176
Responding to, 158–159
Rhyming, 177
Writing, 170–177
Portfolios, 40–41
Posters, 133

Practical writing,
How-to writing, 106–125
Letter writing, 102, 273, 336

Present tense, 230, 232, 295–296, 355

Prewriting, 14–17, 58
Descriptive writing, 66–69
Expository writing, 112–115
Narrative writing, 88–91
One writer's process, 16–17
Persuasive writing, 134
Poems, 172–173
Report writing, 190–191
Response to literature, 144–145, 152–153
Story, 166
Problem (part of a story), 163
Process, see Writing process
One writer's, 16–27
Writing, using the, 14–15
Prompts for assessment,
Expository, 128–129
Narrative, 104–105
Response to literature (a poem), 158–159
Pronouns, 224–227, 293, 369
In contractions, 236
Plural, 223, 226–227
Singular, 224–225
Proofreader's guide,
Capital letters, 275–277, 360, 367, 380–383
Opposites, 287, 392
Parts of speech, 291–297, 353–356, 364–366, 369, 373–374
Proofreader's guide, (continued)
Plurals, 278, 376–377
Punctuation, 270–274, 350–352, 372, 378–379
Spelling, 279–283
Understanding sentences, 288–290, 393–394
Using the right word, 284–286, 389–391
Proofreading marks, 298, 316 and inside back cover
Proper nouns, 222, 276–277, 291, 365
Publishing, 14, 38–39, 59
Descriptive writing, 76–78
Expository writing, 122–124
Narrative writing, 98–100
One writer's process, 24–25
Persuasive writing, 138
Poems, 176
Report writing, 199
Response to literature, 149, 157
Stories, 169

Punctuation, 55, 290
Apostrophes, 236–237, 274, 372
Commas, 272–273, 379
Exclamation points, 55, 271, 288, 290, 352
Periods, 55, 270, 288, 290, 350, 378
Question marks, 55, 271, 288, 290, 351

Question marks, 55, 271, 288, 290, 351

Read/red, 286
Reading, across the curriculum, 102
Reading journal, 242
Reasons to support an opinion, 134
Red/read, 286
Reference books, 181
Reflecting on your writing, 79, 101, 125, 383
Report writing, 178
Library, using the, 180–183
MODELS 189, 199
Process of,
Editing, 199
Prewriting, 190–191
Publishing, 199
Revising, 196–197
Writing, 192–195
Reference materials, 181
Research report, 188–199

Response to literature, 140–159
Assessment, writing for, 158–159
Book reviews,
Fiction, 142–149
Nonfiction, 150–157
MODELS 143, 149, 151, 157
Poem, 158–159
Process of,
Editing, 148, 156
Prewriting, 144–145, 152–153
Publishing, 149, 157
Revising, 147, 155
Writing, 146, 154
Prompt, 158–159

Review, book, 140–159
  Fiction, 142–149
  Nonfiction, 150–157
Revising, 14, 20–21, 59
  Descriptive writing, 72–73
  Expository writing, 118–119
  Narrative writing, 94–95
  One writer's process, 20–21
  Persuasive writing, 136
  Poems, 175
  Report writing, 196–197
  Response to literature, 147, 155
  Stories, 168
Rhyming poem, 158, 177
Road/rode, 286
Rubrics, learning about, 36–37

Science,
  Animal report, 188–199
  Class pet (descriptive paragraph), 81
  How-to paragraphs, 108–111
  Learning log, 210–211
  Nonfiction book review, 150–157

Scope and sequence, TE-44–TE-55
Search, keyword, 182
Selecting a topic, *see* Topics, choosing
Senses, using, 62–63, 81
Sensory charts, 68–71, 250, 334

Sentence fluency (writing trait), 28, 34, 260–261

Sentences, 42–55
  Asking, 54–55, 271, 290, 348
  Complete thought, 44, 53, 288, 341
  Exclamatory, 54–55, 271, 290, 348
  Fluency, 28, 34
  Kinds of, 54–55, 270–271, 290
  Order in, 46–47, 342
  Parts of, 48–53, 367, 342, 346
  Punctuation of, 54–55, 270–271
  Sentence starter, 89, 244
  Subject-verb agreement, 234–235, 289, 394
  Telling, 54–55, 290, 347
  Writing, 52–53

Sentence starters, 361
Series, punctuation of, 272–273
Settings, 163
Short-answer test, 217
Singular nouns, 223, 278, 292, 366
Singular pronouns, 224–225
Singular subjects, 234

Social studies,
  Expository writing, 127
  Narrative, 104–105

Speaking and learning, 200–217
Speaking skills, 200–203
Speech, parts of, 291–297
Spelling, 279–283
  Dictionary, 186–187, 257
Start-ups,
  Descriptive, 62–63
  Expository, 108–109
  Narrative, 84–85
  Persuasive, 132–133
Story map, 91–93, 104, 251, 335
Story plan, 166
Story plot, 163
Story writing, 162–169
  MODELS 164, 169
Struggling learners, 20, 22, 25, 27, 30, 31, 32, 33, 34, 45, 47, 48, 51, 53, 55, 59, 69, 73, 75, 77, 86, 87, 89, 91, 93, 95, 97, 99, 101, 102, 109, 113, 115, 117, 119, 128, 133, 135, 136, 138, 145, 148, 164, 166, 167, 169, 171, 172, 174, 175, 183, 185, 191, 195, 197, 203, 205

Study skills,
  Finding information, 180–187
  Interviewing, 206–207
  Learning logs for, 210–211
  Listening, 204–205
  Taking tests, 214–217
  Viewing, 212–213

Subject card/entry, 182
Subject of a sentence, *see* Naming parts
Subject-verb agreement, 234–235, 289, 394
Support for an opinion, 134
Symbols, correction, inside back cover

Table of contents, 4–10, 185
Teaching tips, 11, 15, 17, 23, 39, 41, 45, 46, 51, 52, 53, 54, 55, 56, 57, 58, 66, 67, 71, 72, 73, 85, 89, 91, 94, 98, 100, 103, 110, 112, 113, 115, 116, 117, 118, 124, 128, 133, 134, 135, 136, 143, 146, 149, 151, 155, 157, 160, 165, 167, 169, 170, 171, 173, 176, 181, 182, 184, 186, 187, 190, 193, 199, 203, 205, 207, 213
Television viewing skills, 212–213
Telling part, sentence, 50–53, 288, 344, 345, 346
Telling sentence, 54–55, 290, 347
Tense of verbs, 230–233, 295–296, 355–356
Tests,
  Responding to prompts, 104, 128, 158
  Taking, 214–217
  Types of, 214–217
Their/there/they're, 286
Thematic approach,
Theme words, 298–311
Time-order words, 95, 111, 116, 260
Title card/entry, 183
Title of a book, 184, 276
Titles of people, 276
  Capitalization of, 276, 380
  Punctuation of, 270
To/too/two, 286
Tools of learning, 200–217
Topics, choosing, 242–247, 357, 362
  Descriptive writing, 66–67, 244, 357
  Expository writing, 112–113, 244
  Narrative writing, 88–89, 244
  One writer's process, 16–17
  Persuasive writing, 244
  Poetry, 170–173
  Report writing, 190–191
  Response to literature, 144
  Story writing, 162, 166
Trait-based approach, 316

Traits of writing, (see also individual entries) 28–35, 65, 87, 111
 Conventions, 28, 35–37, 65, 74–75, 87, 96–97, 111, 120–121, 137, 148, 156, 168, 175, 198
 Ideas, 28, 30, 36–37, 65, 67, 87, 89, 111, 113, 242–247
 Organization, 28, 31, 95, 111, 115, 248–253
 Sentence fluency, 28, 34, 260–261
 Voice, 28, 32, 254–255
 Word choice, 28, 33, 73
Two/to/too, 286

Unit planning sheet, 413
Using the right word, 284–286, 389–391

Verbs, 228–235, 294–296, 353–356
 Action, 228–231, 294–295, 353, 355
 Agreement with subject, 234–235, 289, 394
 In contractions, 237
 Linking, 232–233, 294, 296, 354, 356
 Tense of, 230–233, 295–296, 355, 356
Viewing skills, 212–213
Vocabulary,
 Antonyms, 287,
 Homophones, 284–286
 Using a dictionary, 186–187, 256–257

Voice (writing trait), 28, 32, 254–255
 Descriptive writing, 254
 Expository writing, 255
 Narrative writing, 254
 Persuasive writing, 255

Web diagrams, *see* Cluster diagrams
Web sites, viewing, 212–213
Why write?, 11
Won/one, 285
Word bank, 258–259

Word choice (writing trait), 28, 33, 73, 256–259
 Descriptive writing, 65, 73
 Poems, 173
 Report writing, 196

Words, 218–239
 Learning new, 186–187, 256–259
 Series of, 272–273
 Using the right, 284–286
Working with partners, 26–27
Worksheets, 340–394
Workshop, writing,
Writer's notebook, 66, 67, 172, 243
Writer's resource, 240–267
Writing, 14, 59
 Assessment prompts,
  Expository, 128–129
  Narrative, 104–105
  Response to literature, 158–159
 Beginnings, *see* Beginnings
 Endings, *see* Endings
 Forms of, *see* Forms of writing
 Middle, *see* Middle paragraphs
 Topics, *see* Topic choosing
 Traits of, *see* Traits of writing
Writing a first draft,
 Descriptive writing, 70–71
 Expository writing, 116–117
 Narrative writing, 92–93
 One writer's process, 18–19
 Persuasive writing, 135
 Poems, 174
 Report writing, 192–195
 Response to literature, 146, 154
 Stories, 167

Writing across the curriculum, *see* Across the curriculum, writing
Writing assessment,
 Responding to a prompt, 104–105, 128–129, 158–159
 Rubrics, 36–37
Writing on tests, *see* Tests, taking
Writing process,
 Editing, 14, 22–23, 35, 59, 74–75, 96–97, 120–121, 137, 148, 156, 168, 175, 199
 One writer's process, 16–27
 Prewriting, 14, 16–17, 58, 66–69, 88–91, 112–115, 134, 144–145, 152–153, 166, 172–173, 190–191
 Publishing, 14, 24–25, 38–39, 59, 76–78, 98–100, 122–124, 138, 149, 157, 169, 176, 199
 Reflecting on, 79, 101, 125
 Revising, 14, 20–21, 59, 72–73, 94–95, 118–119, 136, 147, 155, 175, 190–197
 Understanding the, 12–41
 Using the, 12–27
 Writing, 18–19, 70–71, 92–93, 116–117, 135, 146, 154, 167, 174, 192–195
Writing tests, *see* Assessment
Writing with partners, 26–27
Writing workshop, TE-20–TE-21